Off-Centre Stages

THE SOCIETY FOR THEATRE RESEARCH

The Society for Theatre Research, founded in 1948, brings together those interested in the history and technique of the British theatre, and encourages research into these subjects. Lectures are held in London and a Northern group contributes further events. Members receive the Society's illustrated journal, *Theatre Notebook*, as well as (at least) one book annually. The Society makes substantial Research Awards and in 1998 instituted the Theatre Book Prize. New members are welcome. Details of subscription rates and a list of past publications appear on the Society's website – www.str.org.uk – or may be obtained by writing to: The Joint Hon. Secretaries, The Society for Theatre Research, c/o The Theatre Museum, 1E Tavistock Street, London WC2E 7PR.

Off-Centre Stages

Fringe Theatre at the Open Space
and the Round House
1968–1983

JINNIE SCHIELE

UNIVERSITY OF HERTFORDSHIRE PRESS

SOCIETY FOR THEATRE RESEARCH

A joint publication of the University of Hertfordshire Press
and the Society for Theatre Research

First published in Great Britain in 2005 by
University of Hertfordshire Press
Learning and Information Services
University of Hertfordshire
College Lane
Hatfield
Hertfordshire AL10 9AB
and
The Society for Theatre Research
c/o The Theatre Museum
1E Tavistock Street
London WC2 7PR

British Library Cataloguing in Publication Data
A catalogue record for this book is available from the British Library

ISBN 1-902806-42-5 hardback
ISBN 1-902806-43-3 paperback

Design by Geoff Green, Cambridge CB4 5RA
Cover design by John Robertshaw, Harpenden AL5 2JB
Printed in Great Britain by Antony Rowe Ltd, Chippenham SN14 6LH

Every effort has been made to trace the copyright holders for
uncredited photographs

For Eileen

Acknowledgements

For access to the archives of the Open Space and the Round House theatres, I must thank Thelma Holt and Charles Marowitz, who also generously gave up their time to be interviewed by me and to read my manuscript.

Thanks also to John Arden, Steven Berkoff, Howard Brenton, John Burgess, Paul Collins, Robin Don, Walter Donohue, Trevor Griffiths, Jocelyn Herbert, Boris Howarth, Maggie Howarth, George Little, Clive Merrison, Philip Ormond, Alan Pearlman, Tony Richardson, Sue Rose, Nikolas Simmonds, Malcolm Storry and Timothy West, who either wrote or spoke to me about their involvement with the two theatres.

With help in preparing my manuscript, first for a doctorate and later for this book, I am indebted to Eileen Cottis, Peter Cottis, Frances Dann, Laurence Harbottle, Wendy Kolmar, Amy Myers, Leslie Smith, Malcolm Taylor and Peter Thomson; Bill Forster and Jane Housham of University of Hertfordshire Press patiently gave invaluable advice; Malcolm Holmes of the Camden Local History Library provided an expert service for all matters of local history. Thanks, too, to those with better computer skills than me, Graham Catterall, Julian Farrell and Ann Stangar. Nothing at all would have been achieved without the support of Decca Aitkenhead, Michel Chatenay, Susan Donald, Julian Farrell, Sukie Killick, Susan Painter, Shelley Phillips and Marie Rostan.

My greatest debt of all is to Eileen Cottis, who has guided and encouraged me every step of the way.

Contents

List of Illustrations

ABBREVIATIONS USED

OS Archive: Open Space Archive, Theatre Museum, Covent Garden

OS Prog: Programmes in the Open Space Archive

OS 1/3 etc.: File number of material in the Open Space Archive

RH Archive: Round House Archive, Theatre Museum

CF: Contract File, Round House Archive

SF: Show File, Round House Archive

Preface

Fringe theatre of the 1960s and 70s tended to be off-centre both in location and in its remoteness from conventional politics and theatrical practice. Not all fringe theatre was politically committed, but in general its instincts were left-wing; not all fringe theatre was experimental in form, but again its instincts were towards the avant-garde and the offbeat, with support for the marginalised or the revolutionary. Both of the theatres explored in this book are obvious contenders, in different ways, for categorisation as fringe theatres: the Round House, unique architecturally, vast, exhilarating, but incredibly difficult to tame to performance; the Open Space, tiny, intense, flexible, but so small that it had its own inherent problems. Both influenced, and were influenced by, the fringe of the sixties and seventies. It was my good fortune to 'discover' the archives of both theatres and be given permission by Thelma Holt and Charles Marowitz to house them at the Polytechnic of North London (now London Metropolitan University) where I was a research assistant. They have since been placed in the care of the Theatre Museum where they are in the process of being catalogued.

The Round House and the Open Space theatres were both created in the borough of Camden, as it was formed in 1965 from the areas of St Pancras, Holborn, and Hampstead, the outer boundaries of which were linked to form the new borough. By 1945 almost all professional performances in the borough of Camden took place in privately owned, purpose-built theatres which divided into two categories: West End theatres in the south of the borough, and local houses further north. In both areas the average playgoer was very little concerned with the personalities of the management, which remained anonymous. The Unity, a Labour-movement theatre group using a converted mission hall as its theatre, was the only exception to the rule. By 1985 half of the West End houses had fallen to the property developer; even as early as the sixties, local houses had ceased to exist as independent theatres, and by 1985 a variety of venues had arisen in their place, often converted, some of them surviving on subsidy, others struggling without.

In Britain, before 1960, the notion that theatre might happen in any space where people could gather had hardly been explored. In 1964, Peter Brook and Charles Marowitz worked together on the Royal Shakespeare Company's Theatre of Cruelty season at LAMDA (London Academy of Music and Dramatic Art), bringing together two very different talents whose fusion was to produce shockwaves throughout the conventional theatre. Marowitz brought group experiment with him from America, Brook a sound knowledge of commercial West End theatre and its practitioners, and an anarchic drive to escape its limitations. This Theatre of Cruelty season achieved enormous publicity, both good and bad, and it helped kickstart the underground movement of alternative theatre, later to be called 'the fringe'.

The political playwrights of the early sixties (Arnold Wesker, John Arden, David Mercer and others) were to make use of the many small, non-theatre spaces with club status that proliferated. Lunchtime theatre sprang up in pubs and basements, encouraging playwrights such as Howard Brenton, Sam Shepard and John Grillo to write hour-long plays. Community theatre began to flourish in different parts of London. Inter-Action (based in Kentish Town), led by the ebullient American Ed Berman, was a near neighbour of the Round House, and its offshoot, the Almost Free Theatre (Rupert Street, Soho), was just down the road from the Open Space. Berman's enterprise embraced lunchtime and experimental theatre, the Fun Art Bus (which took plays around many London boroughs and further afield to Bath and even Munich) and work with children. Its concerns were as much sociological as artistic.

One building outside London, the old dosshouse in James

Court, Edinburgh, shot into the limelight as one of the new wave of theatre spaces, and has retained its cachet as a prime venue for cutting-edge theatre to the present day (though it has since changed its premises twice): the Traverse. It seated sixty people and, with the help of some private patronage, became the focus of all the alternative venues at the Edinburgh Festival. A charismatic and controversial American named Jim Haynes took it over in 1964 and ran it until 1966 when he was forced to resign. During this time he met Charles Marowitz, who directed Saul Bellow's *A Wen* and *Orange Soufflé* (later to be billed as *The Bellow Plays*) and Peter Barnes' *Sclerosis* for him. Haynes went from Edinburgh to London where he opened the Arts Lab, Drury Lane in 1968 (the year when theatre censorship was abolished in Britain, the students in Paris occupied the Odéon and Jean-Louis Barrault was dismissed from the post of director of the Théâtre de France, which he had held since 1959).

The Arts Lab was a place where all the arts were welcomed, where hippies hung out, and where the *International Times* (London's first underground paper) was sold. It became a centre for American alternative culture, which was to influence so much of what happened later on the fringe. This was a venue for all-comers and inevitably Marowitz gravitated towards it, but, though he loved its spirit, his yearning was for a theatre of his own, with a permanent company able to experiment with and learn from the work it would perform. Very few of the major fringe companies that developed through the sixties and seventies *(Welfare State, People Show, Freehold, CAST,* for example) were building-based and, like others, having established his Open Space, Marowitz found that he had to play host to them. His ideal was to set up a theatre on the fringe: paradoxically he founded the Open Space in the heart of the West End. He was the only one with his own company to do so.

Arnold Wesker's commitment to Centre 42, the first company to use the Round House as a theatre, was as political as it was artistic. The centre was to reach out to the culturally uninitiated and underprivileged, an attitude which would alienate many. Wesker has always been a proselytiser for his socialism (so evident in his early plays), and he, like Marowitz, managed to annoy some who might have helped financially – both could seem arrogant in their convictions. George Hoskins, who had joined the project as Wesker's financial adviser, carried on alone after Wesker resigned in 1970. His policy combined influences from Peter Daubeny's World Theatre seasons and from the 'hippy' sub-culture of such festivals as Glastonbury and Woodstock. Thelma Holt, who took over during Hoskins' illness in 1977, recognising, perhaps, that revolutionary fervour was on the wane, revamped the Round House so that it could easily accept productions from the provinces (notably Manchester). Although she had severed her connection with the Open Space, she nevertheless took in Marowitz's adaptation of *Hedda*, his last attempt to continue his work without a permanent base in the Euston Road. The Round House offered a home to many more experimental companies than the Open Space, with its tiny auditorium, could have hoped to, but if neither was in the vanguard of theatre revolution they both belonged distinctively to the resistance, aiming to provide London with alternatives to mainstream theatre, knowing that their ventures would attract the nation's critics who were all London-based. Both wanted to show how a cultural capital could influence world theatre.

The Round House, a Victorian engine shed and one of the most ambitious conversions in the area, began its new life in the hope of becoming a Government-sponsored arts centre; the Open Space Theatre, situated close to the West End, began as a two-handed enterprise which quickly became identified with Charles Marowitz and, less perceptibly to the public eye, with Thelma Holt. Each represents a considerable achievement on the part of its management, and together they demonstrate a range of different approaches to theatre in the area; they both offered, in their own way, a valuable contribution to the work accomplished by British theatre of the period.

Sources for the materials used are listed in the bibliography, where it will be seen that the facts have been found in different ways for each enterprise. For instance, interviews have been conducted with management and artistic personnel, but only at the Open Space was it possible to speak to a number of artistic directors who worked there – thus in Part 1 there is a greater emphasis on detailed studies of productions. Because the Open Space was a theatre which began and ended with Charles Marowitz, I have selected for detailed study a period which best illustrates his achievements there. The first years are important as context for future development, and the subsequent years, up to 1976 when the theatre in Tottenham Court Road was closed, embody what was most typical and original in the Marowitz/Holt directorship. There was a perceptible development towards a peak of achievement between 1971 and 1973. The high standard was maintained, but with less intensity, until it rose again in 1975, when a new 'permanent company' was formed. Included is all the work done in association with Thelma Holt, who left shortly after the move to the new premises. It becomes clear that without her expertise in raising money and her skill in public relations, particularly with the Arts Council and politicians, Marowitz's fire of enthusiasm for the project was gradually extinguished.

Part 2 outlines the history of the Round House and its origins in Arnold Wesker's Centre 42, which, after a long campaign, failed to emerge. The subsequent management policy was to allow in any production whose backers could pay the hiring fee. As there was no other discernible policy, I have divided the sections up by grouping together the years where a pattern of development can be traced. The first of these deals with the years 1968–71, where I have discussed certain productions in detail to demonstrate the first years of full theatrical activity at the Round House, a growing awareness of its potential, and the influence these productions had on events to come. In the second I have shown the types of production which flourished there during the period 1971–78. This is followed by a discussion of its last years under the new Holt management, with a summary of Thelma Holt's achievements.

The following chapters present a study of two Camden theatres during the first two decades of fringe theatre. The materials chosen contribute to an appraisal of the theatres' histories and repertoires. From this appraisal arise crucial questions about performance space and its influence on the

kind of productions presented, and also about the managements' willingness and ability to exploit prevailing conditions
and trends in dramatic performance.

[Part 1]

The Open Space Theatre

The History of the Open Space Theatre

In 1956 Charles Marowitz came from America to England to study drama at the London Academy of Music and Dramatic Art (LAMDA). In his book, *The Act of Being*, he related the results of his training thus: 'having proved myself a failure at drama schools both in New York and London, it seemed the most natural thing in the world to set up an acting school of my own – if not to edify others then at least to instruct myself'.[1] He decided to stay in England and in 1958 he formed his own company called In-Stage, and with help from the British Drama League in the form of a fifty-seater studio workshop theatre at 9 Fitzroy Square, London W1, he directed a number of British and world premieres, some of them in conjunction with the Traverse Theatre in Edinburgh.[2]

In 1962 Marowitz worked as assistant director with Peter Brook on a production for the Royal Shakespeare Company of *King Lear*, which resulted in the Marowitz/Brook collaboration on the Theatre of Cruelty season at LAMDA in the autumn of 1963. It was during this season that he wrote his first twenty-eight minute version of the collage *Hamlet* which he later expanded to eighty minutes and directed, first with In-Stage for the Literarisches Colloquium, Berlin, at the Akademie der Künste in 1965, and then at the Jeannetta Cochrane Theatre in 1966. Between 1963 and 1966 he spent a great deal of time running acting workshops for professional actors all over the world as well as in England and Scotland. He made important contacts with wealthy patrons such as the impresario Bernard Delfont and the actor Roddy Maude-Roxby, both of whom generously donated money without which the open space would never have got started.

Later he met Thelma Holt, a young Royal Academy of

Dramatic Art (RADA) -trained actress who had already had some success in the West End and, at the Hampstead Theatre Club, in Leonid Andreyev's play *He Who Gets Slapped*. This meeting was to transform what had hitherto been a one-man dream (Marowitz had done all the groundwork of making contacts and raising funds) into a partnership which was to last twelve years. Holt was not only to take the leads in his productions but was also to help him run the new Open Space Theatre. It was she who was to cajole and bully the Arts Council and other private supporters into subsidising it, and it is significant that after she left the theatre in 1977 it managed to struggle on for only two years before closing. Marowitz himself said somewhat prophetically: 'we survive, to a large extent, because Thelma Holt is a witch and a miracle-maker, and without her the wheels that propel the complex machinery of our theatre simply would not rotate.'3

Besides his practical theatre work he also wrote articles and reviews for drama magazines and newspapers, which earned him an international reputation as a perceptive and sometimes acerbic theatre critic. Having established himself in this way with the theatre-going public and more importantly with influential members of the acting profession, he felt ready to launch his own theatre. After looking at many different buildings (among them the Camden Theatre, which they could not afford), Marowitz and Holt finally found premises in the basement of a disused old people's centre at 32 Tottenham Court Road, which, when converted, seated an audience of no more than two hundred. They also obtained part of Flat 1, at 30 Tottenham Court Road, to use as an office.

Marowitz, with Thelma Holt as his executive director, formed a non-profit distributing company known as Camden Productions Ltd. They both put money into the venture and sent out appeals for financial assistance to everyone they could think of. Patrons of the theatre were listed as Lord Birkett, Peter Brook, Bernard Delfont, Peter Hall, Harold Pinter and Michael Winner, and with the help of this influential group a grant of £1,500 was obtained from the Arts Council to help start the project. Nineteen founder members who had contributed £50 or more by the time of the first production

Exterior of the Open Space Theatre, Tottenham Court Road, July 1976, with Thelma Holt and Charles Marowitz

included Sean Connery, David Frost, Bernard Miles and Roddy Maude-Roxby.[4] The benefits of becoming a founder member were: life membership, the right to special ticket concessions for dress rehearsals and opening nights, a bi-monthly newsletter containing articles, reviews and details of forthcoming events, and special invitations to 'sideshows' and exclusive late-night attractions.[5] The theatre was to be a club (membership two guineas per annum) and by becoming a member one was to be entitled to the same concessions as the founder members.[6]

Marowitz and Holt amassed from diverse sources about £5,000 with which to construct their theatre and to mount their first production.[7] Tony Carruthers, who had already collaborated with Marowitz at the Traverse and designed the set for the première of Joe Orton's *Loot*, directed by Marowitz at the Jeannetta Cochrane Theatre for the London Traverse Company in 1966, agreed to design the theatre using mobile rostra for both seating and staging, as suggested by Marowitz.[8] All the conversion work in the Tottenham Court Road building was done by Thelma Holt, Marowitz and friends; for instance, they stuck egg boxes to the ceiling to help soundproofing. The seating and acting areas were left adaptable to the needs of each production. The seats were movable chairs and the acting area could be as big or small as necessary and could be raised or left at floor level, as the director desired. According to a letter (OS 10/8, 23 March 1973) from Thelma Holt to J. Wheeler of EMI Property Developments Ltd, the auditorium area, including the lighting box and stage management room, was 60 feet by 51 feet.

The lease was signed on 30 July 1968, between Gort Estates (Development) Limited and Camden Playhouse Productions Limited, with Island Records Limited as a third party (presumably as guarantors). The rent was £500 per annum and was payable at quarterly intervals. The landlords were required to give six months' notice if the building was to be redeveloped or demolished.[9] In 1973 Holt and Marowitz acquired the shop above at number 32.

In August 1976 the Tottenham Court Road theatre was closed, and redevelopment started on the whole block. From

[2]

Official Artistic Policy and the Permanent Company

In 1968 a publicity leaflet, designed to help launch the Open Space, outlined the aims and policies of the theatre, which amounted to a summary of Marowitz's attempt to put into practice everything he believed theatre ought to be doing.[1] I quote at length so that an evaluation of the theatre's achievement can be made later with reference to the director's stated methods and aims:

> London's newest theatre ... has been created to provide playgoers with genuine alternatives to the commercial offerings of the West End. It will stage the work of new writers, particularly those working in new and different forms, and will eventually house a small permanent company concerned directly with experimental projects. Our first season of plays will include works by writers such as Antonin Artaud, Peter Weiss, Bertolt Brecht, Fernando Arrabal and Norman Mailer, as well as works by relatively new writers like Paul Ableman, Peter Barnes, Jakov Lind, Heathcote Williams and Cecil P. Taylor. Apart from main-bill performances, there will be regular lunchtime shows and midnight matinees. The theatre will feature mixed-media events, environmental-pieces, pop-concerts, poetry recitals and happenings. It will stage regular public discussions on urgent social, political and artistic topics. It will also be a centre for theatre-study and maintain a full-time actors' workshop. Its permanent company will explore new techniques in writing, acting and direction, taking the sort of risks that only an adventurous non-commercial company can take.

The idea of a full-time 'actors' workshop' was elaborated on: the workshop would be divided into the two categories of 'professional class' and 'studio class', each programmed for three nine-week sessions a year at £18 and £25 respectively per session. The former was designed for 'resting actors', 'aimed at combating the artistic fatigue of routine employment and extended unemployment'. The work to be done in these classes was intended to help with 'audition technique and problems of personal interpretation'. The latter was to offer 'a systematic training-course for actors and actresses with some previous acting experience'. Marowitz demanded regular attendance in order to explore with his students the ideas of Stanislavsky, Artaud and Brecht. An impressive 'Guest Faculty' was appended, including Martin Esslin, then Head of BBC Drama, Ralph Koltai, Irving Wardle and Clifford Williams. An extra attraction to the classes was the possibility of being asked to work on one of Marowitz's own productions at the Open Space, and members were also to receive special ticket concessions for performances at the theatre.

The publicity blurb was designed to make it sound as though the enterprise was fully organised along the above lines and that it was only a matter of opening the theatre and everything would immediately be put into practice. In fact Marowitz knew very well that this kind of positive statement of objectives was necessary in order to interest the Arts Council in subsidising them – whether they would be able to realise them was a different question altogether. As he himself has said, policy evolves as a result of work done and does not precede it.[2] It was perhaps incautious of him to sound so definite in the leaflet because it gave critics an excuse to carp every time the artistic policy seemed to get lost as the theatre struggled to keep open. Controversy in one form or another was never very far away from Marowitz; he thrived on opposition born out of his commitment to work in his own fringe theatre. Thus, the idea that any of the listed activities should take place on a regular basis would have been possible only when money became available and the circumstances were right. Of the playwrights listed, only Paul Ableman had a play produced at the Open Space during its first season, though many of the others had works presented at a later date. Lunchtime and late-night shows had periods of popularity, and 'mixed media events', 'public discussions' and so on took place very occasionally.

The most fundamental of the objectives stated in the publicity brochure, and the one which Marowitz himself never tired of restating, was the need for a permanent company, without which he felt none of the other aims could be achieved. He had been given a taste of the kind of ideal conditions which were set up for the LAMDA season of Theatre of Cruelty and of Brook's methods of directing when he (Marowitz) acted as assistant director on *King Lear* in 1962. His interest in the idea of a permanent company was still a major obsession in 1966 when he questioned Peter Hall closely about his views on the necessity for working with actors loyal to him, above the claims of the commercial world.[3] There was no hope of creating the kind of company Marowitz craved without funding (his standards were set by the subsidised Laboratory Theatre in Poland and the Open Theatre in America), as the theatre itself was too small to be self-supporting. Critics might grumble at the lack of experiment in the opening productions at the Open Space, but it was necessary for Marowitz to achieve some kind of box-office success in order to impress the Arts Council with his ability to run a theatre, before the essential company could be formed.

About a year after the opening production of *Fortune and Men's Eyes* by John Herbert, the Wiesbaden Festival management offered Marowitz £2,500 to take his production of *A Macbeth* (adapted and directed by Marowitz himself) to Germany (*Guardian*, 14 March 1969). At about the same time an earlier appeal letter sent out by the company to London Weekend Television bore fruit. From a reply dated 2 February 1969 and signed by Humphrey Burton, it is clear that Marowitz had approached him with the proposal of joining forces on his projected satirical show, to be called *The General Strike*. This had been an idea first publicised in 1968, but it was never to come to anything, and Burton rejected it on the grounds that London Weekend Television was already working on a similar project. However, he hinted that there was a possibility of a general grant in the near future. Marowitz had sent out a letter on 12 October 1968, carefully stating the theatre's position and need for subsidy. It had gone to all the television companies and other influential people such as Jennie Lee (the first Minister for the Arts appointed by Harold

Wilson), Harold Pinter, Martin Esslin and David Frost. Humphrey Burton was the one man who was receptive to the plea, and on 5 May 1969 the Open Space received a cheque for £2,600.

With this financial help Marowitz was able to move one step closer to his ideal of experimental theatre, which resulted in the kind of production preparation that had hitherto not been possible. Although the company formed for this production was not yet a permanent one, certain actors were to appear there again later, giving a kind of continuity to casting which meant that audiences would begin to recognise and associate names and faces with the Open Space. There was also a continuity in the designers Marowitz used before he set up his permanent company, and it was here that both John Napier and Robin Don started their careers. Nikolas Simmonds and Thelma Holt were cast in the second collage to be presented at the Open Space, to play Hamlet and Gertrude (they had previously played Macbeth and Lady Macbeth together), and now *Hamlet* received praise for its ensemble acting: 'the painted cast ... show that they as much as any company in Britain understand how to exploit group technique' (*Guardian*, 11.7.69). If this had nothing to do with the fact that these two actors had worked together with Marowitz before, the production undoubtedly benefited from the group exercises that formed part of the rehearsal routine, and which under unsubsidised circumstances would not have been possible.[5]

By the end of 1970 there had been an increase in the number of productions presented, especially at lunchtime, but there was still no extra Arts Council grant. During this time the majority of the productions were brought into the theatre and were not chosen for their suitability but because the companies wanted to hire the theatre. Towards the end of 1971 there were more of Marowitz's own productions and more by young British writers, some of whom were later to be numbered among Britain's leading playwrights. Two plays in particular caught the public's attention, and their reputation and success helped the theatre into its next stage as a fully subsidised company: Picasso's *The Four Little Girls* and *Sam,*

Sam by Trevor Griffiths, presented on 15 December 1971 and 9 February 1972 respectively. Between these two dates Marowitz decided to go ahead with his plan to audition actors to form a repertory company, and for two days he had over a hundred actors together participating in improvisation exercises, games, acrobatics and so on until he finally whittled down the numbers to ten actors whom he wanted for his revival of *Hamlet* and who were to stay as a permanent company at the Open Space. They then went on to the Edinburgh Festival at the Traverse Theatre with *Hamlet* and *Ham-Omlet*, a lunchtime show consisting of improvisation exercises which were part of the main production's rehearsal process. After that they toured in Holland for several weeks. When they returned to England those who wished to stay on, and were needed, rehearsed for *An Othello*.

All this was arranged before the end of the financial year (4 April 1972) while Thelma Holt was still waiting for news from the Arts Council as to whether they would increase the grant from £5,000 to £19,500, which would cover the cost of employing a permanent company of ten whom Equity insisted should be paid the minimum rates, then £18 a week. This state of affairs was reported in the *Evening Standard* (4 April 1972), and two weeks later the same journalist announced that the Arts Council was willing to give the theatre a £12,000 annual grant, with another £1,000 as guarantees against loss. (The official figures in the Arts Council Annual Report differ slightly from those quoted in the press.) Although this was not as much as they had asked for, it meant that work could proceed along the lines outlined by Marowitz in his first public statement of the theatre's objectives.

Ironically, though, the permanent company, which was ostensibly Marowitz's chief aim and argument for subsidy, never had more than a nominal existence. A core of actors would stay with him for a short time, but he could not afford to guarantee their salaries on a long-term basis. Nikolas Simmonds, who played many leads for Marowitz's productions, claimed that although Marowitz always publicly affirmed his intention of forming a company, he used it rather as a weapon with which to gain financial support than as a real objective in practical terms.[6] Whether or not this is true, Marowitz has always maintained that the Arts Council never really understood what he and Holt were trying to achieve at the Open Space.

Although the idea of a permanent company was firmly conceived intellectually, and the best of Marowitz's work was accomplished with actors he knew well and used many times such as Timothy West and David Schofield, his own personality sometimes militated against long-term group work. His work with actors is theoretically conceived and driven, relying on their ability and intelligence to interpret his demands as a director.[7] Actors joined and left the group depending on how they responded to the Marowitz treatment and he to them. Although he offered a year's contract to some of the first 'company' members in 1972, this was not repeated because the money was not there, though he again worked with a core of actors in 1975.

The aims of the theatre were still ostensibly the same as late as 1977, when it was proposed at a meeting of the Council of the Company, held on 23 September 1977, that a new permanent company should be formed in the fiscal year 1978-79. The same difficulties beset the company then as previously, and the company announced a policy of temporarily bringing in productions as the only viable financial course.

NOTES

1   Leaflet in Cuttings Book 1, OS archives.
2   *Open Space Plays*, pp.10–11.
3   Charles Marowitz and Simon Trussler, eds., *Theatre at Work* (London, 1967), p.154.
4   The exchange of letters is to be found in OS 1/12.
5   Some of the exercises used for the production of *A Macbeth* are included in Charles Marowitz, *The Marowitz Shakespeare* (London, 1978), pp.70–79.
6   Nikolas Simmonds in interview with the author, 19 March 1982.
7   Charles Marowitz in interview with the author, 2 June 2004.

[3]

New Forms: Adaptations and Collages

Marowitz's main interest lay in working on plays which he himself had written or adapted. It was with these works that his talent as director was most evident. He assimilated Shakespeare's imagery into his own theatrical language using highly effective production devices which marked the plays as his. It was not a question of his superimposing a style on a piece of work which could not easily assimilate it (his production of *The Tooth of Crime* (see pp.64–70) showed how his own style could obliterate that of another playwright) but of its becoming an integral part of his conception. He has always maintained a belief in the director's duty to interpret a play as he understands it. In his words, 'there is only reinterpretation not misinterpretation'.[1]

The plays referred to as his Shakespeare 'cut-ups' or 'collages' which were presented at the Open Space are: *A Macbeth, Hamlet, An Othello, The Shrew, Measure for Measure* and *Variations on the Merchant of Venice*. His method of recreating the works was different in each case, but his reasons for adapting them remained the same: they were not reworked in order to provide a new slant upon something already well-known, but to confront head-on 'the intellectual substructure of the plays, an attempt to test or challenge, revoke or destroy the intellectual foundation which makes a classic the formidable thing it has become'.[2] What he seems to have meant by 'confronting the substructure' is that he took issue with Shakespeare's presentation of theme and character and altered it to suit his own interpretation or needs. He objected to the reverence with which he believed the plays had always been treated, and wished to extract something new and pertinent from the old form. Of *A Macbeth*, which was the first of his collages to be presented at the Open Space, he said: 'the different vantage-point of a collage (i.e. an inside view of external developments) can alter the entire resonance of a theatrical experience',[3] and this could well have been said of all of them.

The production of *A Macbeth* was made possible by the Wiesbaden Festival management, which offered Marowitz's company almost £2,500 to take it to the Festival for 14 and 15 May (*Guardian*, 14 March 1969). A cast of eleven took part in *A Macbeth*, the largest used so far in one of Marowitz's own productions. Set design and construction were kept at a lower cost than for productions such as *Fortune and Men's Eyes* and Paul Ableman's *Blue Comedy*, where the theatre itself had been transformed to enhance the naturalistic effect of the stage sets.[4] This production was set in no definite period or place, and the stage was stark and sombre. The unadorned auditorium with its uncomfortable seats merged easily into the acting area and did not disturb the atmosphere created by the actors.

The Marowitz adaptation of Shakespeare's play stressed the occult by cutting and redistributing the dialogue amongst a much smaller number of characters than there are in the original. Marowitz also interpolated scenes of black-magic ritual which adumbrated or interpreted the action. In this way he limited and clarified certain aspects of the play that have always been difficult to present in practical terms. The idea that the play is dominated by the supernatural is not a new one to Shakespearean scholars: for instance, Wilson Knight said of the play that the evil in it comes from 'the abysmal deeps of a spirit-world untuned to human reality', and when describing Lady Macbeth he called her 'an embodiment ... of evil'.[5] Marowitz took and shaped these ideas from the original, giving them concrete form upon the stage. Thus, Lady Macbeth became the head of a coven, and the action of the play was dominated by the all-powerful presence of the devil's servants. The platform stage itself was almost triangular in shape and echoed the shape of the gibbet which appeared with the effigies of certain characters during ritual scenes with the witches. The floorboards were bare and painted black with drawbridge-like structures for entrances and exits at the back of the stage. Very little was used in the way of stage furniture, but all of it was black. In a letter to Herr Antoine (15 April 1969, OS 2/15) at the Hessisches Staatstheater in Wiesbaden, in which arrangements were discussed for the company's visit to the Festival, Marowitz stressed the need for only one indispensable prop, a black, outsize throne. The rest he felt could be improvised without difficulty.

During the blackout, after the house lights had dimmed, the incomplete effigy of Macbeth was set and as the lights came up Thelma Holt, playing Lady Macbeth, was seen standing with her back to the audience in front of the effigy.[6] The three witches entered and added pieces to it until one of them added a crown and the resemblance to Macbeth became clear. Then Lady Macbeth, intoning words used by the first witch in the original, obliterated the wax eyes of the effigy with a poker handed to her by one of the witches.[7] The poker smoked, the eyes melted, and blood gushed from them. It must be noted that for at least three critics in the audience it was not clear that the effigy was intended to be Macbeth, and the implied commentary upon their relationship was lost.

After a ten-second fade the lights were rapidly brought full up on the next scene, with Duncan, Banquo, Malcolm and Macduff. It was played in bright light in order to underline the contrast between the two worlds, the one as yet untouched by black powers, the other menacing, dark and governed by Satan. The brightly lit passages became less frequent as the play progressed. The entrance of Lady Macbeth immediately after the king's entrance was intended to shock the audience into the realisation that it was she who had been seen in the opening tableau with the witches. Thus her complicity with them was made visually clear from the start, though her authority over them was not confirmed in words until she angrily accosted them after the scene of Lady Macduff's murder (p.120).[8]

The play proceeded with a series of visual shocks. As the king and others were making their exits from this scene, Macbeth appeared and stabbed Duncan, Lady Macbeth stabbed Banquo, the lights dimmed and the witches carried away the corpses. After a blackout the lights came up dimly and

Macbeth, with an actor on either side of him representing two different aspects of his personality, rushed towards the audience breathlessly babbling the speech, 'If it were done when 'tis done, then 'twere well/ It were done quickly'. The two other personifications of Macbeth silently mouthed the words with him. Nikolas Simmonds, who played Macbeth himself, directly confronted the audience from the front of the stage with his fear of cold-blooded murder.9 The words of the soliloquy tumbled from him like thoughts flashing across his brain. As the soliloquy came to an end, the lighting changed abruptly and his final sentence, 'He's here in double trust', was spoken directly to his wife in full light. In this scene his fear of not being strong enough for the deed and his abject fear of her were manifested as he grovelled before her words:

> Wouldst thou have that
> Which thou esteemst the ornament of life,
> And live a coward in thine own esteem? (p.83)

In the following scene the audience was reassured to see the obedient subject and reasonable Macbeth assert himself before Duncan. Rejecting Lady Macbeth's taunts for this short scene, Simmonds played a man resolved to remain a loyal kinsman. An abrupt change again took place and a Macbeth unable to control his guilty relish at the thought of being Thane of Cawdor and 'king hereafter' emerged. This was followed by a scene of unrelenting pressure applied by Lady Macbeth which brought Macbeth close to hysteria as he burst out with 'Prithee peace'.

Benedict Nightingale, writing for the *New Statesman* (30 May 1969), missed the point when he complained that the character of Macbeth did not develop. What Marowitz seems to have attempted in this production was not a linear development of his protagonist's character but a series of tableaux showing the disparate and conflicting personality traits that made up the man Macbeth. *Plays and Players* (July 1969) was critical in much the same way, though this critic made the more valid point that 'he [Macbeth] is licked from the start by the witches (malevolent spectators in Shakespeare, malignant adversaries in Marowitz) so his mental processes cease to be interesting.' However, for some critics, attention was kept well enough by the stage effects. 'Patterns of light and sound are striking, shifting identities are stimulating' (*Sunday Times*, 25 May 1969), and 'in his [Macbeth's] dislocated rhythms, his discrepant images and juxtapositions, the colour and line of Shakespeare's text are not simply preserved but shine with a fresh brilliance, casting new and disconcerting, often ravishing reflections' (*Spectator*, 21 June 1969).

Indeed, shock tactics were an essential part of Marowitz's strategy, not simply the shock of violent, visual images in the ritual murder scenes when blood was spilled, nor the shock of hearing well-known lines delivered by characters other than those expected, but the shock offered by the setting up of a character's personality in one scene, only for it to seem to be destroyed in the next. The use of three Macbeths highlighted the different aspects of Macbeth's character ('the Timorous, the Ambitious, the Nefarious'), giving a tangible image to an abstract idea.[10] Robert Cushman thought 'there must be subtler ways of representing a man at war with himself' (*Plays and Players*, July 1969), but in making this criticism did not take into consideration the Marowitz emphasis on the mystic number three, 'the peculiar knot of trinities that winds its way through the play',[11] to which he gave a solid theatrical presence by echoing the groups of three in the triangular form of the stage, the gibbet, and the inevitable triangle formed by having three Macbeths on stage at the same time. Henry Raynor for *The Times* (21 May 1969) complained that they diminished the role of Lady Macbeth by taking her words (he seems not to have noticed that her role here was quite different from the one Shakespeare wrote) and that the two other Macbeths 'dwindle into the necessary murderers, servants and attendants'. It seems unfair to accuse Marowitz, however indirectly, of using any character simply because it was necessary that someone should perform the actions. The two Macbeths took these parts in order to stress the way in which Macbeth committed all the murders himself even though he persuaded others to strike the actual blows.

Within the triangular setting of the play was the black-magic circle which, throughout, suggested the voodoo rites which were central to the play. Whenever the witches appeared they formed a circle at once threatening and ritual-istic. It was not only Duncan, Banquo and Lady Macduff who were enclosed and threatened by the circle, but Macbeth and his lady too. The closing image of the play was of Macbeth, small, powerless and frightened, sitting on his immense throne surrounded by 'a fresco of heads – all characters of the play' (p.124) from whom issued a low sound throughout the ensuing scene, described by Hilary Spurling as 'a beautiful evocation of figments of Macbeth's imagination' (*Spectator* 21 June 1969). During a blackout the cast took up their positions at the perimeter of the stage, facing the audience. 'Wheeling menacingly close', they each turned to Macbeth, stage centre, to deliver their lines and gradually moved closer in to him, until they were finally on him, beating him to death with their broomsticks. The *Observer* (16 June 1969) called it a 'memo-rable' visual effect. As Macbeth was finally killed, Lady Mac-beth struck off the head of the Macbeth effigy, thus breaking the circle formed by the play's structure which began with the same image. At the same time the 'tight circle' (*A Macbeth*, p.131) of actors around Macbeth opened, to reinforce the idea of a fate completed and a return to normality as the witches took off their stocking masks and walked towards the audience in a blaze of bright light.

Whether critics liked the play or not, and there were more who did not than did, it seems to have been a production which impressed at moments with its disturbing and original images. The murder of Duncan was one which drew comment from Hilary Spurling. The scene is described in detail in the published text, but it is clear only from an eyewitness account that the mime is played three times in an unbroken circle. Almost as if it were in slow motion the silent action was finally shattered by a piercing scream from Duncan as Lady Macbeth pushed the daggers into Macbeth's hands, forcing him to stab the king many times. Even Nicholas de Jongh (*Guardian*, 21 April 1969), who did not like the play at all, had to admit to being impressed by this scene. He also mentioned Lady Mac-beth's funeral scene which, according to the critic for the *Aus-tralian* (5 July 1969), was the most powerful image of the play.

Thelma Holt as Lady Macbeth, and, left to right, Louise Breslin, Lesley Ward and Jenifer Armitage as witches, in *A Macbeth* by Charles Marowitz

The scene which was generally criticised was that of the sleepwalking, which Thelma Holt played nude underneath a transparent nightdress. Most critics mentioned it in passing, and most of them wrote dismissively of it as a gimmick – Lady Macbeth in a see-through nightie.[12] None of them discussed it seriously or made any attempt to understand why Marowitz had chosen to have the scene played like this, except the critic for *What's On* (30 May 1969), who came to the heart of the matter, albeit in a facetious manner:

> The view that Lady Macbeth is not, properly, a woman at all, but a man in woman's clothing, can always foment a lively argument among Shakespearean scholars of the more perverse order. Thelma Holt ... makes her own position in this controversy beguilingly explicit by wearing naught but a diaphanous nightie in the sleep-walking bit.

In Marowitz's production Lady Macbeth was seen for most of the time as a demon, devoid of feminine characteristics, but the point had to be made that although she served the devil she was a woman, and the startling image of her naked body in the sleepwalking scene made the point neatly and clearly.

The same critic who complained about the three Macbeths (*The Times*, 21 May 1969) called the play an 'amusing literary game' which meant 'nothing to those who do not know Shakespeare's text'. At a lecture given by Marowitz on 3 December 1981 to students of the then Polytechnic of North London, his reply to this comment was that those who knew Shakespeare's *Macbeth* thought that those who did not must have been confused, whereas those members of the audience he had spoken to who had no prior knowledge of the play were not confused at all. Certainly, if Henry Raynor had been less aware of the original and more open to the Marowitz interpretation, he might have found it a more worthwhile evening.

Box-office receipts were good for this production, and despite high production costs the company lost less than £1,000 on the project.[13] Clearly Marowitz had been right in thinking that this sort of experimental work would be in demand, whatever the critics had to say about it, so he followed it a month later with a revival of his *Hamlet*.[14] In this

collage Marowitz used the same method of textual preparation as he had for *A Macbeth*. The orginal play had been
reduced to an hour and a half's playing time and lines of dialogue had been redistributed amongst a very diminished cast
of characters. Again his aim was similar to those Expressionist
playwrights who wished to externalise an internal state of
mind, and again his intention was of 'transmitting experience
from the play through the eyes of the central protagonist'.[15]

The staging was as bright for this production as it had been
black for *A Macbeth*. The stage was white and gleaming like a
circus ring; a white, rectangular proscenium arch had been
constructed at the back which left a deep fore-stage thrusting
out into the audience. Across the back of the stage and on
either side behind the arch ran a long white rostrum, used
sometimes to suggest a specific location or simply as another
acting level when certain characters were to dominate others.
It was used as a seat for the members of the Danish court
behind the bench which was brought on for Hamlet's trial
scene, and as a schoolroom for Hamlet and Ophelia when
they were taught by Gertrude how to conduct themselves
properly in society (Laertes' lesson to Ophelia in Shakespeare's play); and it was used by Claudius and the Ghost
when they stood back to back as if in a picture frame, while
Hamlet looked up at them from the stage below.

The bare, black side walls of the theatre and the lamps
which hung from the ceiling, the whitened heating pipes and
the ventilation holes in the white flats at the back of the stage
were not concealed, in fact their presence was emphasised by
the stark whiteness of the acting area. Marowitz's Hamlet is an
actor who is unable to concentrate on his role, whose performance is therefore inadequate, and the audience were
constantly reminded of this by the visible traces of the theatre
itself. The circus-like arena and the appearance of the characters, who wore circus costumes and make-up, was borne out
in many of the scenes which used the rhythms of vaudeville
joke routines and the stylised buffoonery of the Clown. All
this, Marowitz claimed, was to be found in the original play,
and certainly the elements he suggests in his introduction to
the printed text are valid.[16] He chose to emphasise them by

setting his play in the ring with all the tawdry glitter associated with circus acts – a visual symbol with the complexity and resonance of a Shakespearean pun.

Only Fortinbras wore natural looking make-up. Hamlet's face was white with a red teardrop painted on his cheek; Ophelia was rouged like a puppet-doll with round red blobs on her cheeks and huge spidery eyelashes painted on the skin all around her eyes; Gertrude's eyes were elongated with silver eyeshadow, sparkling with sequins; Claudius had a green half-mask painted on to his face which covered it from the forehead to the bridge of the nose; the Ghost had a greyish tinged face with heavy black lines around the eyes; the Clown wore a traditional sad circus clown's make-up, and when doubling as Polonius he placed a grey-gloved hand on his chin to denote a beard; Rosencrantz and Guildenstern had half white, half black faces, and these colours were reflected in their costumes (black-and-white sweaters and scarves), and they were linked together with a rope which stressed at once their function as puppets manipulated by Hamlet (not Claudius) and their lack of individuality. Thus each character was defined by his mask and was inseparable from it. Only Fortinbras, the man of action and Hamlet's alter ego, was not masked, and his costume was the only one that might have been seen in a traditional production of *Hamlet*. Hamlet himself wore a sloppy black sweater underneath which could be seen a red t-shirt with a white neckband. His dark corduroy trousers had holes in them and his hair was thick and unkempt. The contrast in character between him and Fortinbras was made immediate through the choice of costume: the one dishevelled ('literally, a mess', as Marowitz described him on page 14 of his introduction to the play) the other neat with clipped hair and gleaming breastplate over his soldier's uniform. The authority figures in the play, Claudius, the Ghost and Fortinbras, were all dressed conventionally but with no attempt at creating a single period. Claudius and the Ghost were both in pinstriped suits, though Claudius was distinguished with a purple shoulder sash which matched Gertrude's.

The characters of the court, all figments of Hamlet's imagination, merged with each other to suggest that they had become, for him, stereotypes and not individuals. So Ophelia, being passionately embraced by Claudius, was replaced by Gertrude as the two figures revolved slowly, clasped together. The two women became one woman and all women in Hamlet's diseased imagination. He watched the action, seated with the Clown down stage, and a strobe picked out the couple as if they were in a clip from an old film. Most of the play was lit simply in bright white light which got brighter as the final scene focused on Hamlet standing in the middle of the circle of prostrate figures. Quick transitions between characters and scenes, which were an essential part of the hallucinatory quality of the action as a whole, were not always accomplished with lighting tricks, but were effected by unexpected or abrupt changes. At one moment Hamlet was being rocked by the mother Gertrude; the next he had the whore Gertrude pushed on to the ground in a kind of rape scene which ended with the appearance of Claudius, to whom Hamlet immediately turned his attention, belittling and threatening him by forcing him backwards across the stage as he held him at arm's length and pushed with his finger against the tip of Claudius's nose. As the watching court cried out for judgment, a white bench was whisked on in front of them so that a trial scene was instantly established.

The film sequence was a lengthy one, and it continued with Gertrude and the Ghost enacting the roles of Player King and Queen. It ended when Gertrude joined Claudius for the murder and together they stepped out of the old film and moved swiftly and menacingly towards Hamlet, reciting between them, 'Thoughts black, hands apt…'. Hamlet, drawn towards them as if hypnotised, was forced to help perform the murder. His terror, which registered on his mobile face beneath the white mask, was transferred to the audience by the giant shadows of Gertrude and Claudius thrown up on the white cyclorama. Briefly they dominated the stage, as Hamlet's obsession and fears were given visual and apparently tangible form.

Hamlet's lack of emotional maturity was dramatised in scenes of childish games with Rosencrantz and Guildenstern and Ophelia, and his mediocrity as an actor was stressed by

Antony Haygarth as Hamlet, Richard Mayes as Claudius, David Schofield as Fortinbras, in the version of Marowitz's *Hamlet* at the Globe Bankside

the Clown, who directed and prompted him for many of his scenes. Aware always of his audience, and usually pitted against a character who did not share his weakness, he failed each time to convince himself of his ability to act. Hamlet had already been seen as a spectator at a film who was drawn unwillingly into the action and as a manipulator of others, notably Rosencrantz and Guildenstern, whom he held on a rope. Then he himself was wound up by the Clown who gradually managed to elicit from him the semblance of a passion, so that as he cried 'Now might I do it pat', the central white flat at the back of the stage dropped to reveal the members of the court seated in a kind of Punch and Judy booth or ornate theatre box, cheering Hamlet as if he were the hero of a melodrama. Their exaggerated response to his 'And now I'll do it' immediately deflated the hero and, his confidence in tatters, he could do no more than mutter 'And so he goes to Heaven/ And so am I revenged'. The courtiers pushed their way out of the box and, sweeping Hamlet aside, rushed to congratulate Claudius. Each time Hamlet, as principal actor, failed to convince, this was monitored by his on-stage audience, who either booed or mocked him. At the end of his trial, having by his ravings emptied the stage of everyone except Fortinbras and having reiterated yet again his intention of avenging his father, Hamlet's confident façade crumbled again as Fortinbras merely sneered at him.

The chaos of nightmare was evoked by the recurring motif of characters falling down, ostensibly dead, though they had not been struck. Meeting for the first time, Hamlet and Laertes engaged in a battle of words (pp.62–3). Although Laertes was holding a sword, he made no move to kill Hamlet, yet Hamlet collapsed and Laertes stepped over him as if he were not there and continued his scene with Claudius. Later Hamlet carried out a ritual killing of Claudius at prayer, rhythmically striking three times, but it was Polonius who dropped. The final violent image of the play showed Hamlet wildly stabbing all the members of the court, touching no one, yet felling them all. But their deaths were as temporary as their wounds were illusory, and the corpses lay there laughing maniacally at Hamlet in his final humiliation.

One of the things Marowitz claimed his collage work accomplished was to find a 'way of transmitting speed in the theatre'. If the play *Hamlet* was to reflect our lives today, he argued, then it must in some way suggest the 'relentless, insatiable motor-power that makes the world move as quickly as it does'. The incessant changing of images, location and personality kept the tension high and demanded intense concentration from the audience. The very opening image with all the characters on stage gabbling different fragments of speeches epitomised the speed at which the play moved and the confusion inherent in it. The critics loved or loved to hate the production, and the show was sold out.[17]

In 1970 *A Macbeth* had yet another revival when it played at the Premio Roma Festival, then went on a four-week tour of Italy and ended in Paris. After this it then played at the Open Space again. It was not until 1972 when the permanent company was formed that Marowitz created a new collage, which followed another differently staged revival of *Hamlet*. The new collage was *An Othello*, which was devised from the original in a different way from the other two. There was a radical

Judy Geeson as Desdemona and Rudolph Walker as Othello in *An Othello* by
Charles Marowitz

departure from Shakespeare's text, with interpolations by
Marowitz written in Black Panther slang. The roles of both
Iago and Othello were played by black actors, and the idea
behind the work was to present the political theme of the
black revolution in America as represented by Malcolm X. As
Marowitz was at pains to point out in an interview with Peter
Ansorge in *Plays and Players* (October 1972), the play *Othello*
does not contain the theme that Marowitz was to impose on
his version of the story. He was, he said, attempting 'to put the
black power cliché into a more interesting, less clichéd context'. The collage was commissioned by the Wiesbaden Festival and Marowitz was under a great deal of pressure to finish
the script, which he completed in two weeks. It was, he felt,
unsatisfactory because he had not had enough time to work
on it, though its success with the public equalled that of his
other two collages.[18]

His work on *The Taming of the Shrew* suffered in the same
way. *The Shrew* was created hurriedly to replace a cancelled
project at the last minute (*The Marowitz Shakespeare*, p.16), and
as usual it was Thelma Holt who spurred him on to do it. It
was premiered abroad at the Hot Theatre in the Hague in

October 1973 (not 1974 as stated in *The Marowitz Shakespeare*), and opened on 1 November 1973 at the Open Space. Although Marowitz himself was critical of the work, it proved very popular with audiences; it toured abroad and had a revival at the Open Space in 1975. Holt played Kate in all performances, though five different actors played Petruchio.[19] Nikolas Simmonds played the first, and reviews of the 1975 revival referred to the original casting, 'The mesmerised disgust which she [Holt] showed for her first and best Petruchio, Nikolas Simmonds, is not shown here. But Malcolm Tierney's Petruchio is an immense improvement on the last' (*Guardian*, 10 December 1975).

Marowitz's play removes all the comedy from the original and shows a Kate subjected to the tyranny of man. He wanted her portrayed as a middle-aged spinster, powerless against Petruchio, and her final speech (which is the same as the one Shakespeare gave her) was delivered by Holt as a 'masterpiece of dramatic irony' (*Guardian*, 2 November 1973), leaving the audience with the impression of a woman unable to break her chains yet undiminished by her ordeal. Marowitz had been inspired by an interview he had seen on television with a woman doctor, then aged about sixty, who had spent many years in a Soviet prison in solitary confinement and whose spirit was unbroken by the experience.[20] The torture of Kate had its source in the atrocities of Northern Ireland, and the technique Marowitz used was to identify 'marriage with a police state dungeon' from which he created a 'black Artaudian fable' (*The Times*, 3 November 1973). All Marowitz's work at this time was influenced by Artaud's 'total theatre' that used sound, light, gesture and visual image, rather than the spoken word, to disturb the subconscious of both actor and audience. The stage for *The Shrew* was bare and grey with only a few essential props. Petruchio's tribunal chair, which dominated the final scene (its shape was repeated in the bridal head-dress Thelma Holt wore), was typical of the effective stage imagery in all the collages. The chair itself stood about eight feet high and Petruchio conducted the trial with Kate standing below him (Marowitz originally had her standing on a podium, but Holt felt the full effect of his tyranny could only be obtained if she was lower than him) looking wasted and white but unbeaten. Glaring white light accentuated her pallor (Holt wore no make-up for this scene – she had just time enough to wipe off what she had had on for the previous scene before she made her final appearance) and the texture of Robin Don's set for Petruchio's dwelling, which was grey, slimy and subterranean, formed a striking contrast to the opulent texture of the set used for the scenes in Katherine's home.

The final image was of Kate standing beneath Petruchio wearing heavy chains – the embodiment of the slavery into which she had been sold when she married him. She was dressed in her bridal robes to the tolling of a funeral bell (according to Holt, the idea was taken from the Russian film of *Hamlet*). As the critic for *The Times* (24 December 1975) said, 'the piece still exhibits Marowitz's best and worst qualities side by side'. The weak link lay with the modern interpolations, with which Marowitz was never happy, though he changed them every time – his strength with the 'awesome stage pictures' he knew so well how to create.

Nikolas Simmonds and David Schofield (he had played the eponymous protagonist in the 1973 production of *Woyzeck*) returned to join the permanent company which would open the new 1975 season with the last of Marowitz's collages to be presented at the Tottenham Court Road premises, *Measure For Measure*. It was inspired by an unpleasant personal experience Marowitz had had of English justice, and he used Shakespeare's play to show that 'the trappings of the law are not synonymous with the functions of justice' (*Guardian*, 28 May 1975). Again he deleted all the comedy and sub-plot, this time also changing the main plot so that Isabella (Ciaran Madden) is seduced by Angelo (Nikolas Simmonds), despite which her brother Claudio (Brian Gwaspari) is executed. Usual characterisations are given a different twist. In an article he wrote for *Plays and Players* (June 1975), Marowitz drew up an ideal cast list for his play which might 'suggest some of the nuances it should contain: Angelo – Richard Nixon; Isabella – Mary Whitehouse; Escalus – Harold Wilson; Bishop – Al Capone; Provost – Pat O'Brien; Lucio – Lenny Bruce; Claudio – Errol Flynn; The Duke – Malcolm Muggeridge. Directed by the CIA

Ciaran Madden as Isabella sees the head of Claudio in *Measure for Measure* by
Charles Marowitz

in collaboration with The Festival of Light'.

The play does not diverge drastically from the original
until Isabella decides to give herself to Angelo, and it is at this
point that the staging (designed with Robin Don) took on a
greater emblematic significance. Already the audience were
seated like a jury at a tribunal. On stage, a huge, vertical scroll
hung at an angle to the audience. On it was written the Duke's
decree against fornication. When lit from the front it looked
solid, and it was framed with panels of high-gloss black per-
spex which reflected the action, distorting and multiplying it.
It rolled up to reveal a gauze screen behind which Angelo was
seen undressing Isabella in silhouette. The love-making was
accompanied by a requiem mass. Immediately afterwards, as
Isabella came down stage from behind the gauze, she flicked
away the cloth from an ornament which was revealed to be
Claudio's head. Lighting was used in this production to give a
cinematic effect and scenes dissolved or merged with each
other. As Isabella screamed on discovering the head of her
brother, so there was a simultaneous black-out over her, and a

'lights up' on the Bishop who was standing down stage. The blending of tableaux, or the abrupt switching from one image to another, was used extensively, and more nightmare/dream sequences were added here than in the previous collages. To enhance this effect and to suggest Isabella's inner turmoil, an echo chamber and recorded sounds were used. Although the play deals with the essentially political theme of corruption in high places, the emphasis as always was on the individual's struggle against corruption, authority and moral weakness.

Variations on the Merchant of Venice and *An Othello* are the most overtly political of all of Marowitz's Shakespeare collages. Both plays superimposed a modern situation on the original. In *Variations* it was the blowing up of the King David Hotel in Jerusalem in 1946. The play was framed with a 'voice-over' reading the news, and slides of the 1946 bombing were projected on to a screen. In this case it was the only modern text added to the play, though the rest of the dialogue was taken from both Shakespeare's play and Marlowe's *Jew of Malta*. Thelma Holt and David Schofield were the only two regular Open Space actors to appear in this production, which opened the new premises in Euston Road. It had a good press and proved a promising start to the new season.

Marowitz adapted four other works which were not Shakespeare's: Oscar Wilde's *The Critic as Artist* and Büchner's *Woyzeck*, which were both presented at the Tottenham Court Road Theatre in 1971 and 1973 respectively; *The Father*, by Strindberg, and *Hedda* from Ibsen's *Hedda Gabler* in 1979 and 1980 at the Euston Road premises and the Round House respectively. From Wilde's essay he cut out a good deal of the purple prose and added a dramatic situation – a first meeting and seduction between Wilde and Lord Alfred Douglas. Only Wilde's dialogue was used, though some epigrams found their way into the text from his other works. The stage was transformed into a sumptuous Victorian sitting room (designed by Philip Reavey and John Napier) and green carnations were handed to the audience as they entered. In order to separate the set from the rather dingy cellar-like surroundings of the Open Space, gauze curtains boxed it in. When the stage was lit, the gauze became transparent, giving a dreamlike quality to the proceedings which put the audience at one remove from the situation. Marowitz had hoped to make the public feel as though they were watching something they ought not to have been, and according to the critics he achieved this effect magnificently. Timothy West played the part of Wilde to the almost unanimous acclaim of the critics.[21] This was not a production in the familiar Marowitz style (the acting and setting were naturalistic), though the green carnations were reminiscent of his 'environmental' technique.

The figures available for this production show that in terms of public response the show was a success and that, on average, houses must have been over half full at each performance; it ran for five and a half weeks (OS 13/31).

The other three adaptations marked a return to Marowitz's visual treatment, where the themes were communicated by a series of stage images which captured the essence of the play, either underlining it or presenting the audience with new insights. The episodic and fragmented structure of the original *Woyzeck* made for exactly the kind of production that Marowitz liked to create. Büchner's text is unfinished (whether by accident or design), and successive editors have juggled with the scenes and arrived at different conclusions about their sequence. Marowitz wrote his final nightmare trial scene with the amplified voices of the characters giving their testimonies whilst the solitary figure of Woyzeck (played by David Schofield) stood on stage, his head caught in two cross lights to emphasise his isolation and spiritual bewilderment. Michael Patterson, who wrote the introduction to the Eyre Methuen edition of the original text, believes it possible that Büchner had intended to write a final trial scene, so Marowitz was for once using an accepted idea for ending the play, though the way it was done was his own.[22]

From the description in the Methuen edition of the play, of other productions of *Woyzeck* (p.xvi), it would seem that Marowitz had taken a lead from Reinhardt's staging in 1921 and allowed lighting to replace scenery and the social message of the play to be subordinated to the spiritual dimension. Marowitz used a bare stage with back and side flats covered with khaki-coloured hessian, so the stage resembled the inside of an empty box. Lighting was used to suggest the pool into which Woyzeck walked at the end (bright white light contrasted with the black surroundings), and although there was plenty of bright colour in the costumes, the final impression was of a monochrome production. Robin Don's first suggestion for the set had involved a series of concentric steel hoops, suspended from the ceiling, which could be raised or lowered as required.[23] They were to have dropped finally like the ripples of a pool on to the stage. Marowitz, however, whether for economic, practical or aesthetic reasons, decided not to exploit this idea and ultimately resisted all Don's attempts to provide a set.

The critics were almost unanimous in their praise of Marowitz's conception of the play and liked the way he had juxtaposed different acting styles. These changed abruptly from the naturalistic to highly stylised or mimed movements, such as running on the spot or round in circles. Sometimes this marked time whilst action took place on another part of the stage; at one point the pace became more frenzied as Woyzeck intoned his autobiographical monologue to the rhythm of the Drum Major's love-making to Marie; and at other points it denoted the tension building in his mind and a vain desire to escape from it.[24] The stage was bare save for a few essential props such as stools or chairs. Personal props often had a symbolic function, giving a surreal quality to the production. In Scene IV Woyzeck took a model of his own head out of a box while the Drum Major (Malcolm Storry) spoke words as if they came from the head. Woyzeck's dagger in Scene XIV was large enough for him to be stretched out on it (like Christ on the cross) and carried out. The military characters were dressed in outsize uniforms which increased their own and diminished Woyzeck's stature and accentuated his helplessness. Harold Hobson was one of the few critics to object:

> Woyzeck was a very good play a century and a half ago, but today it has become dull because its central thesis has been repeated too often ... But even a cliché can seem fresh if it is freshly put. Mr. Marowitz does not put it freshly. (*Sunday Times*, 25 Feb 1973)

David Schofield as the protagonist in *Woyzeck*

It is amusing to note that his one item of praise concerned the symbolic quality of a particular stage effect which was unintentional. After the murder, blood appeared on both Woyzeck's clothing and the Drum Major's, thus highlighting society's implication in the act. According to John Burgess in interview, this had happened simply because the violence of the scene and the quantities of stage blood which were used meant that it was impossible to control the spurting liquid. There was no time to clean up thoroughly before subsequent scenes and the fact that the Drum Major had some on him was mere chance.

The violence beneath the superficial noise and gaiety (e.g. during the fairground scenes) kept the play taut and exciting. The tension did not slacken and no time was lost in scene changes because there was very little to change. Woyzeck played the parts of the horse and the monkey at the fair; the transformation of Marie from the Drum Major's woman to the poor girl who was Woyzeck's mistress was effected by simply casting off a luxurious cape to reveal the poverty beneath; different locations were suggested through the action and acting rather than the set.

Many of the techniques had been seen before: the woman degraded by a man in a scene of simulated buggery (*The Shrew*), the entry into the mind of an individual by surrounding him with other actors who menacingly stared at him, the solitary light which picked out his head, the disembodied voice-over and so on. Later, audiences became used to them but at this stage in the Open Space's lifespan they were still fresh enough to make the impact that *The Father* and *Hedda* failed to produce.

Artaud at Rodez, Marowitz's second original play to be presented at the Open Space (the first was *Sherlock's Last Case*),[25] was a culmination of the Artaudian techniques that he had developed in his earlier collage work. It was shown in repertoire with *The Shrew*, the most Artaudian of all his previous productions, and this pairing could be seen as another of the high spots in the history of the Open Space Theatre.

The play uses information researched by Marowitz when he interviewed Dr Ferdière (the man who was responsible for Artaud's treatment at Rodez) and friends of Artaud (Roger

Blin and Arthur Adamov) in 1966.[26] It shows a man obsessed with a personal vision of what art in the theatre ought to be and driven to madness by his inability to achieve it. This was dramatised through the confrontation between Dr Ferdière and Artaud himself. Ferdière was the personification of conformist values which stifle the artistic temperament, as personified by Artaud. The subject matter (Artaud's life) was particularly well suited to the form that Marowitz gave it, as his behaviour in life imitated his theories on art. It is ironic that Artaud despised the written word whilst Marowitz's collation of material formed a very well-written play. Critics complained that certain invented scenes, such as the kidnapping of Artaud by Blin and the beat poet who seemed to have walked out of the Living Theatre, were poor. Certainly the intended comedy was heavy-handed, and Clive Merrison, who played Artaud, claimed that this was always a weakness in the production,[27] but on the whole the play was much admired.

As with Marowitz's other productions, it was the non-verbal, visual aspect of the show which was most striking. In his Shakespeare collage work he had a text which he commented upon, illustrated, or subverted with the on-stage action or effects. With *The Shrew* he pared down the original to its basic story and provided it with salient images (a woman literally chained in marriage to a man, the man and woman who destroy each other through marriage, the scream of inner pain); with *Artaud at Rodez* he used violence, ritual, the Tarahumara Indians' chant, and disturbed the audience with his penetrating stage imagery: Artaud banging the walls of his coffin from inside it while his so-called disciples walked away; his muse, erotic and seductive, offering opium for inspiration; the final scene where all members of the company 'slowly appear holding a double mask on a stick. Each face on the double mask depicts a slightly unreal staring face with white staring eyes ... actors holding the staring masks slowly turn them around revealing the reverse-side which contains a wry, cruel smile' (*Artaud at Rodez* p.65).

Michael Billington, writing in the *Guardian* (10 December 1975) of *The Shrew* when it was premiered in Rome, commented:

'seeing this piece in the midst of a foreign audience does remind you how strong are its visual emphases' and the same could be said of *Artaud at Rodez*. Irving Wardle went so far as to say that Artaud's theories had become part of a 'powerful house style' – and at this period this was also true of Marowitz's own work, if not of other works appearing at the Open Space.

Artaud at Rodez did not depend on a clear chronological narrative line; the scenes were harsh, crude and dislocated. The speed with which images followed each other was pre-saged in the opening scene where Artaud was wheeled rapidly round on a hospital trolley. The stage was bare and black, so the impression was of a great deal of central space. While he was wheeled about, two doctors were administering ECT treat-ment. The sense of ritual was achieved through the accompa-niment of Artaud's taped voice chanting like the Tarahumara Indians. Lighting was bright white, and strobes were used to suggest frenzy. Clive Merrison played Artaud at a consistently high pitch, and the critic for *Plays and Players* (February 1976) said of the role that it 'requires a performer who can meet the challenge of the punishing vocal and physical experiments Artaud undertook as an actor. Clive Merrison, in a finely uni-fied peformance, often comes close.' Merrison, describing his rehearsal process in interview, said that he approached it by reading all Artaud's writings, after which he immersed himself in the appropriate acting and vocal imagery. He studied pho-tographs of Artaud and would try to imitate the pose, freeze, and start to act from there. What he created was a memorable physical performance, 'eyeballs seemingly fixed in an attitude of cross-eyed mania, voice garbling [sic] out in strangulated form a torrent of words' (*Guardian*, 17 December 1975). In the same review Marowitz is quoted as stating that his idea was 'to perform a specimen of Artaudian theatrecraft' and only one critic found the claim specious. This was Harold Hobson, who attacked play, performance and Marowitz's integrity (*Sunday Times*, 21 December 1975).[28]

Marowitz must have felt vindicated by most of the other reviews, which spoke highly of his achievement. The reviewer for the *New Statesman* (26 December 1975) remarked that

Clive Merrison as Artaud in *Artaud at Rodez* by Charles Marowitz

'Charles Marowitz's productions often suggest that he's the only man in London who actually understands Artaud; and now he has confirmed it.' Hobson had praised Jérome Savary's Grand Magic Circus for its truly Artaudian qualities to the detriment of Marowitz's production (Savary had opened with *Les Grands Sentiments* at the Round House on the same night). However, Savary's work, like Ken Campbell's and Lindsay Kemp's, only employed certain Artaudian characteristics. All three directors desired to escape from the confines of naturalism, but their theatre was not really disturbing or dangerous. In the production of *Artaud at Rodez* Marowitz had not been able to do group exercises or improvisation; there had not been enough time, as Marowitz was still writing the script when they went into rehearsal. In the production of *Woyzeck* the actors had enjoyed juggling with the scenes themselves and had contributed positively to the final form of the play.[29] In that respect *Artaud at Rodez* cannot be said to have been a group effort.

The major features of Marowitz's collage work and adaptations might be described thus:

An emphasis on speed which necessitated a film-like technique to enable him to switch from one image to another, often dazzling an audience with its unexpectedness and lack of rational explanation. This gave a natural place to the evocation of dream or nightmare, in turn a method of exposing what was happening in the mind of a character.

Shock tactics, both verbal and visual, as an integral part of his means of expression – so, well-known characters in a Shakespearean play would speak the wrong lines (e.g. Hamlet) or those present at the trial scene in *Variations on the Merchant of Venice* were gunned down by Shylock's men for the production's finale.

Simple or bare sets, essential to facilitate quick changes, which were usually effected by the cast themselves.

Lighting as the chief means of suggesting a different realm from the real world (e.g. the red lighting stipulated in *The Father* which was a signal for both actors and audience that a different style was required).

The productions encompassed many different themes but the one which was common to all was that of the struggling individual, bound by the strictures of a conventional society and isolated from the rest of humankind because of a desire to elude them.

NOTES

1   Charles Marowitz in conversation with the author, 2 June 2004.

2   *The Marowitz Shakespeare*, p.24.

3   *The Marowitz Shakespeare*, p.15.

4   The cost of the sets for *Fortune and Men's Eyes* and *Blue Comedy* can be found in OS 13/12.

5   Wilson Knight, *The Wheel of Fire* (London 1961), p.158 and 152.

6   OS archives, Director's Copy and lighting plot, *A Macbeth*.

7   References made to Shakespeare's text are taken from *The Arden Shakespeare* (Chaucer Press, Suffolk, 1972).

8   All page references to the play *A Macbeth* are taken from *The Marowitz Shakespeare*.

9   All interpretations of Simmonds's characterisation are taken from the annotations in his rehearsal script, OS archives.

10   *The Marowitz Shakespeare*, p.15.

11   *The Marowitz Shakespeare*, p.14.

12   *Guardian*, 21 May 1969, *Plays and Players*, July 1969, *Daily Telegraph*, 21 May 1969, *Tribune*, 6 June 1969.

13   Accounts can be found in OS 13/12.

14   First performed in a shorter version for Peter Brook's Theatre of Cruelty, 1963.

15   *The Marowitz Shakespeare*, p.14.

16   Charles Marowitz, *The Marowitz Hamlet*, (London, 1968), pp.11–50. All other references to the text are taken from this edition.

17   A condensed version of this production was filmed at the Open Space for 'Late Night Line-Up', and transmitted on 30 December 1969. It is stored by the BBC at Television Centre.

18   *An Othello* has been fully documented by John Burgess in an article for *Theatre Quarterly*, 2(1972), no.8, pp.68–91 which was later reprinted in *The Act of Being*, pp.163–196.

19   Thelma Holt in interview, 21 February 1984.

20   Thelma Holt in interview with the author, 19 February 1979.

21   Favourable reviews from *Evening Standard*, 27 May 1971, *Financial Times*, 27 May 1971; less favourable or ambiguous reviews, *Guardian*, 27 May 1971, *The Times*, 27 May 1971.

22   Georg Büchner, *Woyzeck* (Eyre Methuen London, 1979), p.xxii.

23   John Burgess in interview with the author, 25 July 1985.

24   Scene ix, p.14; scene xii, p.19, prompt copy OS archive.

25   Marowitz wrote *Sherlock's Last Case* at very short notice to fill an unexpected gap in the theatre's repertoire. He used the nom de plume of Matthew Lang, keeping his identity secret until the play's Broadway opening in 1984. A full account of its genesis is to be found in *Burnt Bridges*, pp.121–126.

26   Charles Marowitz, *Artaud at Rodez* (London, 1977).

27   Clive Merrison in interview with the author, 10 April 1985.

28   Marowitz's full reply can be found in OS 10/7. An abbreviated version appeared in *The Sunday Times*, 4 January 1976.

29   Malcolm Storry, in interview with the author, 17 May 1985.

[4]

Environmental Pieces

In a discussion of his production of *The Four Little Girls* by Picasso, Charles Marowitz comments on 'environmental theatre' thus: 'an environment inside a theatre is only a fancy name for a stage setting – even if the setting happens to overflow into the house'.[1] It was a method of staging that he had used several times before the Picasso play in different ways, and the above quotation does not give an insight into these differences. The object of creating productions in this way was not always the same, and the final result of involving the audience by immersing them in the world of the play was different in each case.

Fortune and Men's Eyes, by John Herbert, attempted, by the transformation of the theatre into another kind of institution, to recreate an actual prison with real inmates who included not only the actors playing the scripted parts but also the audience. The play opened on 11 July 1968 to enthusiastic audiences.[2] Reviews were mixed and press coverage was not really comprehensive until the play transferred to the West End. However there were enough good reviews to bring the audiences flocking in, and the run was extended until 4 October.[3] On 17 October it was transferred to the Comedy, where it was presented by Michael White and Larry Parnes.

The play is set in a Canadian reformatory and deals with the corruption of a new inmate by his fellow prisoners. Its atmosphere is claustrophobic, and Charles Marowitz's production made the most of this by treating the audience as inmates. The main entrance to the theatre was not used: instead the public were ushered in through the fire exit. They were immediately confronted with iron fire-escape staircases and narrow passages along which the audience were ordered in single file. A barred door was opened by a guard who took the tickets whilst flashing lights proclaimed, 'This Way'. Two inmates stared out silently from behind iron bars as the public filed in, and another guard equipped with a sub-machine gun watched from above. The audience were fingerprinted (according to Oliver Pritchett of the *Guardian*, 12 July 1968, 'everyone submitted like lambs' on the opening night) and were then pushed into a cell until twelve people had accumulated. Then they were allowed to pass across the set to their seats. Loudspeakers blasted out prison information until the play was about to begin, at which point the guards silently disappeared and the play opened with the sound of a shower and the appearance of the four characters who make up the play.4

As B.A. Young said (*Financial Times*, 24 July 1968), ' "What is theatre?" is a question that concerns Mr. Marowitz's new undertaking, the Open Space Theatre.' The production attempted to break down the traditional barriers set up by the proscenium arch theatre, and to implicate the audience directly in the action of the play. Thelma Holt's claim in her introduction to the published text, that it was the first production to 'use environment as an integral part of stage-design' is not quite accurate; for instance, the idea had been used in a production of John Bowen's *After the Rain* at the Hampstead Theatre Club in 1966, where the audience was assigned the role of students attending a lecture, and in John Arden's *The Happy Haven*, performed in April 1960 at the Drama Studio, Bristol University, on an open stage, the audience received similar treatment. Although neither of these plays can be said to have created the environment with such detail (it is much easier to make a theatre auditorium look like a lecture theatre than a prison cell), the idea is the same.

The Marowitz production was successful, though critics could not agree on where its success lay. Oliver Pritchett of the *Guardian* (12 June 1968) felt it was 'an effective way of setting the scene', but that the play 'didn't really convince on human relationships'. Jeremy Kingston, writing for *Punch* (24 July 1968), felt that the story 'grips attention from the start and seldom lets it go'. Michael Billington for *The Times* (18 October 1968), after the play had transferred to the Comedy, declared, 'to me the play fulfils one of drama's most basic functions: it tells us about an area of life that few of us will ever experience at first hand.' Both he and Kingston agreed that Marowitz's direction was impeccable.

Only two reviews wholeheartedly condemned the play. One was published in *The Stage* (18 July 1968), where the reviewer was clearly offended by the homosexual subject matter, and he ended by blaming the director. The other, by Harold Hobson, was a tougher attack altogether on the theatre enterprise as a whole, as experienced through this play.

From the dark, claustrophobic atmosphere of the Open Space club setting, *Fortune and Men's Eyes* transferred to the pink and genteel Comedy Theatre in the West End. It received a great deal of publicity as it was only the second play since censorship had ended on 26 July 1968 to show male nudity on stage (the first having been *Hair* at the Shaftesbury). The *Daily Telegraph* (12 October 1968) claimed that it was the first time a male nude had appeared in full lighting on the West End stage. The nudity, the homosexuality and the scatalogical language were what now concerned the tabloid reviewers: 'Nude actors come into the light' (*Daily Mail,* 4 October 1968); 'Strong stomachs and broad minds only' *(Evening Standard,* 18 October 1968). Emphasis was laid on the fact that the Lord Chamberlain had previously forbidden the play performance rights in its original form. Many mentioned the number of people who walked out from the first night performance, and Milton Shulman (*Evening Standard,* 18 October 1968) added: 'I doubt if there is a viable commercial audience for this kind of outspoken social realism.' It seems he was right: the play lasted only until the end of November.

Undoubtedly the club theatres of the 1960s had a different clientele from the West End theatres, and this possibly accounted for certain production changes which Marowitz allowed. Although the play itself was largely unchanged, the audience was not subjected to any of the physical discomfort which it had experienced at the Open Space. The public was no longer fingerprinted as it came in, nor was it exposed to anything resembling prison procedure. The sirens and loud-speakers still blared across the auditorium to remind the audience of the prison setting, but the sensation of being trapped in it with the characters was no longer felt to the same extent. According to John Higgins (*Financial Times*, 18 October 1968), Al Mancini, who played the part of Queenie the transvestite, was allowed to overplay his drag scenes, which, while remaining highly comic, were not in tune with the other performances. This would seem to be borne out by the number of reviewers who referred to the acting in terms which suggested caricature and high camp.

It is also true to say that Marowitz's production had been specifically tailored to fit the Open Space's auditorium and the building as a whole, so it was natural that there were difficulties when the play transferred to another venue. The production used the entire theatre building to create its effect, and since the Open Space itself was suitably dingy, uncomfortable and altogether suggestive of the penitentiary, the creation of a 'total environment' was successful. (By contrast, in a production of Racine's *Britannicus* at the Studio, Lyric Theatre, Hammersmith (27 May 1981), directed by Christopher Fettes, the same effect was attempted – a darkened auditorium with armed guards marching up and down while the public waited for the action to begin – but it was not entirely successful since the audience had just walked in from a foyer which looked very like a plush hotel lounge.) Simon Trussler for the *Tribune* (25 October 1968) commented that the transfer 'has transformed the production's eye-witness intimacy into more or less conventional proscenium-archery – with the audience as targets instead of participants'. At the Open Space Marowitz had achieved a startling and dramatic entrance for his characters, where actors and audience suddenly became almost indistinguishable, such was their proximity. The tiny space and stage with audience on three sides had been an integral part of the director's conception of the play, which was inevitably lost when it transferred to a traditional theatre.

No other environmental production was attempted until 1970, for although it had proved a popular experiment, it was also a very expensive way of setting a play. In 1970 Marowitz decided to try it again, with two productions running one after the other. The first of these was a charity performance of a dramatised reading of the transcript of *The Chicago Conspira-cy* (published in *Open Space Plays*, pp.77-149), compiled by John Burgess. It had two showings on 24 August (originally only one performance had been scheduled, but the demand for tickets was such that it was presented to two full houses on the same day). The cast was an amateur one headed by the writer William Burroughs in the part of Judge Julius Hoffman and included victims of the McCarthy investigations such as Larry Adler, Carl Foreman and Clancy Sigal. All proceeds were to be sent to the 'Chicago Conspiracy Trial Fund' to help those who still had appeals pending. According to Irving Wardle (*The Times*, 25 August 1970), Marowitz, who directed the production, deliberately chose non-professionals for the parts because he felt that the most appropriate people to speak for the participants were members of the American public and, where possible, Americans who had suffered at the hands of the American judicial system.

The text of *The Chicago Conspiracy* was taken from literature already published about the notorious trial which had taken place after the riots following the Chicago Democratic Con-vention of 1968. The defendants were accused of trying to ini-tiate a revolution which would overthrow the government, and Burgess's reconstruction of the salient points of the trial sought to show that the court proceedings were corrupt and that the true conspiracy was created by the government itself. In Wardle's introduction to the published text and in his review of the production he stated firmly that the dramatisa-tion was not concerned with finding villains, but gave a fair hearing to both sides of the question. As proof of this he cited the scene where the actor playing Bobby Seale, a black defen-dant, sitting in the audience at the Open Space, was bound and gagged in a most savage fashion because he kept demand-ing his rights. Although the audience's sympathies were with Seale, he said, the production also showed his 'thunderous self-righteousness' *(Open Space Plays, p.80)* so that there was a feeling of relief when his tirade was forcibly stopped. The judge too had his moments of pathos, apparently due to William Burroughs' rendering of the role (*The Times*, 25 August 1970). Wardle claimed that the production was open-minded without an over-emphasis on the martyrdom of individuals. This must have been a result of sensitive direction from Marowitz, because a reading of the text arouses a feeling of horror at the perversion of justice at every stage of the proceedings, and there seems to be no kindness shown to the prosecuting counsel or the judge.

The parts were read, and although the cast seemed underrehearsed at first (*Daily Telegraph*, 25 August 1970) the audience rapidly became engaged with the events. Marowitz used his by now familiar technique of making the audience feel part of the action. The production attempted to set up trial conditions, so that the public were frisked by 'American police' as they entered to take their places as spectators at the original trial. Recorded crowd sounds helped to create the atmosphere of a busy courtroom, and members of the cast planted in the audience encouraged verbal reaction from the spectators. The brutalities that the actual trial practised on some of the accused were not shirked, and fighting was effectively simulated in the 'courtroom'.

The adaptation began with a loudspeaker announcing the sentences of each of the defendants, accompanied by a photograph of the relevant person flashed onto a screen. Each of the characters summed up in a few sentences what he felt about the court proceedings. Then followed a series of scenes which led up to the end of the trial, each preceded by captions projected onto a screen which revealed the content of the scene to follow and in some cases commented on it. This Brechtian narrative technique did not appear to create a sense of detachment in the audience, but simply clarified and linked each separate scene.

Although there were only two performances, the press was unanimous in its opinion that Marowitz had staged a valuable documentary play which ought to have reached a wider audience than a small club could hope to accommodate. In its theatrical context it resembled its predecessor, *Fortune and Men's Eyes*, but its substance was more radical and subversive. In the 1990s the Tricycle Theatre in Kilburn, London would follow suit with its celebrated productions of trials or inquiries: *Nuremberg War Crimes Trial, Half the Picture* (a dramatisation of the Scott 'Arms to Iraq' Inquiry), and *The Colour of Justice* (based on the Stephen Lawrence Inquiry); in 2003–4 *Justifying War: Scenes from the Hutton Enquiry and Guantanamo.*

The second major production was *Palach* by Alan Burns, directed by Marowitz and presented for four weeks from 11 November 1970. Alan Burns had written his first novel in 1961 and had already established a reputation for himself as a novelist before he met Marowitz in 1969. In the *Guardian* (30 April 1970) Angus Wilson had referred to him as 'one of the two or three most interesting new novelists working in England'. Marowitz asked him to write a play for the Open Space, which he subsequently did, but the production was shelved for a time because money for it could not be found. The Arts Council refused a request for extra subsidy, and it was not until an anonymous donation of £500 was sent for the production that work could be started on it.

In his play, Burns had tried to recreate the atmosphere and theme expressed in Breughel's picture *The Fall of Icarus.* Just as no one takes any notice of Icarus as he disappears beneath the waves and the rest of the world goes about its business, so Jan Palach, the Czech student who burned himself as a protest at the Soviet invasion of his country, perished in what seemed to be a futile and despairing gesture forgotten as soon as it had been made. This self-sacrifice, at the heart of the play, was inspired by the protests of monks in Vietnam: what had seemed (to audiences of the period) far away, and something that could not happen here, suddenly shifted closer to home. The self-immolation, however, was not allowed to take a central position in the structure of the work. The production focused for only a few moments on the letter that Palach had written to his countrymen, after which his words were swallowed up by other events happening elsewhere in the auditorium. At no point in the production was there any attempt to show the physical act of martyrdom on stage. Burns was making the point that the essence of the martyrdom lay in the futility of the act, and that the 'knowledge' which Palach expressed in the letter, that his would not be the final sacrifice if the people did not respond to his plea to help create freedom for Czechoslovakia, was false. The villains of the piece

Nikolas Simmonds as Palach, with Penelope Nice as Girl, Liza Hughes as Mum, Henry Soskin as Dad, in *Palach* by Alan Burns and Charles Marowitz

were not the invading Russians, nor the characters on stage, but the media who control our responses and who decide how much importance they will allow us to attach to a political act. The critic for the *Guardian* (12 November 1970) felt that, because of the writer's treatment of the martyrdom, the play foundered for want of a centre, whilst others felt that the chaos evoked by the production was not helpful in establishing its point.

In keeping with the spirit of the play, Ian Brakewell, the designer, had the walls of the theatre covered with random lists of words beginning with P. The name of Palach was included amongst them, but it was not given prominence (*Open Space Plays*, p.195). Four stages were set against the walls, connected to each other by planks. The audience sat in the centre so that they were surrounded by the action.[5] Often, different scenes were being enacted at the same time on different stages, and as the audience entered to take their places, televisions were blaring out random programmes. The playwright's initial idea had been to recreate something of the atmosphere of a fairground, with music and bustling activity surrounding the spectators, who would themselves wander round the different 'booths'. The idea of the audience moving about as well as the actors proved impracticable in the small theatre, but the feeling of intense activity was maintained. The idea of enveloping his audience in a total environment was one which appealed to Burns, but which he warily chose to stand back from during certain moments of the play. As soon as the audience had assembled, the various activities which had been going on before the dimming of the house lights ceased and a long blackout ensued, with a recorded dialogue between director and playwright as they mulled over their forthcoming play, *Palach*. A totally realistic conversation was given another dimension by virtue of the fact that it was disembodied and that none of the points made was actually concluded, so that the voices faded out as another thought started. This perhaps superfluous piece of Brechtian distancing (the device is not used anywhere else in the play and seems to be largely irrelevant) served the purpose of explaining what should have been evident without explanation by the end of the play. The voice of Burns was heard to say:

> The characters occupy their time in chat, which is 'not communica-
> tion, comprehension, understanding, but rather indicates a particu-
> lar style of life. Their idle talk is the sign of alienation, an incapacity
> to relate to anything at all'. The action occurs off-stage and creates
> forebodings which 'cast their shadow over idle talk'. (*Open Space
> Plays* p.197)

If, however, the message that the play was to communicate was unambiguous and straightforward, it was what made for clarity through the seeming chaos of the action. In *Confessions of a Counterfeit Critic* Marowitz was later to acknowledge his un-Artaudian tendency to wish to 'cleanse the corruptions of society', but being attracted towards some of Artaud's theories of staging he felt that it ought to be possible to reconcile a 'high styled theatre' with one 'which isn't decadent, arty or ballsless-ly aesthetic'.[6] An attempt to realise this synthesis was made by using Artaud's idea of an acting area surrounding the audience, with much of the effect of the ensuing scenes created by the growing noise level where the coherence of language was lost. Indeed some of the scenes employed only sound and mimed movement, such as the simultaneous scenes with the students maintaining 'a quiet background of rhythmical sounds', the boy and girl miming a factory routine with 'appropriate sounds', and Mum and Dad who conversed in advertising slogans (p.202). In the scene which followed the reading of the letter, a visual image of the boy's decision to go through with his self-immolation was accompanied by finger snapping and a 'rapid pattering of hands on thighs' (p.227), which built the tension to breaking point before the scene switched abruptly to something else. Even when language was used in a recognisable form, it was given a new shape. In order to demonstrate the monotony and triviality of their lives, Mum and Dad were given Ionesco-like conversations which consisted of groups of, what were, for them, key words :

> DAD [*reads newspaper*]: Paper, paper, paper, paper, paper
> ...
> MUM [*washes dishes*]: Dishes, dishes, dishes, dishes, dishes
> ...
> [*pours coffee*]: Coffee, coffee, coffee, coffee, coffee ...
> (p.200)

or they conversed in advertising slogans:

> *These are spoken with great variety of tone and emphasis, follow-ing the course of domestic rows, reconciliations, etc.*
> MUM: What makes a shy girl get intimate?
> DAD: What we want is Watney's.
> MUM: Don't say brown, say Hovis.
> DAD: Bovril puts *beef* into you.
> MUM: Bovril puts beef into *you.*
> DAD: *Bovril* puts beef into you. (p.202)

Through the clichés used by the members of the family and the vicious and vulgar jokes of the priest, a developing line of coherent thought gradually emerged through the character of the boy who eventually adopted the persona of Palach. He was the only character in the play who tried to understand the motives of the young Czech, and his thoughts had to be discerned through the jumbled conversations of the other characters. Finally, simultaneous action on all four stages ceased, and a spotlight was focused on the boy/Palach. The students drew lots, a voice gave an eyewitness account of the situation, and the boy read out the letter. After that moment of clarity, confusion took hold again until the end, where the boy gave up trying to make people listen and sat down in the audience and hopelessly observed the continuing turmoil onstage.

The first performance of this 'happening' presented the focal scene differently. Instead of creating the one moment of indisputable truth, however quickly it might have been concealed again, as the second version did, it disguised the letter in the same way that the characters' previous thoughts had been delivered, i.e. amidst the cacophany of other monologues taking place simultaneously. Whatever were the reasons for changing the scene after the first night, the re-working of the scene quite clearly gave the production the focus that so many of the critics thought it lacked.

Nikolas Simmonds, who had already played Marowitz's Macbeth and Hamlet, besides small parts in various other Open Space productions, played the boy, and gave, according to Harold Hobson (*Sunday Times*, 15 November 1971), a superb performance as the 'quietly desperate Palach'. Most critics gave reasoned accounts of the show, and most were impressed by the director's handling of the four stages and the simultaneous acting on them. Only *The Stage* (19 November 1970) carried a vitriolic attack on what the critic called 'a garble of words, tricks, exercises'; together with the critic for the *Daily Telegraph* (12 November 1970), he found nothing original in the methods of staging. Yet what Marowitz had done with this production was to move away from an environmental presentation which stressed the convention of experiencing reality at first hand to a more expressionistic form which suggested the essence of a confused and confusing world, with a population at once alienated from any real moral values and yet ultimately unable to escape their implications. This final point was admirably exemplified by trapping the audience physically in the middle of the action.

The move away from the realistic culminated in the

Marowitz production of Picasso's *The Four Little Girls* in 1971. The production was originally conceived as a way of participating in the festival arranged to celebrate Picasso's ninetieth birthday. Money was slowly raised, but not in time to open for the birthday on 28 October.[7] The target of £6,000 was eventually reached (the Open Space's total grant for the year was £5,000), and for a week the theatre was closed in order to transform its interior into the dream world which the four little girls of the play inhabit.

Picasso and Artaud had been friends, and they had shared many artistic ideals, which to some extent explains Marowitz's interest in the play. He draws an analogy between the stage directions used in *Les Cenci* and *The Four Little Girls* and describes the feel of the play as surrealistic.[8] Most critics were captivated by Marowitz's 'imaginative response' (*Sunday Telegraph*, 19 December 1971) to the problems inherent in the text, and described at length the startling images such as the cage which descended to incarcerate the girls, the chalice of wine which also descended from the roof at the end of the play, the different coloured spots which covered each girl in turn as she expounded the importance of colour, and so on. None of them mentioned the acting except to say that it was just what was needed. Marowitz was praised for shaping the play, not only by cutting but 'by polarising its emotions between the gay and the sinister, and sustaining this contrast even in the straight nursery games' (*The Times*, 17 November 1971).

Although the 'environment' for the production was ostensibly the work of three designers, Robin Don, Carolee Schneemann and Penny Slinger, it was Don who took the initiative in the impossible situation which inevitably arises when three creative artists are asked to design one set. Don had a deep-rooted concern with the texture of a stage set (clearly seen in his later design for *The Shrew*), which blended with Marowitz's conception of the production as a whole and which he [Marowitz] clarified in *The Act of Being* (p.159).

Marowitz had forced the audience to enter the theatre in an unconventional manner for both *Fortune and Men's Eyes* and *The Four Little Girls*. In the first he made them descend a

Suzannah Williams, Ann Holloway, Susan Penhaligon and Mia Martin as the four girls in *The Four Little Girls* by Picasso

fire-escape, and in the second he had had made an especially small entrance to the auditorium so that people should feel a little like Alice entering Wonderland. The first was, however, dependent on good naturalistic acting from the cast which involved the audience in their emotional conflicts, leaving nothing to the imagination. *The Four Little Girls* relied upon the set to interpret in visual terms the poetic imagery used by the girls.

The audience, who sat upon the pink plastic grass where the girls played, became a part of their inner life; the landscape which described the limits of their world was both easily visible and tangible. The effect was more like experiencing a kinetic Chagall painting (demanding an imaginative leap on the part of the audience), which a thoroughly naturalistic production like *Fortune and Men's Eyes* did not. Unlike any of the other environmental pieces, it was the artificiality of the setting that was most important. As Marowitz said, it was necessary to 'obliterate the theatre' (*The Act of Being*, p.159). The production demonstrated Marowitz's ability to respond poetically to the challenge of a poetic play.

NOTES

1   *The Act of Being*, p.159.
2   Not 10 June as stated by Catherine Itzin, *Stages in the Revolution* (London, 1970), p.366.
3   For the financial position at the end of the production see OS 13/12.
4   Introduction to *Fortune and Men's Eyes*, in *Open Space Plays*, pp.15–16.
5   It is interesting to note that the Théâtre du Soleil's production of *1789*, which used similar staging techniques to the playwright's original intentions, opened in Milan on 10 November 1970.
6   Charles Marowitz, *Confessions of a Counterfeit Critic* (London, 1973), p.8.
7   Full production details are contained in *The Act of Being*, Appendix 3, pp.148–162.
8   *The Act of Being*, p.150.

[5]

New American Writers

In the first four years of the Open Space's existence Charles Marowitz welcomed a large number of American plays into his theatre, sometimes directing them himself, at other times making his theatre available for other companies bringing in productions that interested him. He is quoted in *Plays and Players* (October 1972) as having said, 'I've kept wanting not to do American plays', though the number of productions perhaps belies this claim (out of 33 programmes between 1968 and 1971, 19 were American). There is no doubt that Marowitz was interested in importing the best of Off-Off-Broadway (the term for theatres set up in tiny basements or cafés), where the fringe tradition was firmly established, and his comment in the introduction to his *Off-Broadway Plays 2* seems to be more to the point: '[The Open Space theatre] rapidly became a kind of extra-territorial Off-Broadway out-post'.[1] The kind of plays that he chose to present were written to be performed in conditions very like those provided by the Open Space, and the plays' influence was bound to be felt by British playwrights who were only just beginning to explore the possibilities of fringe theatre. By 1972, when Marowitz was able to set up his permanent company, many more British playwrights were making contributions to the repertoire, with plays that were also tailored to performance conditions.

The overriding concerns of the American works presented at the Open Space were disillusionment with America's values and a criticism of its imperialistic wars and of war in general. The form of the plays tended to be conservative in that a small number of characters were presented naturalistically and with great psychological minuteness. In the *Plays and Players* article,

Marowitz said of the American tradition in drama, 'One always feels that every new play is some little wriggle in an individual's psychoanalytical development.' His description fitted most of the plays that formed the American season at the end of 1969.

The first main-house programme of American plays, both directed by Marowitz, was made up of two one-act plays, *The Fun War* by Geoffrey Bush and *Muzeeka* by John Guare; both presented themes in an anti-naturalistic fashion. *The Fun War* dealt with the Spanish-American war, and in a programme note Marowitz explained that:

> a large part of the text ... is drawn from actual historical
> sources. None of the events depicted are fictitious. All of the
> characters represent real people. Every seeming absurdity of
> 'invention' actually happened during the years when America
> embarked on the foreign policy which has led – inexorably – to the
> Korean 'police actions', Latin American 'interventions' and the
> Vietnam War. (OS Progs)

The critic for the *Financial Times* (26 February 1969) felt that the programme note was more stimulating than the play, which did not present a clear picture of the history.

Muzeeka, an Off-Broadway award winner in 1967, was reviewed more favourably and was generally considered the better play of the two. It is about a young man, Jack Argue, destroyed by American society and more specifically by American materialism and the Vietnam war.[2] After finding out that he enjoys killing, he kills himself. The staging of the play anticipated Complicite (founded in 1983): four stagehands were used as props; they formed chairs for the characters to sit on, they carried on posters, made sound effects and sometimes joined in the action. Paul Jones, then a pop singer, played the part of Argue, but even his presence did not draw the audiences. For a publicity stunt before the opening, he and another actor, Chris Malcolm, were pulled along Tottenham Court Road in the bathtub used in *The Fun War* to represent the American fleet. The *Daily Mirror* (22 February 1969) carried a photograph, but the plays closed after eleven performances. John Russell Taylor pinpointed the reason for *Muzeeka's* lack of appeal when he said:

> Mr Guare depends too heavily on a set of specifically American con-
> ditioned reflexes for his dramatic effect, instead of giving his hero
> ... any very vividly individualised life of his own ... I suspect this is a
> brand of domestic wine which just does not travel. (*Plays and Players,*
> April 1969)

Taylor's criticism suggests that lack of detailed characterisation was what led to the confusion that the second play generated. The comment that it was too American to be understood
by the English was a recurrent one in the reviews of the productions which came afterwards, most notably Sam Shepard's
The Tooth of Crime.

Because these were Open Space productions they lost the
theatre a great deal of money (obviously the production costs
were incurred by the management), but this did not deter
Marowitz from presenting a whole season of American plays at
the end of the year.

One of his reasons for forging ahead with the American
season was the sponsorship offered by the American Embassy
in London. It was arranged that the actors should be paid on a
profit-sharing basis.[3] Each of the eight plays was to have been
performed on six consecutive nights, which, if done under the
terms of the Esher Standard Contract, would have cost the
management more than £3,000. Equity decided to threaten
the actors with a three-month suspension if they played for
anything below the minimum rate, and Marowitz was forced to
cancel the shows. Marowitz and Ed Berman of Inter-Action
decided to join forces in a formal protest (Berman had also
been involved in profit-sharing productions), in order to give
fringe theatre the special status which it so clearly lacked. The
main points which they drew up were:

a. All the actors had been in unanimous agreement with the
   deal, and under Equity's conditions the season could never
   have been undertaken.
b. It was vital to recognise that the dozen or so fringe theatres,
   which often seated only fifty people, were not able to operate like the commercial theatres.
c. The special status of these theatres had been tacitly
   acknowledged by Equity since they had often in the past

knowingly permitted their members to work for very small wages and often for nothing at all. By doing this they had recognised the fact that in an overcrowded profession any opportunity to work might create subsequent opportunities for paid work.

In the draft copy of the statement prepared for the Department of Employment and Productivity, Marowitz intimated that Equity was run along totalitarian lines which implied that the union's members needed protecting against themselves, and he cited Russia's occupation of Czechoslovakia as an example of this argument put into practice. Actors themselves were afraid of challenging a union that could deprive them of work, and therefore he wished, as management, to help bring this problem of fringe-theatre work out into the open, and to help push Equity into the drafting of new and more appropriate regulations. Unfortunately for fringe theatre the whole project got no further than the draft stage and a little publicity, because, almost as soon as the threat to suspend the actors had been publicised, Equity decided to withdraw the ruling and instead simply cautioned the actors not to work under such conditions. The productions were on again, and at the end of the season a triumphant statement appeared in the *Evening Standard* (27 August 1969), 'The actors have earned more than double the amount they would have received from the flat rate.'

The season finally started on 12 August with two one-act plays by Mike Weller, which were to be the most successful of the collection. The plays were all chosen as representative of the Off-Broadway writing of the previous five years, and Marowitz considered that collectively they gave a clear idea of what was happening on the American fringe (*The Times*, 18 July 1969). Of the two Weller plays, *The Body Builders* and *Now There's Just the Three of Us,* the latter claimed most critical attention and most reviews spoke enthusiastically about it.

The overall effect was naturalistic: the set depicted a rather dilapidated flat with a view of other apartment blocks from the window. The dialogue, however, was far from naturalistic. Although full of colourful American slang, it was heightened and exaggerated as the situation became more overtly sexual. In both plays the artificiality of the language was underlined by the style of acting which accompanied it. *The Times* (13 August 1969) described it as comedy dependent on 'bold exaggeration', but it also remarked that 'it never severs its contact with naturalistic situation'. This gave a feeling of the extraordinary within the ordinary which obviously delighted its audiences. Like Joe Orton, Weller had flouted the taboos of language with great gusto and found a poetic idiom within the vernacular, though his plays did not contain the same stringent criticism of society that Orton's did.

The plays ran for two weeks, the second week netting over £500 in box office receipts. This meant that the members of the company earned over £20 a week, and a second season at the end of the scheduled run of plays had a similar success.

The next programme, two plays by Israel Horowitz, *Rats* and *The Indian Wants the Bronx*, was of importance because it introduced to the public a new director who was to have considerable influence on later productions at the Open Space. Walter Donohue, also an American, first impressed Marowitz with his work on a production at Bristol University in 1969 (*Tom Paine* by Paul Foster). His direction had been influenced by Joseph Chaikin's *The Serpent*, which Marowitz also admired.4 He invited Donohue to present the show at his theatre, which he was able to do for one night only because his students were all involved with their final examinations. Nevertheless Marowitz felt that an association between Donohue and the Open Space might be a valuable one, and he next asked him to work as his assistant on the production of *A Macbeth*. When Michael Rudman, who had agreed to direct the Horowitz plays, dropped out at the last minute, Donohue was given his chance to have sole charge of a production. Reviews criticised his direction (*The Stage*, 4 September 1969, called it 'sloppy'), but he was to continue his work for Marowitz until 1972, when he directed his final play there, *The Tooth of Crime*.

None of the plays presented in the American season had the same financial success that the Weller plays had enjoyed, though none of them did badly, and on the whole audiences were glad to see what Off-Broadway had to offer. It is not possible to give accurate box office figures since the records are incomplete, but the general picture is that the remaining plays did about half as well as the first two.5

The controversy over the showing of Andy Warhol's film *Flesh* paved the way for the presentation of Rosalyn Drexler's two plays, *Hot Buttered Roll* and *The Investigation*, which dealt openly and directly with the world of American pornography. Billed as 'An Evening in Bad Taste', they caused considerable dissent among the critics. Opinion seems to have been divided amongst those who thought *Hot Buttered Roll* (the shorter of the two plays) banal and *The Investigation* substantial and rigorously critical of society, those who thought the opposite to be true, and those who disliked both plays with equal vehemence.

Hot Buttered Roll was set against a backdrop of silk and satin pop-art, which the critic for *The Stage* (26 February 1970) described as approaching 'the ultimate in sexual vulgarity'. This critic, together with Nicholas de Jongh (*Guardian*, 20 February 1970), found the play the more satisfactory of the two. Using information supplied by Marowitz in a lengthy programme note explaining and defending the plays (a practice that Marowitz discontinued, as he explained to students at the Polytechnic of North London, 3 December 1981, because it provided an easy outlet for lazy critics), de Jongh described Drexler's world as 'possessed by bad taste of a particular variety: the vulgarity of ham-fisted eroticism and sexual titillation'. He went on to say:

> The manner of suggesting this world is violent caricature, so that there is a nice relationship between form and content, accentuated by Mr. Marowitz's exuberant direction.

The play is set in the bedroom of an old man who makes love to a dummy. He is attended by a transvestite nurse who panders to his tastes because he is after the old man's money. The world of American pornography was represented in the image of the sickroom with its purple pillows and satin sheets, and the play's general air of decadence was clearly to be understood as satire.

Nicholas de Jongh was not as enthusiastic about *The Investigation*, which attacked American justice through the story of an innocent boy charged with rape. The play did not share the grotesque manner of presentation that had characterised the first and relied instead on naturalistic acting and sentimentality. Irving Wardle, writing for *The Times* (21 February 1970), found an uneasy feeling of complicity with the raw material in the first play, but not in the second. The final image of the play was given a typical Marowitzian twist as the brutish policeman slowly turned his pistol towards the members of the audience before the lights went down, thus implicating them unambiguously in the play's message.

Certain critics disliked the plays intensely (*Drama*, Summer 1970, and *Plays and Players*, April 1970), and felt that the greatest display of bad taste was by Marowitz himself, who had chosen to present the works. For plays as controversial as these the critics were unlikely to have been unanimous in their opinions, and the varied and, in the main, favourable criticism must have pleased the management, who were interested in provoking and outraging a complacent public.

Donohue's next work with the Open Space was as co-director on *Flash Gordon and the Angels* by David Zane Mairowitz one year later. In Donohue's own words, the attempt was a disaster (Donohue in interview 14 June 1984). Marowitz was away for the greater part of rehearsal time and when he came back he was horrified at what he saw. By that time it was too close to the opening night for any radical changes to be made, and Marowitz took his name off the credits in the programme. Donohue blames himself for miscasting the play. Instead of using good English actors he had felt it necessary to use an American cast, and had only been able to find mediocre actors. He had no blame for the play, which is a portrayal of the American system and the way that it has used its heroes as puppets to be disposed of when they are of no more use. Although Donohue himself was not satisfied with the production and Marowitz disowned it, a number of critics liked it.[6]

After this production Donohue's work was restricted to the lunchtime shows, which did not have the same prestige value as the main house productions. Here his work developed, so that, in the months before the permanent company was established and just after, some of the most exciting Open Space

Jane Cardew as the Girl and Peter Marinker as the Young Man in *Sweet Eros* by Terence McNally

programmes that were presented were his.

Three months later, another American double-bill showed Marowitz's continuing interest in presenting new American plays to a British audience. *Sweet Eros* and *Next* by Terrence McNally had both run for two years Off-Broadway, but although this might suggest that they had been in some way innovative, there was nothing in their form which could be termed experimental. The first is a monologue by a young man who has captured a girl, stripped her and tied her to a chair, where she sits, centre stage, naked, throughout the rest of the performance. This was of course the factor which labelled the play 'experimental' and caught the eye of the press, provoking critical argument as to the intrinsic value of the play.

The boy's monologue contains criticism of society in general, but he speaks in particular of his fantasy life and personality problems.[7] In a programme note, McNally said the plays are about 'the politics of human relationships' (OS 13/37), but there is little else which links this play to *Next*, which is a revue sketch (according to critics, a very funny one) about a middle-aged man who is called up and has to undergo a humiliating medical examination, at the end of which he is told that he is unfit and will therefore be rejected by the panel. Having started out trying desperately to avoid being drafted, he is paradoxically upset to find that he is considered unfit to join. Both plays show how power struggles might be reversed and how potent a dream is the desire to dominate.

Most critics attributed the success of *Sweet Eros* to the female nude who graced an otherwise unadorned stage. The proximity of the audience to the action caused the sensation, not anything inherent in the text or form of the play. If we are to believe the anecdote printed in the *Guardian* (5 August 1971), it was the nude that attracted the audiences and not the plays themselves:

> Outside the Open Space Theatre in Tottenham Court Road for the past three weeks has stood a life-sized model of a naked blonde ... Sadly, on Sunday, some cad stole the naked model. Houses fell immediately. So few people came that the performance had to be cancelled. Advance bookings plummeted.
>
> It took two days and about £7 to make a new Jane figure. The replacement arrived 45 minutes before Tuesday's curtain-up. The siren went straight outside, and the theatre was back to fifty per cent filled before you could say Lord Longford.

Even if the successful run of this double-bill is to be attributed to its sensationalism, it must be recognised that the intimacy provided by the small stage and auditorium made it particularly suitable for a play which is dependent upon the actor's ability to portray nuances of emotion. According to most reviews, Peter Marinker, playing the young man, gave a convincing performance.

The next, and most interesting, of the American plays during the Open Space's initial years was Sam Shepard's *The Tooth of Crime*, put on by the newly formed permanent company and directed by Marowitz and Donohue.[8] It showed a radical departure from the staging techniques of the McNally plays, even though Shepard himself would have preferred something more naturalistic. The idea for the play was taken from a meeting between Elvis Presley and David Bowie (before Bowie became famous) and subsequently shows what happened to Elvis, whose talent was taken over by the media, in a country where failure is not tolerated. The play is not merely a portrait of this particular star, but a portrait of any man who has been taken over and abandoned in the same way.

Act One creates a character, Hoss, who is continually shifting position: sometimes he is the giant he was in the past, in control and unbeatable, sometimes he is weak and vacillating, but gradually a character emerges who is going through a nervous breakdown as his confidence is slowly stripped from him. This part of the play relies upon an imaginative performance from the actor. The second half of the play dramatises the man's internal conflict through his encounter with Crow, a new kind of 'star', ruthless and lacking in integrity. Shepard develops a series of boxing bouts between the two men, which symbolise and give concrete theatrical form to the anguish Hoss feels.

It was Marowitz's idea that there should be three rounds to the boxing match, one of which Hoss is to win. Originally Shepard had written in only two, both of which Hoss lost. The extra scene he supplied at the time is not incorporated into the rehearsal text but was, according to Donohue, a very important addition. Again it supplied a momentary victory for Hoss: during this round he wins by relating the history of the blues, revealing an integrity which Crow can neither match nor understand. The play ends with Hoss's suicide.

Marowitz had already shown Shepard's play *Icarus's Mother* as a lunchtime performance when it was first put on in London (20 March 1971), and he was very enthusiastic about directing the premiere of *The Tooth of Crime*. He scheduled it for performance in July 1972, but found that pressing engagements were to take him out of the country during the play's rehearsal period. He decided to ask Donohue, who had just assisted him with the revival of *Hamlet*, to co-direct.

Before he left the country Marowitz abruptly stopped work on his very effective pre-play improvisations. Moves were blocked, and a form was rapidly superimposed upon the play that had little to do with the work already done. His rehearsal exercises were loosely connected to the play text and were exploratory by nature, so that the rigid structure which he forced on his actors because of his imminent departure (according to Donohue, often moving his actors contrary to the stage directions implicit in the dialogue) hindered them from understanding and creating the characters that Sam Shepard had envisaged. Donohue found the actors in a state of bewilderment. He discussed the problem with Shepard and decided, while Marowitz was away, to start again from the beginning, allowing the actors to move as they felt the characters dictated and not as the director had ruled.

On Marowitz's return Donohue explained how he had altered the production, and the company did a run-through for him. Marowitz would not, however, agree on the change of emphasis which Shepard himself wished to see, and the production was altered yet again. Shepard had attended rehearsals to begin with, but he began to absent himself when he found Marowitz unwilling to listen to him, or to re-think his conception of the play.

The rest of the production time was very tense, with Marowitz refusing to listen to anyone, even when the play was patently not working. His mistakes were two-fold. Firstly he wanted Hoss, played by Malcolm Storry, to project the image of a superstar, a giant of his time, who falls at the first knock his confidence receives. Without the feeling of the character teetering on the edge of failure and breakdown the play loses all suspense. According to Donohue, Marowitz realised this, but because of company tension he saw it too late, and although he tried to do something about it at the preview stage it was not possible to do anything substantial.

Secondly he chose a set which was much too gimmicky and cluttered to allow the essential human emotion to communicate itself to the audience. Shepard stipulates in his text that there should be 'a bare stage except for an evil looking black chair with silver studs and a very high back, something like a pharaoh's throne but simple, centre stage' (p.1). At the Open Space the throne was placed beneath a giant theatrical mirror frame which was studded with coloured light bulbs. Behind it

David Schofield as Crow in *The Tooth of Crime* by Sam Shepard

was a reflecting substance which also carpeted the floor, suggesting the actor in his dressing room faced with a reflection of himself which he cannot escape because everything reflects his image. It is a nightmare world where the real self has been lost. The chair which dominates the scene was very ornate, looking like a medieval state throne. The design for the play is difficult to acccomplish since it must appear futuristic, bizarre and sinister without diminishing the actors. The world which the characters inhabit is a combination of the pop world, the

[67]

drug culture and gangster land. Later productions failed to realise all this in their sets or to retain the simplicity which the text demands. Jim Sharman directed it at the Royal Court a year later, and The Performance Group in New York did a revival in 1973, but according to Donohue neither of these was any nearer a correct realisation of Shepard's work.

Donohue's view was that there should be something about the throne to suggest the electric chair. Hoss says at the end of the play, with a gesture indicating the stage in general, 'You win all right ... All this collection of torture' (pp.19-20). Hoss is king and the stage is his kingdom, the central symbol of which is the chair/throne which has him trapped and writhing. His costume, black and studded with silver, is an extension of his throne as a reminder of how far he has identified himself with his public persona.

The musicians were not placed behind a screen as the stage directions suggest, but at the side of the stage on a rostrum where they could be seen as part of the act. This was a factor in helping to create the atmosphere of the play. Electronic music is essential to it: not only does it recreate the rock era, but it also hints at a technological wilderness which is the future (Shepard said to Donohue that the whole play was electric). The New York production failed in part because the group refused to use electric guitar music since none of them could perform it and they would not bring in an outsider. At the Open Space the audience responded to the music as if they were at a live rock concert; it played a vital part in generating the frenetic excitement that is a part of Hoss's lifestyle.

The play opened with a view of Hoss standing with his back to the audience and his profile showing in dim light. Nicholas de Jongh felt that this image was representative of the general line which the directors had taken on the production as a whole, and that, like the central character's obsession, the concern was with the presentation of an image or a series of images rather than with the human beings depicted (*Guardian*, 18 July 1972). Shepard believed his play was dependent upon characterisation; Marowitz had denied this fundamental concern of the play and tried to develop instead a stylised pattern of images which had nothing to do with the

personal conflict being fought out within the central character, Hoss. This conflict in Act 1 is expressed through soliloquy,
song, monologue and dialogue with his retinue. At one point
he adopts his father's voice and, alternating it with his own, he
creates a conversation in which he attempts to reassure himself of his humanness. He is a man who has lost his sense of
self and has allowed himself to be manipulated by the world
he functions in:

> They're all countin' on me. The bookies, the agents, the Keepers.
> I'm a fucking industry. I even affect the stocks and bonds. (*old*)
> You're just a man, Hoss.

In the second act the isolation of certain images worked well
in the context of the action. The strip which Betty, Hoss's old
girlfriend, performs towards the end began at the back of the
stage in its own light as she moved slowly forward until she was
very close to the audience. The final suicide of Hoss with his
back to the audience was subdued, with the gunshot fired off-
stage. No extra means were used and the intensity of the emotion was generated through the actor's performance. Many
critics were bemused by the strange language of the play,
which Shepard had created in order to suggest a sub-culture,
and the critic for the *Financial Times* (18 July 1972) concluded, as Taylor had suggested of *Muzeeka,* that the play was
aimed at an American audience.

Sam Shepard did not see the production as it was presented to the public. He had booked his sailing back to America
on a date that ought to have enabled him to see the opening
night, but when Marowitz saw that his first night was to clash
with another, he postponed it, so that Shepard was on his way
home before it had opened. He attempted to persuade
Marowitz that he was not within his legal rights to postpone
the opening, but Marowitz prevailed, and after much
unpleasantness Shepard departed, leaving the critics and
public to misunderstand his play, as he saw it, yet ironically to
some critical acclaim and box-office success.[9]

In many ways these American plays were eminently well
suited to the Open Space environment, with their small casts
and tendency to explore states of mind induced by external

influences. From the selection of plays presented here it is impossible to generalise about what effects were most successful – whether it was the naturalistic setting of the Weller plays or the theatrical symbolism of the sets for *Hot Buttered Roll*; whether it was the presentation of the minutiae of a young man's psyche in *Sweet Eros* or the complex symbolic language and form of *The Tooth of Crime*. It is clear that the British plays that followed *Blue Comedy* had assimilated some of these techniques, culminating in *Sam Sam,* in which Trevor Griffiths forged something of excellence which was peculiarly British.

NOTES

1   Charles Marowitz, ed., *Off-Broadway Plays 2* (Harmondsworth, 1972), p.10.

2   John Guare, *Muzeeka*, in *Off-Broadway Plays 1* (Harmondsworth, 1970), 1970, pp.139–161.

3   All the following information is taken from publicity leaflets and a draft copy of the statement made by Marowitz for the Department of Employment and Productivity, OS 13/40.

4   For a description of this production, see Peter Ansorge, *Disrupting the Spectacle* (London, 1975), pp.28–29, and John Lahr, *Acting Out America* (Harmondsworth, 1970), pp.122–135.

5   OS 9/6. For a list of the plays included in the American Season, see Appendix.

6   *The Times*, 17 February 1971; *The Stage*, 25 February 1971; *Sunday Times*, 21 February 1971; *Financial Times*, 17 February 1971.

7   Terrence McNally, *Sweet Eros*, in *Off-Broadway Plays 2*, pp.43–56.

8   All references to the play are to the unpublished text, used for the Open Space production: Sam Shepard, *The Tooth of Crime*, OS archives.

9   Marowitz's own account of the production of *The Tooth of Crime* can be found in *Burnt Bridges*, pp.200–204.

[6]

New British Writers

Although it was part of the official policy at the Open Space to present the works of new writers, most of the new British plays written by playwrights who have since become famous were relegated to the lunchtime spot with minimal publicity. Many of them received excellent direction, supported by good performances, but they were not allowed to develop into anything more than interesting examples of new plays, and there seemed to be no real attempt to publicise the Open Space as a theatre that nurtured new talent. The plays selected for discussion in this chapter illustrate two aspects of the Open Space's repertoire. Firstly, there is a clash between the prevailing British taste for naturalism and the innovative use of music-hall and other techniques. There was much critical debate about the suitability of the Open Space both for naturalism and for modes of presentation which consciously attempted to subvert it. Secondly, new plays were put on there that were overtly political and broke into territory that the censorship of the stage had been set up to protect. However, the Open Space became associated with productions that were criticised for taking full advantage of the new freedom from censorship, but were not in other respects particularly experimental.

Of the forty-eight main house productions during the first four years, only seven plays were by British playwrights, and the first of these was by Paul Ableman, who had written his first successful play, *Green Julia*, in 1965, and who had also worked with Brook and Marowitz on the Theatre of Cruelty season. His *Blue Comedy* sparked off a controversy amongst theatre critics about the kind of plays an avowedly experimental theatre ought to be presenting. *Blue Comedy* consisted of two one-act plays, *Madly in Love* and *Hank's Night*; they were billed as sex comedies and as such received pre-performance public-ity because the lead actress, Sarah Atkinson, refused to appear naked at the end of *Hank's Night*. This play is a farce about two wealthy suburban couples who end a conventional dinner party with an orgy suggested by one of the guests. The play shows how the suggestion is taken by the different characters and how the desire for it fluctuates until the orgy finally hap-pens at the end of the play. The nude scene would have been the final fling before the blackout to show that the orgy was about to happen. Equity had not yet stepped in to help actors and directors over the question of nudity on stage, and although Marowitz said, 'I asked Miss Atkinson to remove her underclothes only because that is what the script requires' (*Sunday Telegraph*, 13 October 1968), she was not obliged to and did not. It could not be said to have ruined the show, though it perhaps added a coyness where none was intended.

The other play, *Madly in Love*, is about a male virgin who, desperate to lose his virginity, persuades a psychiatrist friend to allow him to treat a schoolgirl who suffers from a compul-sion to obey orders. It is a slight story with great potential for farce, and most of the critics enjoyed it for its sparkling dia-logue and smooth action.

The plays were a financial success, and the four-week run was extended by two weeks, with the last performance on Sunday 1 December. The box office returns had started at £320 2s 6d for the first week and dwindled to £156 os 6d by the end of the fourth week, but it was nevertheless decided that the plays should continue to run. The total box office returns for the six-week period were £1,270 4s 6d. Out of this, actors' salaries at £7 a week for the rehearsal period and £12 a week for performances had to be paid, plus 5% for royalties due to the playwright. After deducting the other running costs it can be seen that the theatre could not exist without help from other sources and that a £100 guarantee against loss from Camden Council was a help, but not sufficient. The plays did however sell to Bernard Delfont and Donald Albery for presentation in the West End, and although they were not actually performed until 21 April 1970 (and then at the Yvonne Arnaud Theatre in Guildford), the Open Space received £1,000 as a non-returnable advance on account of any sums which might become due in the event of a transfer.[1]

The two plays that followed, written by Stanley Eveling, were of a much more serious nature, though they broke no new theatrical ground. The programmes for the two shows were printed as one to encourage those who saw the first to see the second. In order to emphasise the seriousness of the plays, a long dialogue between Marowitz and Eveling was printed in the programme, discussing the nature of this playwright's art and his attitudes towards the problems expressed in his plays. The first, *The Lunatic, The Secret Sportsman and the Woman Next Door,* was described by Eveling as

> a kind of summation of the absurdity of our cultural inheritance. On the one hand you have the idealised man as the aggressive, liberal, self-assertive, dominating, masculine figure – the Sportsman ... and on the other hand, you have this extraordinarily spiritualised ideal ... of the Untouchable Man, the man who is beyond the body ... It seemed to me that I could present these like symbiotic twins who could never escape from each other and who never wanted to be together.

If this sounds a prolix and weighty summary of the play's theme, the production itself was, according to Irving Wardle in *The Times* (4 December 1968), 'almost a clown show'. If the programme notes suggested pretentiousness (*Daily Telegraph,* 4 December 1968, and *Punch,* 11 December 1968), Wardle made the opposite claim: 'The objection, indeed, is not to its pretensions but to moments of vaudeville banality.' The play was directed by Max Stafford-Clark, first at the Edinburgh Festival, then in Amsterdam at the Mickery Theatre, before coming to the Open Space.

The second play, *Come and Be Killed,* directed by Michael Blakemore, was written in a naturalistic manner and was likened to *Look Back in Anger* by more than one reviewer.[2] To begin with, press reaction was slow, and a letter was therefore sent out to all the critics who had failed to attend the opening, re-inviting them (OS 10/19). The result was that the critics eventually came, their reviews were good, but the public did not respond as well as the management had hoped and the play came off after 11 January 1969 instead of at the end of the month. It did marginally less well than *Lunatic* in terms of box office returns, but the expense of the naturalistic set was £451 as opposed to the £20 used to create the scene in *Lunatic*.3 Perhaps the subject matter and conventional structure of *Come and Be Killed* was not appealing, but it is most likely to have failed to attract because of the late press recognition and because it was Christmas, a notoriously bad time for theatres that do not offer specifically seasonal entertainment.

The play was about the moral implications of abortion and the ways in which human beings usually avoid confronting the important issues. In his programme interview, Eveling said that he had used a naturalistic style, 'because I wanted to make people smell the blood; to make them experience the dead, decaying foetus'. This he appears to have achieved, but at the expense of alienating potential audiences.

Just as the Off-Broadway playwrights had found that performance conditions similar to those at the Open Space were particularly well suited to plays depicting emotional conflict between characters, so British playwrights exploited the same idea. *Come and Be Killed* was followed by *Find Your Way Home* by John Hopkins (1970) and *Curtains* (1971) by Tom Mallin, two more examples of small-cast plays presenting intense and passionate situations. Hopkins had written extensively for film and television, but this was only his second stage play; the first, *This Story of Yours*, was performed at the Royal Court in 1968. *Find Your Way Home* dealt with a marriage destroyed by a male homosexual affair. It revealed at length the feelings of the three people involved, a technique that some critics found cliché-ridden and others painfully true to life. Most critics found it necessary to comment on the homosexual content of the play because Hopkins had opposed the conventional moral position which treated homosexuality as a disease. Again critics could not agree on the relative strengths and weaknesses of the production. The critic for the *Financial Times* (13 May 1970) liked the portrayal of the heterosexual relationship but not the homosexual one, and the critic for the *Guardian* (13 May 1970) took the opposite view. Simon Trussler for *Tribune* (22 May 1970) felt that the Open Space

Theatre was too small to take the melodramatic quality of the play, but Irving Wardle in *The Times* (13 May 1970) commented that the Open Space was well suited as 'a compression chamber for the passions'. This was the sort of constructive controversy on which an experimental theatre could thrive, and houses were good.

Curtains received similar notices, with critics responding well to the 'probing psychological drama' (*The Times*, 20 January 1971), but objecting to any departure from the naturalistic illusion. More interesting were three plays that were written in a different mode, using music-hall techniques which were built into the plays' structure. They were all directed by Charles Marowitz, whose inclination was always away from naturalism. The first two were one-act plays by Peter Barnes, who had previously had a success with *The Ruling Class* at the Nottingham Playhouse in November 1968 with a subsequent transfer to the Piccadilly Theatre, London (26 February 1969).

Barnes and Marowitz were very close friends long before either achieved any recognition. As a critic for *Encore* magazine, *Plays and Players*, and on BBC radio, Marowitz constantly championed Barnes' work and had directed his very first play *Sclerosis* for the Traverse in Edinburgh where it opened on 1 June 1965, transferring for a single performance at the Aldwych in London on 27 June 1965. The closeness of the friendship resulted in Marowitz being asked to direct the premiere of *The Ruling Class* in Nottingham. Unfortunately, the dates of the premiere conflicted directly with the West End transfer of *Fortune and Men's Eyes* and Marowitz felt he had to forego the assignment, despite the fact that he had consulted at length with Barnes on cuts and alterations to be made to the script. This caused a rift between the two men that the production of the double bill of one-act plays helped to heal.[4]

Leonardo's Last Supper and *Noonday Demons* were written especially for the Open Space in a spirit closer to the provocative nature of experimental theatre than any of the other new British plays so far presented. In his introduction to the play text, Barnes wrote:

> And so the aim is to create, by means of soliloquy, rhetoric, formal-
> ized ritual, slapstick, songs and dances, a comic theatre of contrast-
> ing moods and opposites, where everything is simultaneously tragic
> and ridiculous.'5

John Napier, who had designed the set, had created 'a ghost-
train setting of cobwebs, bones and spidery tentacles' *(Sunday
Telegraph,* 7 December 1969). At the theatre's entrance hung a
golden skeleton amidst cobwebs, and one reviewer likened the
theatre's appearance to Count Dracula's castle (*The Stage,* 11
December 1969). The feeling of the unexpected, heralded by
the set, was immediately followed up in the action and language of the plays. *Leonardo's Last Supper* opened with a
modern-sounding lecture on the Renaissance in Italy coming
over loudspeakers, followed immediately by a cortège of four
cantors chanting the 'Miserere' over a corpse. The bier was
laid on stage, and with an abrupt change in the lighting the
actors performed a thoroughly modern and jazzy knees-up. By
contrast, the set for *Noonday Demons* was entirely dominated by
a mound which was later revealed to be the excrement of
Saint Eusebius (played by Joe Melia). The language used by
the play's only two characters was a mixture of modern slang
and mock medieval prose.

Unlike the Hopkins and Mallin plays, the imaginative theatrical form of these plays made up for any lack of thematic
content. These seemingly lightweight farces were characterised by an emphasis on the grotesque, as taboos of language and action were broken.

In 1972 Trevor Griffiths' play *Sam Sam* used music-hall
techniques to convey serious political statements of the kind
that were to characterise all his later work.[6] This was his first
full-length play (though the second, *Occupations,* had been
performed previously, at the Stables Theatre Club, Manchester, in 1970, and also by the RSC at The Place in London,
1971); it was so well received by the public that its run was
extended. The play uses a blend of naturalistic and non-
naturalistic techniques, though the naturalism of the second
half has been chosen to represent and reflect the bourgeois
values which the play attacks. However, as so often in this theatre, it seems to have been the non-naturalistic first half that

appealed to the critics, several of them failing to identify the inherent parody of the naturalistic form in part two. Griffiths himself has said that the second half of *Sam Sam* was 'to a certain extent, an attempt to have a critical discourse with that form'.7

The play dramatises the lives of Sam 1 and Sam 2 who are brothers – they are both played by the same actor. The first half depicts a working-class Sam through a series of monologues presented as music-hall turns together with sketches of his life with his wife and mother. The second half shows Sam 2 who has, through his education and ambition, attempted to reject his origins for a middle-class lifestyle. His wife and in-laws form the conflicting groups for the second half.

Act I creates the working-class environment of Sam 1. Although the stage directions require a bathroom set, it was the 'essence without superfluous detail' (*Guardian,* 10 February 1972) which John Napier provided. What the critics did not mention was the comic effect caused by the trucking in of the complete bathroom set. According to Griffiths, it became a 'mobile mise-en-scène in the variety show tradition' which contributed to what he referred to as the 'cartoon element in the production'. It creaked and groaned its way onto the stage in semi-darkness (it was not possible, in any case, to black out the stage area completely) and no attempt was made to hide the mechanics of the setting from the audience. Marowitz again used the lack of sophistication of his theatre facilities to comic advantage so that even the off-stage whispers of the actors became a part of the total comic effect. Some of the older actors had difficulty in adapting to the working conditions at the Open Space, and every night they would let the audience know that they were unhappy with the lack of facilities when their off-stage voices could be heard complaining as they bumped into each other or knocked things over. It was not that these interjections were incorporated into the production; they were there simply because you could not eradicate them, and to the delight of Griffiths and the audience they added to the atmosphere of music-hall comedy which he had hoped to convey through the play. However, though he found this technique of 'cartoonising' one of the most successful elements of the production, he also felt that it was not balanced properly against the realistic mode which was also part of the play's structure. The final result was that there was not enough realistic context against which to set the cartoon, in order to clarify the playwright's targets.

Lighting was used to give fluidity to the changes from one dramatic mode to the other, and by using bright spotlighting, six or eight different playing points were picked out. In the first act, Sam (Nikolas Simmonds) performed like a stand-up comic and his routines were lit in this way. He addressed the audience directly, and according to Griffiths the audiences both loved it and were wary of being drawn into the action. They were audiences who had in the recent past experienced the work of Pip Simmons, so that when Sam handed a bowl of batter to a member of the audience sitting in the front row there was a frisson of expectation and anxiety as he wondered what the next move might be.[8] Griffiths' use of this technique is dramatic and apt: content and form blend, and it foreshadowed his later and more successful play *Comedians* (successful in that it reached a wide audience through the West End stage and television adaptation). Griffiths said in an interview in *Time Out* (4 February 1972) that through *Sam Sam* he wished 'to hit somebody – it's got to leave blood on the face', a comment that is given a visually dramatic image in *Comedians* as Gethin Price pricks his dummy, a representative of the bourgeoisie, with a pin, and it begins to bleed.

Trevor Griffiths has referred to the structure of *Sam Sam* as 'two slabs', and he discussed at length with Marowitz the possibility of writing a bleak but funny scene around the grave of Sam's father with the two Sams present, in order to tie the two halves together. However, the difficulties inherent in a final scene of this nature led him to abandon the task and to trust to the tenuous links already present. Act II starts in a similar way to Act I. This time Sam 2 is not doing a music-hall act, but rehearsing a speech he is going to make as a politician. A spotlight was used against a darkened stage to pick out Sam, just as it was in Act I, but this time the technique disappeared after the first scene. Sam's mother from Act I returned to make an appeal on behalf of her other son, Sam 1, and Sam 2's voice is said in a stage direction to move 'closer to Sam 1's though the distance is not entirely spanned' (p.28). The stormy relationship between Sam and his wife in Act I is mirrored by the equally disastrous pairing of the couple in Act II, with the lack of understanding between both sets of parents stressed in both acts. However, Griffiths gives the first half of his play an extra dimension as he makes Sam point to and comment upon the techniques he is using:

> Sam (*directly to audience*): You can clear off for a bit if you like. See what we're up to, can you? Both of us talking away, neither of us listening, makes the point very nicely, no communication, you know the stuff. (pp.11–12)

Later he does an imitation of a 'Hampstead-intense voice' and at the end of the speech he says, 'all right then, let's try someat else then, shall we? How about this', and he leads into a flashback scene between his drunken father and beaten-up mother (pp.18–19). It is a clichéd scene which is given validity by Sam's comment at the end, 'How's that then? That a bit better? That a bit closer to your authentic working class drudgery is it?'

In the second half the clichéd scenes are left to speak for themselves, as if the playwright is now determined to take himself and his characters seriously, and consequently the majority of the critics felt that the play had lost its originality and had lapsed into sentimentality. This seems to be what the critic in *Plays and Players* (April 1972) meant when he said 'the surrender to form is ultimately self-defeating'. Griffiths found the audience's attention upon the play was intense and focused, but although they were engaged with the play from the beginning to the end, they were more attuned to the methods of the first half which comments directly upon itself than with the less reflexive and more realistic second half. Marowitz complained that England had never had an avant garde, but he had already earned himself the reputation of promoting experimental theatre, and his audiences and the critics were eager for plays with a critical approach to form.

According to Griffiths, the aspect of the play that had attracted Marowitz's attention was the Strindbergian element in the second half, the conflict between the male and the female. For Griffiths this was only one aspect of a play which was essentially about class conflict and 'the illusory nature of so-called class mobility', and he felt that the production lacked social specificity. Nikolas Simmonds was acclaimed unanimously by the critics and was described in *The Times* (10 February 1972) as an 'actor of prodigious emotional intensity and grasp of character'. This was precisely what Griffiths thought was missing from the performance. Though he does not deny Simmonds's technical achievement, he found that the performance was only 'adjacent' to the part. Simmonds had the knowledge and experience of Sam 1's class, but somehow suppressed or refused to acknowledge it. According to Griffiths, Simmonds missed the pain and tended to patronise Sam 1. There was a feeling that as an actor he was saying to the audience, 'I know this character and I will mediate the play to you accordingly.' Simmonds got the part because he was at the time the first actor in Marowitz's newly, but not yet officially, formed repertory company, and Griffiths had to accept a casting he would not necessarily have chosen. Even if this prejudiced his view of the production, there was no lack of commitment to it on his part, and he regularly attended rehearsals, where he was impressed with Marowitz's disciplined approach to his work as director and with his dedication to the play.

One other play of predominantly British origin deserves mention for its attempt to fashion a new style of playing, and that is *Lay-By*, created by the Portable Theatre Company, originally for the Edinburgh Festival. In the group were Trevor Griffiths, Howard Brenton, David Hare, Snoo Wilson, Stephen Poliakoff, Hugh Stoddart and Brian Clark, though according to Griffiths ninety per cent of the writing was done by Hare, Wilson, Brenton and himself. Brian Clark walked out after two or three weeks of working on the project.[9] The story, taken from an account in the newspapers, recounts in its own way the elements surrounding a motorway rape case. The play is aggressive and angry. It attacks complacency about corruption and injustice in society by depicting realistically (though comically) scenes of sexual perversion in the pornography trade.

During the performance the audience were made to feel implicated in the seedy voyeuristic society as house lights went up and pornographic photographs (pasted onto four-foot boards so that it would be difficult to remove them from the theatre) were handed round for their scrutiny. According to Brenton and Wilson (*Plays and Players*, November 1971), even in a theatre the size of the Royal Court this implication was lost, and the play degenerated into a small revue. In the Open Space Theatre where there was no proscenium arch to hinder audience/actor contact, the play became much more 'dangerous' (Brenton). The very dinginess of the theatre and its position in the run-down area of Tottenham Court Road, lent a feeling of the play's environment to the production.

One of the complaints made by the critics was that there was no unity of style in the production as a whole, reflecting sharply the fact that the play was written by seven authors. However, it might well be argued that the mixture of styles was used deliberately to confound the audiences' expectations in order to attack their complacency. The characters are not given psychological consistency; they are there simply as pawns in the playwrights' game to demonstrate a point of view by word or action. The final image is of bodies being pulped, a shocking but comic visual symbol of what becomes of people and their reputations after death. The play was not mystifying: its very lack of subtlety was a part of its intention. It was meant to shock and alienate its audiences. Snoo Wilson in interview (*Plays and Players*, November 1971) claimed, 'We have alienated permanently a section of the British theatre-going public.'

The conspicuous lack of new British writing in the evening presentations at the Open Space was to an extent compensated for by the work put on in the lunchtime spots. Those British plays provided a greater variety of form and content than the American ones had, and Marowitz could be considered to have been at fault in not giving a more prominent status to new British playwrights, who were ready and eager to use his kind of theatre.

NOTES

1   A full breakdown of income and expenditure can be found in OS 13/12.

2   *Tribune*, 3 January 1969, *The Stage*, 24 December 1968, *Sunday Telegraph*, 5 January 1969.

3   Accounts for this production can be found in OS 13/12.

4   Charles Marowitz in interview with the author, 2 June 2004.

5   Peter Barnes, *Collected Plays* (London, 1981), p.122.

6   All references to the play are to the unpublished text, used for the Open Space production: Trevor Griffiths, *Sam Sam*, OS archives.

7   Trevor Griffiths in interview with the author, 4 December 1984. All his other comments on this production are taken from the same interview.

8   The Pip Simmons Group first tried out its anarchic brand of performance art at the Arts Lab in 1968. Its method was to create a wild atmosphere of hysteria with pop music and comic-strip characters, and then force the audience into participation. It had brought a production of *Superman* to the Open Space in 1970.

9   For information on the genesis of the play see *Plays and Players*, November 1971, 'Getting the Carp out of the Mud'.

[7]

Lunchtime and Late-Night Theatre

As soon as the Open Space opened, the management decided to launch lunchtime theatre, and an improvised play called *Come* was directed by Marowitz during the run of *Fortune and Men's Eyes*. Lunchtime theatre was a fairly new phenomenon in London, and it was clear from one critic's reponse that this was his first encounter with it: he was much more concerned with the 'bizarre idea' of eating and watching a play at the same time than with the play itself (*Plays and Players*, September 1968).

The production was sparsely attended, and the idea was dropped in favour of late-night theatre. Again the intention was to show plays which featured experimental staging techniques, and much of the work performed was developed through group exercises. Even though the Open Space received good publicity for its attempts to open up a new market, the public could not be persuaded to make late-night visits a habit. Some of the plays were interesting (for example, Mike Leigh, who had been assistant director at the RSC in 1967 and who became well-known for his BBC studio plays in 1975–76, devised an entertainment for the Open Space called *Bleak Moments*), and reviewers were willing to acknowledge the importance of this new departure. However, in common with the rest of London theatre, the Open Space failed to recruit new audiences, and the experiment was abandoned in 1972 after a substantial effort had been made.

A year after the initial failure to launch lunchtime theatre, the management tried again, but with no better result. Nevertheless, the notion of lunchtime theatre was beginning to take a hold on the British public's imagination. *Plays and Players* had sporadically run a column entitled 'Lunch and Late-Night

Line-Up' since 1969. In the latter half of 1970 it appeared every month, and by 1971 'Late-Night' had been dropped from the title, leaving the new heading 'Lunch Line-Up' to appear regularly until September 1971. After that, lunchtime shows continued to be dealt with under the more general designation, 'Fringe'.

The first success that the Open Space had with its lunchtime presentations was in February 1971 when the RSC brought in three plays, one British and two American. This prestigious company gave impressive performances and a necessary boost to the Open Space's fortunes, even though most critics did not like the plays. The first, *Gum and Goo* by Howard Brenton, was a good choice since Brenton's work was already well-known to reviewers (he had been awarded an Arts Council Bursary and was joint winner of the John Whiting Award for *Christie in Love* in 1969), and the play itself benefited from the intimate and bare surroundings. The other two, *Icarus's Mother* by Sam Shepard and *Grant's Movie* by Mike Weller, also dramatised the theme of violence in society as *Gum and Goo* had done, thus setting a trend of dealing with political matters in the lunchtime theatre at the Open Space.

These three were followed by a spate of American plays, so that Jonathan Hammond (writing for *Plays and Players* in September 1971) might be forgiven for assuming that there was a clear-cut policy of turning the Open Space into an off-Broadway cellar. Even the main house programmes at this period were American. Marowitz confounded all such surmises by subsequently presenting, with the exception of one or two productions, nothing but British plays at lunchtime. In fact, as Walter Donohue explained[1], he and John Burgess were reading the new scripts which came in to the Open Space and they were allowed to put on what they liked. It is for this reason that British playwrights were given a chance to show their work: Donohue felt very strongly that one of the Open Space's prime objectives should be to promote new native writing. Both men were interested in political theatre, which explains the new emphasis on left-wing plays. Amongst those which they chose were works by some of today's most celebrated British writers: Howard Brenton, David Edgar, William Trevor and Howard Barker. They represent the best of the lunchtime output at any time during the history of the Open Space.

Donohue's first British play was *Ritual of the Dolls* by George McEwan-Green, a violent and acute study of the emotions. It had been premiered at Sheffield, having won the NUS award for Leicester University under the title *Out of the Box*. Under Donohue's direction in the tiny basement its effect was devastating. The set, which was adapted from the one used for the current main-house production of *The Critic as Artist*, created the illusion of a giant toy-box which housed the dolls who were to enact the drama. The action itself was a mixture of the naturalistic and the stylised; the actors' movements were choreographed so that they looked like toys. Donohue attributes the success of the disturbing moments in the play to the naturalistic way in which he treated those parts of the story which dealt with the true events being re-enacted by the dolls. In order to reach the heart of the emotion, he had used improvisatory techniques with his actors before finally using the script. A measure of his success in finding and exploiting the tensions within the text can be judged from the following anecdote. The author, who had not been present during rehearsals, sat in on one of the final run-throughs. At the end of the performance he left without a word to anyone. Two days later he returned to apologise for his lack of comment and explained that he had been deeply shocked by the extreme violence inherent in a play which he had written. He was appalled at his lack of awareness, yet fully cognisant of Donohue's achievement. Only one review of the play appears to exist, and the reviewer nominated it 'lunchtime play of the month' (*Plays and Players*, August 1971).

Donohue's other two productions were of plays by Howard Brenton. The first, *A Sky Blue Life*, was found by Burgess in a pile of scripts submitted to the Open Space for reading. The play was a combination of a biography of Gorky and extracts from his works, and it was decided that it could be produced on a budget of £10 for the set. Wardle called it 'poverty theatre' in his review (*The Times*, 20 November 1971), perhaps without realising quite how little Donohue had had with which to create a set. The bare floor and back wall were painted black. Slogans were chalked up on the wall by various characters to provide any necessary information for the audience during the performance, and any props were brought on by the actors. The physical feat of crossing the river Volga was accomplished through mime; the different locations were indicated upon the back wall. Donohue was described by Nicholas de Jongh (*Guardian,* 19 November 1971) as resourceful in his use of lighting, but most critics were impressed by the very strong cast of six actors, and Donohue himself has said that the play was successful because the cast was outstanding both at creating character and at suggesting its surroundings.[2]

The second of the Brenton plays, *How Beautiful With Badges,* was commissioned for the Open Space and was therefore written with its stage space in mind.[3] The play concerns two pairs of characters: two Hell's Angels, who are discovered as the play opens reclining centre stage on a bright green ramp of artificial grass, and a boy scout and his companion. The result of their meeting is a violent clash and the play ends with a ritualistic flaying of the scout and his friend by the Hell's Angels. The play shows how people erect defences: in this case the badges they wear are emblematic of the uniforms behind which they hide. Humanity is forgotten and the violence becomes anonymous. It was a very powerful production which did not leave its audience indifferent. At least one person known to the author fled from the auditorium vowing never to return.

Robin Don, who designed the set, took his inspiration from the paintings of Francis Bacon that depict a man trapped in a cage, screaming with pain and horror, unable to escape from life.[4] He designed a cube made from white elasticated ropes (like those used to strap luggage onto the back of a motorcycle) which was suspended on thin black chains from just below the ceiling to just above the floor. It hung free and was flexible so that it might be twisted into any desired shape. The white of the ropes was stark against the black flat which covered the back of the stage. The centre area of the flat dropped down like a drawbridge to reveal upon its surface bright green artificial grass, and leaving an area behind the flat which was bright blue with clouds floating by. At one point in the play the cloud answers a question put to it by Molester (one of the Angels): a taped voice was used which was put on a reverberator to make it sound supernatural, as Molester by this time was high on drugs. The white cube which encompassed the action ensured that the focus of attention was the man caught in the trap. It also enhanced the artificiality of the action, the theatrical image which was being used to counterpoint the reality of the viciousness of fanaticism. Sound effects such as the birds singing were deliberately made to sound realistic in order to contrast with and create a tension between the real world and the strange surreal things which were happening on stage. At certain points during the action Jesus was seen staggering across the back of the stage carrying a large and heavy cross (approximately fifteen feet long). He never spoke, but appeared to be a hallucination of Molester's. Images like this were so bizarre that they became comic; in fact the piece of stage business that always produced the greatest laugh of the performance was when Jesus lay on the cross and with his hammer knocked a nail through one hand, only to find that he was unable to hammer one in through the other. The action was also extremely realistic, with a quantity of blood spurting over the audience, who were only two feet away. Horror and comedy (the hallmark of Brenton's style in his early plays) were blended in this symbolic action. When discussing the production with the author, Walter Donohue said that he had been unable to capture satisfactorily the comic surface of this very serious play.

The play moved towards its climax where Gut and Molester (played by Malcolm Storry and David Schofield), standing on either side of the ramp, rhythmically beat the two others (played by Antony Milner and Ian Flavin) with chains. Donohue enhanced the tension with the use of strobe lighting, which gave the action a feeling of frenzy. Garry O'Connor, writing in the *Financial Times* (3 May 1972), disliked the lighting effects, complaining that they hurt his eyes, and the critic for the *Daily Telegraph* (3 May 1972) was glad when it stopped – a tribute indeed to the author's and director's intention. Nicholas de Jongh (*Guardian*, 4 May 1972), on the other hand, praised the 'superlative visual energy and excitement in the strobe-light fighting'. At one point a piece of flesh appeared to be cut from one of the victims, and a piece of raw and dripping meat was handed into the action. It was not meant to trick the audience into thinking that a piece of flesh had actually been torn from the man's body, but to present a clear and apposite image of the brutality that was taking place on stage. Brenton's writing is compressed, pared down into strong visual images, and is extremely effective in an acting space which is small and 'dangerous', with the minimum of scenery and only a limited capacity for creating illusory effects. It was this aspect of the production that so impressed Irving Wardle (*The Times*, 3 May 1972). The very end of the play was unnaturally quiet as the character Tone delivered a monologue about the past which had formed him. Even those critics who did not like the play acknowledged its peculiar force.[5]

Judging from the regular lunchtime reviews which appeared in *Plays and Players* during 1971 and 1972, the quality of lunchtime theatre at the Open Space was higher than at other venues. While Jonathan Hammond and Nigel Andrews were giving good notices to plays presented there (*Plays and Players* for July, August and September 1971), Andrews was also defending the poor quality of some of the other lunchtime shows by talking of the need to take risks:

> Any alternative to West End theatre is welcome, not because West End theatre is bad but because it has to play safe … Bad plays are a natural hazard if we wish to create an effectively wider choice of available theatre. (*Plays and Players*, August 1971).

Marowitz himself had written an article in spring 1971 for *Ink* in which he attacked the plays performed in lunchtime cellars as 'tame slivers of old telly plays, toss-offs by writers too under-nourished to provide full-length work'.[6] He had picked on a real weakness of lunchtime theatre but his comments led to a rebuttal by John Ford in *Time Out* (7 May 1971), accusing Marowitz of sour grapes because he had not been granted the finances to run a permanent company. It is curious that Marowitz should have found it necessary to condemn so wholeheartedly the work done at his own theatre, particularly when he took no active interest in the choice of lunchtime repertoire. During 1972–73 and 1975–76, when he had formed a company, shows appeared with regularity, and their standard was high. On the whole, the lunchtime productions during the latter part of the Open Space's term at the Tottenham Court Road theatre were not as adventurous as the earlier ones, and critics did not give full support. Even for the revival of Brenton's *Christie in Love* (first performed on 23 November 1969 at Oval House) there were very few reviews, though Nicholas de Jongh in the *Guardian* gave it an enthusiastic write-up (22 July 1976). Only one play, *Split*, by Mike Weller, was given a lunchtime showing at the new premises in the Euston Road, on 19 July 1977, and despite Weller's earlier successes only four reviews are to be found in the cuttings book for that period.

In 1972, lunchtime theatre had been given a fillip with the formation of ALT – the Association of Lunchtime Theatres – whose aims were: 'to promote lunchtime theatre, to present principally new and neglected plays and playwrights, to provide alternative venues for actors, directors and designers, and to encourage audiences by making theatre more accessible.'7 However, by 1976 general interest in lunchtime theatre had dried up and this, together with the theatre's less central position in the Euston Road, was what made Marowitz give up the lunchtime presentations. In times when resources were scarce they were a luxury the management could not afford, especially since the work could not be defended on the grounds of an overwhelming demand.

NOTES

1   Walter Donohue in interview with the author, 14 June 1984.
2   No script has been traced. Actors appearing were Ian Flavin, Susan Levy, Antony Milner, Stephen Moore, Diana Quick and Donald Sumpter.
3   A photocopy of the unpublished manuscript is in the OS archives.
4   Robin Don in interview with the author, 5 June 1982.
5   *The Stage*, 18 May 1972; *Guardian*, 4 May 1972.
6   This article has not been traced, but it is extensively quoted in *Plays and Players*, July 1971.
7   Quoted in *Stages in the Revolution*, p.136.

[8]

Personalities of the Management

In the world of theatre it is almost always the name of the artistic director that is remembered for the success or failure of a production (in the 1960s and 70s they were nearly all men), and it is, of course, on his productions that a theatre's reputation is based. It is therefore not surprising that the Open Space became synonymous with the name of Charles Marowitz even though it was publicised at the beginning as a joint venture of Marowitz's and Thelma Holt's. Marowitz himself was, then as now, a journalist and writer as well as a director, which meant that his name was brought more often to public notice than hers was, and since he hesitated neither to go into print about any grievance that he had nor to support a controversial issue over the law and theatre in general, he quickly brought to the Open Space a sense of adventure and notoriety which was at once its glory and its downfall.

It has become clear through conversations with those who worked at the Open Space that without the work of Thelma Holt the enterprise would never have run for twelve years. It is significant that the theatre survived for only two years after her resignation, and that the final year limped along with her help as administrator of the Round House. She helped build both theatres, recruited support from wealthy patrons, and kept relations between the actors and Marowitz sweet during their many difficult moments. Marowitz was then, and still is, passionate about good and committed acting, but when he sensed mediocrity or laziness could be devastating about his actors.[1] Holt would help ease these frictions, she kept him up to schedule with his written work for the theatre, she took up the actors' cause when accommodation on tour was appalling, she even sent two men packing who tried to extort protection money from the theatre, and as she was present at the time of a police raid (described below) during the showing of Andy Warhol's *Flesh* (3 February 1970), dealt with it efficiently.

Her approach towards people (colleagues, the public and authorities) was fundamentally different from that of Marowitz, which was often high-handed and tended to alienate those who were initially his most ardent supporters.

This assertiveness worked both for and against Marowitz and the work he was trying to do. It meant that he was willing to go against popular opinion in an attempt to bring new life to West End theatre. He thrived on outraging complacency and was always willing to present plays that set themselves against accepted values. In *Fortune and Men's Eyes* he had been quick to exploit the theatre's new-found freedom from censorship, and actors had appeared naked on stage. The play dealt openly with homosexuality, a theme which was pursued again in *Find Your Way Home* by John Hopkins (12 May 1970).

Critics' opinions of the play's worth clashed, and this had the advantage of enhancing the theatre's reputation for presenting slightly risqué pieces. Two other events before and after this production developed into public debates over censorship which have rumbled on over other plays ever since 1968. The first of these was concerned with the controversial *Flesh*, the second film to be shown in a season of late-night programmes which had opened with Norman Mailer's *Beyond the Law*. Before coming to England and while he was writing for *The Village Voice*, Marowitz had met Andy Warhol, who had already achieved iconic status in America. He agreed to show his film at the Open Space, which gave the theatre a very welcome financial boost, and for three weeks *Flesh* had an uninterrupted run. Then suddenly, on the evening of 3 February 1970, thirty-two policemen burst into the auditorium, seized the screen and projector, confiscated all the club membership files, and took the names and addresses of all those present. Jimmy Vaughan, the film's distributor, who happened to be present that evening, immediately phoned the film censor John Trevelyan, who came round directly to see what was happening. He arrived after the police had left but made his position clear to Thelma Holt and others present: he had permitted and encouraged the showing of the film on club premises, though he had not granted it a certificate for general release. Later, when the court hearing took place on 15 May 1970, obscenity charges were dropped, but Marowitz and Holt were fined £200 for breach of licensing regulations. It was alleged that only a very small number of those present at the film showing were members of the club, and the directors of the company pleaded guilty to this charge.[2]

These events received huge publicity from the press, and the question of censorship, and of this police raid in particular, was raised in the House of Commons. *The Times* (13 March 1970) printed a report of the debate where James Callaghan, then the Home Secretary, supported the police action (according to the *Spectator*, 21 March 1970, because of the forthcoming elections). Callaghan's view was opposed by Michael Foot, who spoke in favour of a more liberal attitude towards the arts, but the Home Secretary would not be moved.

In an article printed in the *Guardian* on 6 March, Marowitz clarified his own attitude. He did not believe that the repressive forces in Great Britain were in a majority, nor did he wish people who disagreed with him any ill-will. What he wished to draw attention to was the fact that the repressive minority was well-organised, with a great deal of money and power. He saw the need for a similarly well-organised and well-financed body to combat their attempt to limit the freedom of the arts.

Although he was unable to continue showing the film immediately, and this inevitably meant loss of income, the publicity his theatre received can only have helped his cause, and the audiences came in force to see the film when it returned to the Open Space on 17 March. The £200 fine, which the magistrates had ordered to be paid within twenty-eight days, could have threatened the company's trip to Italy, which was planned for May, but the papers announced on 18 May that Andy Warhol had offered to pay the fine for them and that this had been gratefully accepted.

After being the centre of a debate which actually saw the two principals in court, they were involved in another where, although the law was not invoked, considerable press coverage was generated. The production which caused the furore was *A Nativity Play*, staged by Wherehouse La Mama, an English off-shoot of La Mama, led by Beth Porter. In this play the part of God was taken by a nude actor and the Holy Family was represented as a 'set of swingers' (*The Times*, 17 December 1970). The play was the alleged cause of an outburst by Lord Eccles (Minister for the Arts) at the City of London Conservatives' forum, when he announced that he was to have talks with Lord Goodman, chairman of the Arts Council, to devise a system to deal with pornographic and blasphemous productions performed under the auspices of theatres that received Arts Council grants (*Guardian*, 26 January 1971). Nicholas de Jongh's *Guardian* article went on to analyse the implications of Eccles' remark that it was perfectly all right if people wanted to go into a cellar and see 'some revolting extension of striptease' if it was a privately funded show. He roundly condemned Eccles' position, and was seconded by Marowitz in a *Guardian* article (28 January 1971) where he called for more support from the bigger, 'better-heeled' companies such as the National and the RSC.

Many of the critics disliked the production, and Harold Hobson added his voice to the clamour of those who wished to see the Arts Council's support withdrawn. Reasons for the dislike were diverse: the critic for *Plays and Players* (February 1971) felt the company was not as inventive as it had been in the past. Irving Wardle (*The Times*, 17 December 1970), while treating the show seriously, thought that it was the 'Beth Porter Show' and not an ensemble piece of work, whilst Nicholas de Jongh found it 'too infantile and too stupid to review'. However, as de Jongh so rightly pointed out, the Eccles proposals meant that these respected critics were not to be allowed to differ in their points of view, and companies, such as this one, which had done good work in the past, no longer had the right to fail. In the *Evening Standard*, 22 January 1971 Marowitz was quoted as having said that Lord Eccles did not make it clear whether or not his attack was simply provoked by stage nudity, but that it seemed obvious to him that it was 'a form of political censorship aimed at removing subsidies from groups that are not establishment orientated'. It was an indictment of a theatre, he said, if it had not produced anything which could be described as inflammatory. In his opinion theatre ought always to move away from established values to question and to re-assess, and a theatre that shied away from any controversy which might arise from this was not fulfilling its most valuable function.

If the tone of Marowitz's article here was reasonable, it was perhaps because the discussion of censorship was broadly based and not specifically an attack on his theatre. When defending his own theatre his tone was often more belligerent. In the programme for *Find Your Way Home* he attacked the Arts Council for effectively refusing to increase its grant from the previous year's £3,000.[3] In 1969 they had been given a grant of £1,500 with guarantees-against-loss which brought it up to approximately £3,000. In 1970 the Arts Council withdrew the guarantees and increased the grant to £3,000; Marowitz accused it of 'patent arithmetical deception'. He then sniped at the Arts Council policies in general and suggested that the theatres which received subsidy were those that had representatives in the Arts Council's 'inner circle'.

This was a charge that Marowitz made in his exposé of the Arts Council printed in the *Guardian* (19 November 1971), where it formed the crux of his argument condemning the body for being run by board members who were also major recipients of subsidy, i.e. people voting themselves grants. His opening paragraph stated that he had undertaken some research into the mechanism of the Arts Council because of his own sense of frustration at lack of subsidy. Having declared his emotional involvement with the facts he was to expose, he chose a rhetorical and heavily ironical form of address: 'If, by justice, we mean the hidden use of influence in order to obtain public monies, then the Arts Council of Great Britain is a just organisation. If, by justice, we mean the making of arbitrary decisions under the guise of democratic procedure, the Arts Council of Great Britain is a just organisation', and so on. He then named people and organisations of whom he was critical, and in doing so made some mistakes for which he was quickly taken to task in the stream of correspondence that followed. For instance, Moran Caplat (General Administrator,

Glyndebourne) corrected his allegation that the Glyndebourne Festival was state-subsidised (*Guardian*, 23 November 1971), and Hugh Willatt (Secretary General for the Arts Council) pointed out that Chairman Lambert had served only three years and not eight as Marowitz had suggested. His exaggerations and distortions, though few, were enough to discredit the article to a degree, but they were not sufficient to detract from the importance of what he had to say. The correspondence that followed was by no means entirely unsympathetic, and in *Plays and Players* (January 1972) an article lamented the fact that 'so far no-one has really picked up the gauntlet that he [Marowitz] so angrily flung down'. The reviewer also called him 'a persistent thorn in the side of the Establishment', which aptly describes his relationship with all official bodies during the lifetime of the Open Space.

Hugh Jenkins, MP, chosen by Jennie Lee to sit on the Arts Council, and who later became Minister for the Arts, wrote a generalised rebuttal of Marowitz's charges, stating that 'his conclusions are muddled and many of his facts are wrong' (*Guardian*, 25 November 1971). He did not make a detailed defence and finished by asking Marowitz to look at his own achievement to find the reasons for lack of subsidy. Marowitz's reply to this was to mention the awards his productions had received on the continent and to remind Jenkins that for one production he had received £2,600 from Wiesbaden, more than his annual grant from the Arts Council of Great Britain (*Guardian*, 30 November 1971).

Marowitz ended his article by saying that he was sending a report of his findings to Sir Alan Marre, Ombudsman and Parliamentary Commissioner for Administration. The outcome of this appeal was recorded in the *Guardian* (3 December 1971), where it was stated that the Ombudsman could do nothing since the act appointing him to his position excluded the Arts Council (appointed by Royal Charter) from the bodies whose actions he could examine.

Marowitz's calculated attacks on the Establishment were always couched in highly emotive terminology. Here he had referred to the members of the Arts Council as the 'cultural mafia', and in his tussle with Equity in 1969 over the American season he had drawn an analogy between those who run Equity and the Russians who had sent in the occupying forces to Czechoslovakia. He was quite capable of infuriating those he attacked, but if he was looking for support then it was not necessarily the best way of finding it. In the Arts Council exposé, before officially enlisting the help of the Ombudsman, he announced that he was preparing a submission of charges against the Arts Council, in the full knowledge that he was appealing to a government agency, 'without teeth or temperament to attack'. In the event the Ombudsman was legally unable to help, but it was this sort of aggressiveness, together with the presupposition that everyone was ill-disposed towards justice, that often alienated those who might have helped.

Marowitz's response to people and situations was always vigorously spontaneous and extrovert. His meeting with Alan Burns illustrates his impetuosity and the way in which it could generate creative energy. The story is told in the *Guardian* (30 April 1970) of a local dignitary at the Harrogate Festival in 1969 who spoke at a public assembly of the need for modern artists to remember the affairs of the spirit, and, as an example of one who needed to be reminded, cited Alan Burns. Burns, who was present, leapt from the audience, snatched the microphone from the speaker and recited Artaud's poem 'Shit to the Spirit' (*'Chiote à l'Esprit'*, 1947). At this, Marowitz, also in the audience, strode across the stage, crying 'I commission you to write a play'. Marowitz himself has no memory of this dramatic intervention, but whether or not the story was embellished by the journalist's imagination, the production of *Palach* was created a year later.[4] This characteristic of acting on the spur of the moment was also responsible for his enthusiasm and tenaciousness in the choice of new plays such as *Sam Sam* and *The Tooth of Crime*, where he stuck with determination to his initial reaction, until he was finally able to present them.

This impetuosity sometimes generated hostilities, particularly when working intensively with a group of actors. Malcolm Storry, one of the longest serving actors of the permanent company which was formed in 1972, told how this company came to an untimely end.[5] Candida Fawsitt, who was playing in Arrabal's *And They Put Handcuffs on the Flowers*, injured herself and was unable to perform. The actors wanted to cancel the show; Marowitz wanted to tape her voice so that the others could act around it. Ian McDiarmid, Malcolm Storry and Tony Milner all said that they were unwilling to do this; no compromise was reached, and what had been a very stimulating year's work for the actors (of whom Storry, at least, had been totally committed to the enterprise) ended with deep bitterness on all sides. Unfortunately, it destroyed a company that had produced the most consistently good work which this theatre ever presented.

Marowitz was always one hundred per cent committed to his view of a play, which meant that he sometimes quarrelled with writers and directors, with some more bitterly than with others; he and Sam Shepard could not agree on how his play should have been directed, which meant that Shepard absented himself from rehearsal as much as possible; Ableman had problems with Marowitz's attitude to cutting and altering his text (OS 13/12); Andrew Carr blamed Marowitz for the failure of his play *Hanratty in Hell*; Walter Donohue was not asked to direct again after his part in the production of *The Tooth of Crime*, and so on.

Perhaps because of his reputation as a pugnacious critic of those who stood in his way, and even of those who did not – witness his attack on some lunchtime groups which had appeared with some success at his own theatre (*Plays and Players*, July 1971) – other reviewers were sometimes unjustly hostile towards his work. John Higgins of the *Financial Times*, one of the few critics to attend the first night of Stanley Eveling's play *Come and be Killed*, wrote a sarcastic review because of a mix-up over performance times (19 December 1968). He was patently too annoyed by it to give the play any serious consideration; only the last part of the article bothered to mention it, and that was written in the same flippant tone as the rest of the article. Higgins' opening sentence asked, 'Has success spoiled the Open Space?' – an exaggerated response to a trivial error and a damaging question to put before the public for a theatre struggling for survival. Marowitz was quite naturally incensed, and he wrote to the Editor trouncing Higgins for his unfair article. It is worth quoting in full since the *Financial Times* did not publish it:

> Dear Editor,
>
> Does John Higgins, your erstwhile and hypersensitive drama critic, really believe that readers of the *Financial Times* prefer a description of a first-night ticket mix-up to a critical appraisal of the work of a new playwright? Reading his account of events, it would appear that the Open Space elaborately devised a diabolical stratagem specifically designed to harass the press. The facts are that letters announcing a 7.30 opening went out with all press tickets and the rest was left to the adapting-intelligences of the reviewers all of whom, Higgins included, managed to make this herculean rearrangement. But it really is obscene that three quarters of a drama review should be devoted to whimsical putter concerning front-of-house trivia instead of exploring the implications of a play which, in my biased opinion, is the best yet written by Stanley Eveling; a play which concerns the vast question of moral responsibility in regard to life (birth) and death (abortion) and which is treated seriously and, in my opinion, tellingly by an author writing out of personal conscience. Criticism has reached a sorry state of affairs when these matters can be dispensed with while a critic indulges a strained sense of humour in a vain attempt to divert his readers. If Higgins loathes the play, let him reason out – both the play and his loathing of it, but let's have an end to critical twaddle for the sake of its own puerile self.[6]

A member of the public who wrote a letter to *The Stage* (20 March 1969) making a similar complaint was treated in much the same way as Higgins had been, but with less justification. Marowitz seized the opportunity of replying (2 April 1969) and was not in the least apologetic to those who had been inconvenienced by administrative inefficiencies but merely emphasised the need for subsidy, without which the theatre could not really be expected to run smoothly. His comments may have been justified, but perhaps a less antagonistic tone would have helped his relations with the theatre-going public. His response to this situation was typical of all his dealings with adverse criticism; he never humbled himself before the public or the critics to gain their support but was always direct where it might have been more useful to be tactful. It was usually left to Thelma Holt to make good any damage, as she did in 1977 when Marowitz publicly announced that he was banning Bernard Levin from the first night of his production of *Variations on the Merchant of Venice* (*Sunday Times*, 15 May 1977) in support of a production of *The Devil Is an Ass* at the RSC. Levin (one of the most prestigious critics of the 1970s, who had become a household name in 1962 with his controversial contributions to the satirical television show *That Was The Week That Was*) had condemned the production because some of the dialogue had been updated to make it comprehensible to a modern audience. Marowitz, along with Trevor Nunn and Stuart Burge, rounded on Levin for his reactionary view, and, because of the nature of his own collage work on Shakespeare's play, Marowitz mockingly withdrew his invitation to its opening night. He was forced to submit to theatre critics, led by Milton Shulman, who threatened to black the Open Space if Levin was not invited, and it was Holt who wrote the conciliatory words in the papers revoking the ban.

One of the reasons that his theatre ran so long (many fringe theatres have a much shorter life than the Open Space had) was his willingness to engage in battle with authority. He used shock tactics in his productions and in his dealings with public and press. His criticism was always vigorous and entertaining though sometimes misguided (the reviewer in *Plays and Players* for January 1972 said 'the English theatre would certainly be a lot duller without Charles Marowitz') and it was perhaps his enjoyment of the squabbbles in which he became entangled that sometimes led him to kick harder and more indiscriminately than he ought.

The demise of the Open Space was finally accelerated by events that had nothing to do with the theatre's output. As a courtesy, an actor who had been helping with the reconstruction of the new theatre was auditioned by Marowitz for a part in one of his forthcoming shows and was bitterly disappointed when he was not offered the role. This triggered the so-called 'pink bath scandal'. A story was given to a journalist on the *Evening Standard* alleging that Marowitz had misappropriated funds from the Open Space to buy a pink bathroom suite for a flat he was furnishing with his new bride Julia Crossthwaite. An investigation was set up, the story proved untrue, and the

Charles Marowitz

minutes for the Advisory Board, held on 15 July 1977, stated that 'a proposal was put to the board by Patrick Graucob that the board were satisfied that there had been no misappropriation of Open Space funds by the Artistic Director. The proposal was seconded by Brian Stone and carried without dissent.'[7]

In retrospect, the joint venture can be seen to have been highly productive, even though criticisms have been made of different aspects of it. It was an interesting partnership with both the artistic director and his leading actress as associate directors of the whole enterprise. This pattern was followed after Thelma Holt left, with Nikolas Simmonds taking her place (he had directing as well as acting aspirations), but by this time the Open Space was already beginning to fold. Holt's ambitions as an actress did not seem to stand in the way of her managerial responsibilities (or vice-versa) and she never took on a role which she could not successfully accomplish, though she confessed in interview that she never felt happy with Portia in *Variations on the Merchant of Venice*. When Marowitz's work elsewhere took him away from the Open Space, Holt would control everything, though she never directed any shows. Though they no longer work together, Holt still expresses her admiration for Marowitz's work and ideals, and pays tribute to his qualities as a director by saying she never will act for any other.

NOTES

1   Charles Marowitz in interview with the author, 2 June 2004.
2   There is a detailed account of the *Flesh* raid in *Burnt Bridges*, pp.139–48.
3   OS Progs. Marowitz's figures do not correspond exactly with the official figures.
4   Charles Marowitz in interview with the author, 2 June 2004.
5   Malcolm Storry in interview with the author, 17 July 1985.
6   A copy of the letter can be found in OS 10/19.
7   A copy of Thelma Holt's letter to the members of the Advisory Board, 15 August 1977, can be found in OS 10/19. Marowitz's own, full account of the incident is in *Burnt Bridges*, pp.216–8.

[9]

Summary of the Theatre's Achievement

Charles Marowitz had always complained that there was no theatre movement in England which could be described as avant garde, and he publicised his intention to rectify the situation at the Open Space. This naturally laid his work open to criticism of a specific sort, and he was continually forced on to the defensive by theatre critics who felt that he had done nothing to further truly experimental theatre.

The first two productions, *Fortune and Men's Eyes* and *Blue Comedy* (comprised of two short plays, *Madly in Love* and *Hank's Night*), were particularly vulnerable to attack on this account, because the first production was naturalistic, the second a West End sex comedy, more risqué perhaps than most but with no real surprises in its form or content. In fact, according to Irving Wardle, 'commercial comedy has repeatedly broken the rules; but Mr Ableman sticks to them as firmly as ever' (*The Times*, 22 October 1968).

Both Harold Hobson of the *Sunday Times* and Irving Wardle of *The Times* joined in attacking Charles Marowitz and his enterprise on the grounds that he had led the public to expect experimental theatre and instead was offering 'wholly old world stuff' (*Sunday Times*, 14 July 1968). Hobson criticised the content of *Fortune and Men's Eyes* for being sub-Genet, and went on to say that in any case Genet was not a fit model for experimental theatre. Naturally Marowitz did not submit quietly to the criticism and he firmly rebuked Hobson for his inaccurate judgment of the play's prescriptions. The work was, he stressed, 'a straightforward naturalistic play with absolutely no experimental pretensions' (*Sunday Times*, 28 July 1968). Hobson had argued that 'an avant-garde theatre does exist, both on stage and screen, and it has definable

characteristics', but subsequently gave only an imprecise definition of what he meant, that is that experimental drama must
take account of the violence that has entered our lives in the
last ten years. In his reply Marowitz was able to argue with
some validity, therefore, that the play did fulfil Hobson's personal definition of the avant garde since it had come to terms
with 'the violence prisoners inflict upon one another because
of the values society inflicts upon them'.

Perhaps because of the pre-performance publicity that *Blue
Comedy* had received, the management tried to raise the status
of the two sex comedies by writing a note in the programme
defending them and drawing parallels with Shakespeare and
Molière.[1] The author of the note (signing himself 'Jack
Point') acknowledged the fact that the plays needed defence
only because of prevailing attitudes and the connotations of
the term 'sex comedy'. The management were obviously
aware that they were vulnerable to attack from those critics
who were waiting to see adventurous work performed at the
Open Space, and the claim that these two plays were an example of the 'prancing little steps in a direction the theatre can
take' now censorship had been abolished, was an attempt to
counteract such criticism. Point's final comment, 'It will be
interesting to see if, as a result of the greater freedom he can
now exercise, the English Playwright will tackle the situations
which, ostensibly, have been denied him', certainly echoed
the hopes of serious theatregoers after the abolition of censorship, but seems in the light of the two plays in question a pretentious and unsuitable remark to make. Wardle voiced the
objection, as Hobson had done in his reaction to *Fortune and
Men's Eyes*, that these plays were 'appearing at the wrong
address' (*The Times*, 22 October 1968). A few days later he
related his criticism of the two plays and of the Open Space
Theatre to theatre in general and its 'new-found freedom of
speech':

> There seem at present to be acres of new expressive territory avail-
> able; theatrical radicals have been demanding it for years, but now it
> is theirs they seem uncertain of how to fill it. The conquest was
> worth the effort and long overdue: but it would be sourly ironic if a
> determination to exercise its new rights led the experimental stage

merely into projecting the salacious vacuities of commercial entertainment on a larger scale. (*The Times*, 26 October 1968)

In their reply (*The Times*, 8 November 1968), Holt and Marowitz re-stated the case they had previously put to Hobson:

> one cannot begin to talk about 'experimental' theatre unless there exists a permanent group of actors conducting the experiment. There is no such thing as an 'experimental show' outside the context of a permanent group of actors. If there is, it is a novelty or a calculated piece of unorthodoxy. Experiment, either in science or art, is predicated on continuity. (*Sunday Times*, 28 July 1968).

In the letter to the *The Times* they stressed, in addition, the need for 'aesthetic breakthrough', a point that Wardle's comments only implied. Throughout the history of the Open Space Marowitz was to argue that lack of funding led him away from his objectives – he was continually attacked for it, even by those who eventually held the efforts of the Open Space Theatre in esteem; witness Wardle, who in a review of *The Difference* by Peter Bergman (1971) spoke worriedly of the theatre's

> split personality. For behind the bold radical figure it normally cuts, there lurks a hack comedian awaiting his chance to torpedo the enterprise with a string of feeble wisecracks (*The Times*, 26 April 1971)

In 1976, just before the theatre moved to the Euston Road, Marowitz outlined what, in his view, were the aims and the achievements of the Open Space Theatre (*Plays and Players*, October 1976). It was still his contention that the Open Space had failed to produce the experimental theatre it had striven for because it was not properly funded. He extended here his definition of what he felt his theatre ought to have been: 'a theatre which is more concerned with process than product; more intent on exploring techniques and evolving material'. Yet in 1969 his collage *Hamlet* had brought together the process and the product in a work which was generally admired for its originality of content and presentation, and the funding for this had been minimal.

At the end of 1968 Irving Wardle (*The Times*, 21 December

1968) had been pessimistic about the future of experimental theatre in England. Because it was, he said, merely 'an extension of the American underground', he did not see much hope of its flourishing in a country whose 'imagery and rhythm' was 'entirely alien'. He saw the Americans as having a tradition of acting ensembles behind them (he mentioned the Becks' Living Theatre and Chaikin's Open Theatre) which meant that they had something to build on in the future. England, he claimed, had nothing except the music-hall tradition to fall back on for improvisatory techniques. For this reason he felt that Marowitz, in hoping to create an acting ensemble 'pledged to rescuing the theatre from literature', had simply created a myth 'to provide hope in playless times'.

Marowitz's collage *Hamlet* proved Wardle wrong. The play, which he had already directed in 1965 and 1966 for performance abroad, and which had followed its Italian tour with a run at the Jeannetta Cochrane Theatre in London, was revived and played to an enthusiastic public and press in July 1969. Only Thelma Holt remained from the original cast, but Nikolas Simmonds, who had previously played Marowitz's Macbeth, took on the role of Hamlet, a continuity in casting that merely suggested the beginnings of a permanent company. The critic for *Plays and Players* (September 1969) had this to say about the play: 'The cast ... achieve the type of assured ensemble discipline that would probably be the talk of the town if they came from the Continent or America.'

Fringe theatre and the Off-Broadway productions and happenings that seemed particularly suited to the unconventional venues which housed them were treated with scepticism by most critics, and their attitude to these imports was paradoxical. On the one hand there were those who, like Wardle, felt that the English could never hope to emulate them, whilst there were others who patronised the productions and the writing. B.A. Young had this to say of Mike Weller's work: 'The plays are neat little squibs, uncommonly well composed for the work of a young American' (*Financial Times*, 19 August 1969), and Helen Dawson in the *Observer* (17 August 1969) paid the actors this doubtful compliment for their parts in *Now There's Just the Three of Us*: 'The acting ... is above average for a studio production.' If major critics were reacting to fringe theatre in this way it is not surprising that the Arts Council was to prove so tentative with its financial support.

One of the English groups of the period whose influence was felt by playwrights and directors was the Pip Simmons Group, formed in 1968. They were more popular with audiences on the Continent than in Britain, perhaps because of their choice of American subject matter: when they brought a production, *Superman*, first devised in 1969, to the Open Space in 1970, most critics were mystified by it. On the night the critics went, audience numbers were very small; the resulting reviews could not have helped to attract a larger public. It appears that although the play copied the American cartoon style of characterisation (grotesque figures with comic-strip dialogue) the play as a whole lacked the clarity and simplification of narrative and message that a good cartoon offers. Later Peter Ansorge in *Disrupting the Spectacle* (pp.30-33) treated the show sympathetically, but those working at the Open Space continued to experiment with Simmons' methods despite lack of critical support.

Marowitz's production of *Palach* used stereotyped, cartoon characters and was misunderstood by at least one critic, who talked of the play as being 'all message, at the cost of character, plot, dialogue and drama' (*Daily Telegraph*, 12 November 1970). He complained that he was wearied by the 'superannuated techniques' the play employed. This would appear to be a misguided criticism since there had been no concerted attempt in England to break through the naturalistic form of staging which prevailed, and the influence of groups like the Living Theatre and Pip Simmons was relatively little known. Companies such as Le Grand Magic Circus and Mnouchkine's Théâtre du Soleil had not yet performed in England, and Barrault's adaptation of *Rabelais* had not at this time been seen in its English version at the Round House.[2] To talk, therefore, of techniques as 'superannuated' when they had neither been exploited in Britain nor absorbed the full impact of similar work from the continent seems a premature and unjust attempt to discredit the originality of Marowitz's work.

Burns had provided a somewhat literary scenario for *Palach* that Marowitz decided they needed to work on together, with the actors improvising dialogue and sound. Some of the dialogue was confirmed as text, some remained improvised on the night of performance. For instance, the published text describes a scene where a character is questioned by the rest of the cast, in response to which the character picks out answers from a bowl with slips of paper in it.[3] The stage direction tells us that a different set of answers was produced each night and that all answers were optional. The onus on the actors themselves to produce useful material for the 'happening' was greater than that put upon them by Marowitz in his production of *A Macbeth*. Although in that play they had worked towards their goal through improvisation, the actual text of the play was supplied in its final form by Marowitz. In reference to *Palach*, Marowitz is quoted as having said to Ronald Hayman, 'The actors in this show have probably made a greater contribution than any group of actors, with the possible exception of Littlewood's, have ever made to anything' (*The Times*, 7 November 1970).

The other major influence on British writers and directors reflected in the work presented at the Open Space during its first years came from the group called the People Show whose productions depended upon 'a bringing together, or clash of opposing images and styles'.[4] Howard Brenton, who had four plays presented at the Open Space (*Gum and Goo, A Sky Blue Life, How Beautiful with Badges* and *Christie in Love*), was an exponent of this method. In his production note to *Christie in Love* he described his dramatic devices: 'a kind of dislocation, tearing one style up for another, so the proceedings lurch and all interpretations are blocked'.[5] The People Show was not at the time a new phenomenon (it had been in existence since 1965), but when it put on a show at the Open Space press coverage was very sparse with only a couple of reviewers to enthuse over it (Irving Wardle in *The Times*, 20 August 1971, and David Jay, *Times Educational Supplement*, 17 September 1971); although critics kept calling for experimental work they were often unwilling to go and see it.

The People Show used no set, only a number of props scattered about like so much old junk. Any suggestion of locale was created, as the play progressed, by one of the actors, who chalked up cliffs, waves, and so on, on any available surfaces. An audience had to be willing to make the same sort of imaginative leaps as the actors were continually making, with their unconventional use of the props. In such a tiny theatre as the Open Space there was no place for members of the audience who were not prepared to enter into the spirit of the production. In this respect *A Sky Blue Life* showed the People Show's influence, and though it was probably unintentional on the part of the Open Space management, it is possible to trace in 1971 the emergence of a house-style which had broken away from naturalism and overcome the theatre's limitations with regard to that form, by creating an approach to the space which elicited a different response from audiences and required a different attitude to the material from actors and directors. Both the plays introduced by other companies and those inspired by Marowitz showed an awareness of alternative techniques which had hitherto been missing from the year's programme as a whole. Twelve out of the twenty-two productions in 1971 used anti-naturalistic devices, whereas in the previous year only four had done so, one of which was the Pip Simmons show, so much disparaged by the critics; two of the others were Marowitz's own productions.

Marowitz himself had always eschewed naturalism. In 1978 Alan Pearlman, who was then his associate director, said, 'Our basic commitment is to new writing of a non-naturalistic kind, although we do not exclude naturalistic plays from the repertoire since very often that is all that is available.'[6] The Open Space was, because of its physical peculiarities (its size and lack of sophisticated equipment) well suited to anti-illusionist theatre, though that is not to say that naturalism of a certain kind did not flourish there. Simon Trussler, writing for *Tribune* (3 January 1969) about Stanley Eveling's play *Come and Be Killed*, said:

> the Open Space Theatre, for all its experimental intentions, is in fact an uncannily appropriate environment for the intellectual squalor of John Napier's naturalistic setting. The audience neither looks through a fourth wall nor a picture frame, but practically rests its feet on the domestic hearth

The same was true of many other productions which were intense studies of emotional relationships. The overwhelming sense of grief produced by David Rudkin's *Ashes* is a case in point, where the set was required to be sordid and the theatre's own limitations did not pose an awkward contrast to the desired illusion. The audience's proximity to the actors and action could not fail, if the production and the acting were good, to generate an intimacy and involvement with the play which was totally subjective. A play such as *Blue Comedy*, which was presented there basically as a potential West-End transfer, needed a conventional drawing-room set with the audience seated at a distance in order to help preserve the illusion. The production failed to take into account the requirements of the Open Space, even down to the detail of allowing the actors 'to project as though they were playing to the upper circle at Drury Lane' (*Plays and Players*, December 1968). Conversely, the impact of the naturalistic production of *Fortune and Men's Eyes*, which had thoroughly exploited the Open Space environment, was considerably lessened when it transferred to its West-End venue.

Between 1968 and 1976, when the Open Space was at its Tottenham Court Road premises, the new kinds of drama presented there might be summarised thus:

1 Productions of the classics treated in a radical, and sometimes unrecognisable, way.
2 American imports from off-Broadway, only a small number of which used new forms.
3 New British writing which tended towards cartoon characterisation and political content.
4 Productions which used the whole theatre building to create an environment which was part of the play.

The Open Space did not have any particular commitment to political theatre, though there were periods in its history when several plays of a political nature came together. *The Chicago Conspiracy* was the first play with an overtly political concern to be staged there, and it received an enthusiastic response, even though it dealt with a specifically American event. A production in 1969 of David Mairowitz's *Law Circus*, a satire on justice, did not capture the public's imagination in the same way, partly because it had no specific trial on which to base its satire; a reconstruction of facts which have their own satire inherent in them is a very forceful comment upon the times. A play which was given as little exposure as *The Chicago Conspiracy* could not be seen as directly influencing the course of English political theatre, but it did mirror a growing interest in such work. In December 1970, Joan Little-wood was prevented from presenting a production at Stratford East dealing directly with what she believed were the fundamental causes of the Ronan Point disaster in 1968, because of the risk of libel. Instead she had to disguise her concern in a supposedly eighteenth-century satire called *The Projector* where, according to most critics, the satirical point was largely lost.7 The Open Space, as a club theatre, had been able to present its material in a straightforward manner, and because the issues were American, no authorities objected to it.

Billington wrote in the *Guardian* of 25 October 1971 that there was at that time a lack of political theatre in England, and cited the Open Space as being one of the few theatres that had shown any engagement with political matters. Together with *The Chicago Conspiracy* he mentioned *Palach*, the play produced by Marowitz and Burns, but although the subject of the play was ostensibly Jan Palach who had burned himself to death to express his hatred of the Russian occupation of Czechoslovakia, the play did not in any way concern itself with the political situation there, it merely used the situation for its own ends.

It was not until new British playwrights were featured in lunchtime theatre at the end of 1971 that any consistent pattern of left-wing political writing could be discerned at the Open Space. This was mainly instigated by Walter Donohue and John Burgess, who were reading and choosing plays for performance. They were given complete freedom of choice for the lunchtime spots as long as it did not interfere with Marowitz's own ideas for the main house shows. Burgess was allowed to commission plays from any playwrights he cared to approach as long as he offered no more than £1 to the writer. The guarantee of a production at the Open Space was the bait offered in return for a new play, and this is how David Rudkin's *Ashes* came to be written for them, as well as John Arden's *The Ballygombeen Bequest*, which Marowitz insisted on reading himself. He deemed it too political, so Arden took it elsewhere.[8] Marowitz liked to put on controversial plays, but evidently had no wish to become known as a director specialising in left-wing material, though he later chose to present *Claw* by Howard Barker (1975), which was a passionately political and moral story about a man involved, as one of the under-privileged, in the class war after the Second World War.

It was Donohue who commented in interview that Marowitz did not give the same publicity to plays by playwrights other than himself. As a journalist he had access to means of publicising productions which others had not, and he exploited them at every opportunity for his own work. Other plays, such as *Claw* and David Edgar's *Excuses Excuses,* succeeded despite his lack of interest in them, and in Donohue's view it was a pity that he did not do more to promote new playwrights as well as his own stylistic advances. Much of the best of the new writing was relegated to lunchtime performance, and it was, to a certain extent, the view of Thelma Holt and Nikolas Simmonds (who later became an associate director) that Marowitz ought not to have neglected his role as promoter of new writing.

Charles Marowitz's fundamental concern was with breaking down the conventional presentation of character. Although he wished to create a central character in his works (e.g. Hamlet, Macbeth, Woyzeck, Artaud, etc.) he chose means other than the conventional naturalistic ones to do so. So he used three actors to convey Macbeth's tormented personality; he disrupted the sequence of events in *Hamlet*; he created modern scenes in *The Shrew* which paralleled the Shakespearean ones, and so on. The one technique that remained constant in all his own works was a strong emphasis on visual images which economised on action and dialogue and which provided a clear indication of the play's theme. Thus, in *Hedda*, the play opens with an image of Hedda's father standing sternly downstage right; this is followed by a silent scene between the two of them, first with

Hedda dominated physically by her father, and secondly with her father subjugated to Hedda's whip; *A Macbeth* opens with Lady Macbeth performing a black magic ritual on an effigy of Macbeth; *Hamlet* with Fortinbras standing still in front of Hamlet like a mirror image. Sometimes the visual symbols would consist of whole scenes representing a particular aspect of the play's theme, and these aspects would be presented in a non-naturalistic fashion. At other times it would be an extended moment which might recur at key points throughout the play. A favourite device was the spotlight on one character, which would slowly tighten until the only part of the body which could be seen was the head. This created the sense of isolation which engulfs most of his leading characters (Hamlet, Woyzeck, Artaud, etc.) and at the same time suggested the drama which is occurring in the mind of the character.

In his own work these kinds of technique worked very well for a time, though over the years there seems to have been very little progression from the initial idea, and what was once new and impressive partly lost its impact. Marowitz was also inclined to use the same techniques indiscriminately for plays that arguably needed another style of production. For instance, having been attracted, initially, by the stylised second half of *The Tooth of Crime*, he decided to ignore its other qualities and to present it in terms of external images which were both literally dazzling and also confusing. The *Guardian* review (18 July 1972) commented that the production 'concentrates superbly with lights and artifice on the projection of externals', but unfortunately it concealed the meaning of the play. It is not surprising, then, that Irving Wardle was wide of the mark when he said: 'I think I know what it is getting at. The play is about the use of style as a weapon' (*The Times*, 18 July 1972). He went on to say that style was used as 'an instrument of assault', which was true of the boxing-match sequence but ought not to have been allowed to obscure the rest of the play.

Despite the fact that it had not been possible, during the years that the Open Space premises were in Tottenham Court Road, to adhere to a policy of what plays should be presented there, a certain pattern of characteristics emerges in retrospect and it becomes clear that there were themes that attracted Marowitz more than others, and conversely that those offering the plays for presentation were attracted by his theatre because they knew what Marowitz liked and knew his theatre space would suit them.

Of his own works (his adaptations and *Artaud at Rodez*), the two themes that dominate are the conflicts aroused between men and women because of their driving sexual instincts and the isolation of man from, and disillusionment with, his society. Sometimes treated separately, these themes are usually linked and interwoven. In 1982 Marowitz published an anthology of three adaptations of modern classics by Ibsen and Strindberg entitled *Sex Wars*, which is a heading under which most of his own work might be listed.9 Plays by other people which he chose to direct (there were twenty of them at the Tottenham Court Road premises) reveal his interest in sexual politics rather than social or party-political concerns and, even in plays which were perhaps more angled towards other issues, the sexual implications were often given greater emphasis (witness the production of *Sam Sam*).

The alienation of man from his society and his concomitant sense of isolation is present in all of Marowitz's protagonists. The most familiar figure in his collage work is that of the small and insignificant individual beset by a hostile world. This image was given powerful theatrical form in his production of *Woyzeck*. Malcolm Storry who played the Sergeant is well over six feet and, by his towering over David Schofield who played Woyzeck, the threat of the establishment over the individual was given nightmarish proportions and emblematic significance.

The crushing or the constraint of the individual by superior forces was given expression in the many plays performed at the Open Space which used a prison setting. The opening production of *Fortune and Men's Eyes* was followed by others such as *Grant's Movie*, *Hanratty in Hell*, *And They Put Handcuffs on the Flowers*, and finally the Swedish play *Seven Girls*, about girls in a reformatory, which brought this era of the Open Space to a close. In these plays, prison in one form or another was the literal location for the action. Many others used a metaphorical prison as their main theme, and so we see men and women depicted as being trapped by their own tortured and often obsessive perception of life (outstanding examples here are *The Four Little Girls, Ashes, Sweet Eros, Christie in Love* and *How Beautiful with Badges*). Marowitz was greatly helped by having Robin Don as his designer (Don was not employed on a permanent basis, but nevertheless from 1971 onwards he designed a significant number of productions); Don's concern in his stage design was to show man locked in a self-constructed cage.

Together with the idea of man's literal and metaphorical prison goes Marowitz's own sharpened awareness and criticism of so-called justice. It was not only in the productions at the Open Space that this theme predominated, it also governed his response to many of the situations he generated while he was director there. His cry was always for fairness in the allocation of subsidy for fringe theatre, in Equity's dealings with actors, in his tussles with the law over what material might be presented at his theatre. His scepticism about the law was confirmed in 1974 when he was arrested for loitering with intent in a department store after having watched a make-up demonstration attended solely by women shoppers. In 1975 he wrote an account of the experience for the *Guardian* (28 May 1975), and described how it influenced his treatment of *Measure for Measure*. 'A healthy disrespect for the law is the best way of combating its tendency towards human corruption' is how he summed up the situation, and it is, he claimed, what the play *Measure for Measure* is about. A 'healthy disrespect' for establishment authority in general characterised all Marowitz's dealings during the years at Tottenham Court Road. Although this attitude eventually led to the demise of the theatre project altogether, while the theatre flourished controversy was what gave the enterprise its artistic energy, in tandem with the steadying influence of Thelma Holt's unstinting support.

NOTES

1   OS archives, Cuttings Book 1.

2   First performances by Le Grand Magic Circus in England, 20 December 1972; *1789*, 12 October 1971; *Rabelais* at the Round House, 18 March 1971.

3   *Open Space Plays*, p.220.

4   *Disrupting the Spectacle*, p.39.

5   Howard Brenton, *Plays for the Poor Theatre*, (London, 1980), p.26.

6   Alan Pearlman in interview with the author, 15 November 1978.

7   Howard Goorney, *The Theatre Workshop Story* (London, 1981), p.137.

8   John Burgess in interview with the author, 25 July 1985. The first professional production of *The Ballygombeen Bequest* was by 7:84 Company, Edinburgh Festival, 21 August 1972.

9   *The Father* was presented at the Open Space in the Euston Road theatre on 7 November 1979, and *Hedda* at the Round House on 5 August 1980.

[Part 2]

The Round House

[10]

The History of the Round House

The history of the Round House as a theatre began with playwright Arnold Wesker and his dream of an arts community for the people, which would encourage and develop their active involvement in the artistic life of the country. He first came into the spotlight with his plays: *Chicken Soup With Barley* (1958), *Roots* (1959) and *I'm Talking About Jerusalem* (1960) which were taken up by the Royal Court as a trilogy after individual successes at the Belgrade Theatre in Coventry. Their subject matter, the hopes and aspirations of an East End family dedicated to the promotion of socialism, set against a historical and political background from the 1930s onwards, put Wesker firmly in the camp of the new political playwrights of the period. He blamed public apathy towards the arts on an educational system that did not sufficiently nourish an interest in the many different art forms and, more importantly for the genesis of Centre 42, on those public institutions which boasted of their concern for working people. In his *Encore* article 'Let Battle Commence' he attacked the *Daily Mirror* for ignoring its responsibility to enrich people's lives and challenged it to sponsor 'a film by Lindsay Anderson or a play at the Royal Court theatre, for its own readers'.[1] His most serious challenge, however, was to the trade unions who were already formed into groups and who were therefore in a strong position to help their members experience fuller lives through the arts.

Wesker's vision of a fully subsidised workers' theatre was already being realised in 1958 in France by Roger Planchon, who had moved his company to Villeurbanne, a suburb of Lyon, where he took his work into the local factories and encouraged the audiences' participation in choosing the material for presentation. In 1960, when Wesker's campaign to persuade the trade unions to take a financial interest in a community arts centre for the people was well under way, he wrote an article for the *New Statesman* (3 September 1960) which praised Planchon's efforts and pointed out the difference in subsidy between Planchon's theatre, which received £30,000, and Joan Littlewood's Theatre Workshop, which received £1,000 from the Arts Council in 1960. His article contained not only praise for Planchon's efforts but also a criticism of the nations' attitudes towards the arts as reflected in their responses to the two ventures. He felt that neither France nor Britain had understood or attempted to establish the principle that the arts are a nation's heritage and therefore for everybody and not the privileged few. In his view it was this that allowed both the companies to become fashionable and their work to become elitist entertainment.

Wesker's aim in writing his plays was

> to write ... not only for the class of people who acknowledge plays to be a legitimate form of expression, but for those to whom the phrase 'form of expression' may mean nothing whatsoever. It is the bus driver, the housewife, the miner and the Teddy Boy to whom I should like to address myself ('Let Battle Commence', p.96).[2]

This opinion informed his concept of what an arts centre ought to be and, together with his experience of having plays performed in the provinces and the West End, made him in many ways, an ideal person to run a cultural centre at the Round House. However, his passion for his subject matter drew from many quarters criticism that he was patronising the workers. He was aware of the criticism even at this early stage of his campaign and he acknowledged it in the article. Nonetheless, his belief in the necessity for someone to teach the world proper values and his faith in his own role as teacher remained unshaken for the time being.

At the end of the fifties Wesker was not alone in his anxiety over the state of the nation's culture. Not only were many playwrights, novelists and other artists creating works which attempted to define and comment upon working-class life, but others were analysing it. In 1957, Richard Hoggart had published his book *The Uses of Literacy*, in which he examined changes in working-class culture during the preceding thirty or forty years. Hoggart's main anxiety was 'the division between the technical languages of the experts and the extraordinarily low level of the organs of mass communication'.[3] Wesker's emphasis was not so much on this division but on the 'low level' itself, and his concern was to elevate standards which were implicit in the machinery of 'mass communication'.

In April 1960 Wesker addressed students of Oxford University and participants in the *Sunday Times* Student Drama Festival on the reasons for Britain's lack of interest in the arts. Because in the lecture he accused the trade unions of neglecting their responsibilities towards the people in this respect, he had the lecture printed and sent to every trade union in the country. It was his first direct attempt to involve the unions in his vision of a country where arts of all kinds are considered a necessary part of life. People, he believed, needed to be told about it and the trade unions, as representatives of the people, ought to have been the ones to do it; their failure to do so amounted to 'almost immoral' neglect: 'I believe socialism ... to be not merely an economic organisation of society but a way of living based on the assumption that life is rich, rewarding and that human beings deserve it.'[4]

Wesker did not at this stage make any practical suggestions as to what the unions might do to help, but two months later he sent another pamphlet to them which outlined some positive proposals. The most important suggestion was that the TUC should 'set up a commission to investigate and discuss what relationship the Trade Union movement should have to the cultural life of the community' (p.87). This was followed by a list of organisations that the unions might sponsor, such as a National Trade Union Orchestra, theatres for new industrial areas which had none, a grant system for the children of their members who showed a particular talent, and so on. Four unions replied, ACTT, NATSOPA, and two smaller ones (*New Statesman*, 30 July 1960). A press conference was held after the *New Statesman* article appeared. According to Frank

Coppieters, the general secretary of NATSOPA 'thought that a resolution containing the essence of the venture might get the support of Congress' (p.91).[5]

A week before the resolution was presented to Congress, the *New Statesman* (3 September 1960) ran an article written by five artists who gave their views on how the trade unions could best help the arts. The contributors to the article were Victor Passmore, J.B. Priestley, Angus Wilson, Feliks Topolski and Alexander Goehr. Only Alexander Goehr, a composer of modernist music, disagreed with the whole idea because he could not visualise financial support from an official socialist body, without political interests attached. Nevertheless, the largely sympathetic bias of the long article must have helped promote the cause, and the resolution (number 42 on the agenda), worded as follows, was passed on 8 September:

> Congress recognises the importance of the arts in the life of the community especially now when many unions are securing a shorter working week and greater leisure for their members. It notes that the trade-union movement has participated to only a small extent in the direct promotion of plays, films, music, literature and other forms of expression including those of value to its beliefs and principles.
>
> Congress considers that much more could be done and accordingly requests the General Council to conduct a special examination and to make proposals to a future Congress to ensure a greater participation by the trade-union movement in all cultural activities. (Coppieters, p.93)

Wesker's activity did not stop at this first tangible sign of success. He lectured to trade unions all over the country and continued to bombard the press with articles in support of his aims. At this same period a group of artists had banded together to discuss ways of reaching new audiences; they included John McGrath, Doris Lessing and Shelagh Delaney, and they invited Wesker to join them. It was agreed that Wesker should head the group and the result was to be the formation of Centre 42, which took its name from the resolution passed in 1960. In his dissertation, Coppieters quotes the published aims of Centre 42, which were outlined in the *Centre 42, Annual Report 1961–1962*:

Centre 42 will be a cultural hub which, by its approach and work, will destroy the mystique and snobbery associated with the arts. A place where artists are in control of their own means of expression and their own channels of distribution; where the highest standards of professional work will be maintained in an atmosphere of informality; where the artist is brought into closer contact with his audience enabling the public to see that artistic activity is a natural part of their daily lives... The Fortytwo movement is a bid by a new generation of writers, actors, musicians, painters, sculptors, architects to relieve commercial managements of the burdens and responsibilities in shaping our culture; to assume this responsibility themselves and place art back into the lap of the community where, through familiarity and participation, they can revitalise their work by confronting a new audience and turn their art from a purposeless mess into a creative force. (p.101)

On 4 September 1961, Centre 42 was incorporated as a Company Limited by Guarantee and on 6 October 1961 it was granted charitable status as a National Charity.

The Centre needed a building from which to operate, a place where people might meet for purely social as well as artistic reasons, or where the public might meet the Centre 42 artists. It was also to provide the base for events that would ultimately make their way to the provinces until centres were established all over the country. However, before acquiring such a building, the Centre was invited to set up a festival by Wellingborough Trades Council, and the committee decided, despite all the practical difficulties, including no money, to accept. As a result of this, five other Trades Councils asked them to mount similar festivals in 1962 and they decided to postpone the founding of an actual centre in order to do so.

The festivals generated enthusiasm in the provinces for the ideals of Centre 42 but proved disastrous in financial terms – so disastrous, in fact, that neither Centre 42 nor the Round House Trust, which was formed later, could wipe out the debts incurred at this time. According to Coppieters, the net cost of mounting the festivals was £48,700 and the box-office receipts were £3,215. They were given some assistance from trade unions, local councils, and so on so that their final debt stood at £39,639. The Gulbenkian Foundation gave a generous grant of £10,000 over two years and a further £3,000 in 1963 but other financial help was slow in materialising.

It was decided that as its next priority a home must be found for Centre 42. The lease on the Round House, in Chalk Farm, came up for sale and was being bought by Selincourt and Sons. Louis Mintz, already a well-known patron of the arts and managing director of Selincourt, was persuaded to donate the sixteen-year lease to Centre 42; they obtained it in July 1964.

Meanwhile Wesker managed to interest Harold Wilson in the project. He recommended that George Hoskins, an economist and businessman, should become Centre 42's fund-raiser and financial adviser. Hoskins remained until 1977 when Thelma Holt took over after leaving the Open Space Theatre. His first job was to launch an appeal, and this he did on 17 July 1964 when the lease was handed over. Despite enormous efforts and £10,000 from Wesker, who sold the film rights to *Chips With Everything*, few were willing to donate. Loans were not forthcoming because Centre 42 possessed neither the freehold nor the promise from British Rail that they would sell it to them. In 1965 the Round House Trust was set up with Wesker as artistic director and Hoskins as administrator, but it was not given official status until 10 November 1966. Many eminent and wealthy people acted as trustees, including Peter Hall, Louis Mintz and Eddie Kulukundis. The trust was established in order to separate fund-raising from debts so that any money raised would not automatically be used to pay back debts incurred by Centre 42. As Coppieters explains: 'there were two organisations: Centre 42, which aimed at the creation of a cultural/social centre functioning at a high artistic level and the Round House Trust, which existed in order to raise and administrate the funds necessary to bring into being and retain Centre 42's existence' (p.140). In 1967 they obtained the freehold for £27,500.

The building, an old Victorian engine shed, could not be used without costly improvements and it was evident that there was not enough money to make it into the versatile arts community centre that Wesker wanted. *The First Report December*

1965–31st March 1971, compiled by George Hoskins, has a description of the building as published in *The Builder* 1847: 'This building is a circular form, 160 feet in diameter in the clear of the walls. The roof is supported on 24 columns at equal distances, and forms a circular 40 feet in diameter (they mean radius: GOH) from the centre of the building.'[6]

Designed in 1846 by Robert Benson Dockray and W.J. Normanville and subsequently approved by Robert Stephenson, it had ceased to function as an engine shed by 1856 when it was turned into a goods shed. It was leased to W.& A. Gilbey Limited as a liquor store in 1869 and it is thought that the company added the wooden balcony which was still there when Thelma Holt took over in 1979. The total floor area of the Round House is '20,000 square feet of which 5,000 square feet is inside the pillars ... The floor area of the gallery is 15,000 sq. ft.' (*First Report* p.8).

By March 1967 staircases had been built, essential repairs carried out and simple lighting had been installed. The GLC granted a licence for pop concerts to take place, so a certain amount of money came in from such events straightaway. It was, however, clear at this stage that the funds available were not enough for the necessary conversion work to take place. In August 1964 Wesker had written to René Allio, the designer who had worked with Roger Planchon on his theatre project, outlining what he wanted from the Round House building. The letter is printed in *Fears of Fragmentation* (pp.52–62) and it demonstrates clearly how ambitious Wesker's expectations were. In summary, his requirements were that the building should provide: a flexible performing area; large and small, fully equipped rehearsal rooms; a gymnasium for the artists; a games room; dressing rooms; showers and bathrooms; dark room and cutting room; workshops to accommodate exhibition material; a large separate exhibition area; administrative offices; committee rooms; social area for youth clubs; a restaurant, a bar and a series of small lounges. He even wanted living quarters for resident artists but saw that they would need other buildings for this. There was recognition in the letter that his aims were idealistic but also a feeling that a degree of idealism was essential, if they were to get anywhere at all.

Hoskins decided that a new approach was necessary, that the conversion of the building should take place over a period of seven years (a strategy referred to as 'the seven-year plan'), and that no immediate attempt should be made to implement the changes necessary for turning it into an arts complex. One area was to serve all purposes, so exhibition and theatre space was also to act as a meeting place for those wishing to have a social evening. He also suggested that groups outside Centre 42 should be invited in to help out with cultural events.

Commercial events such as rock concerts were to be a major funding resource so that the centre's own work could gradually develop as the financial position improved. This decision worried Wesker on two counts. He saw his grand vision of an arts centre dwindling into what he had earlier called 'simply another little artistic project'.[7] He was also afraid that if Centre 42 allowed other organisations to take a major share of the programme the centre itself would not be able to establish its own artistic identity and it would be too easy for it to drift into becoming just another building to house commercial enterprises.

In 1969 the first drama productions were brought in, and in 1970 Wesker formed a company to perform his play *The Friends*, which he himself directed. It was a disaster both financially for the Round House and personally for Wesker.[8] It was booked in at the Round House for twelve weeks but, according to Hoskins, after a two-week run the losses were so heavy that the backers wanted to close it, which they did after six weeks. *Oh! Calcutta!* was brought in and Wesker resigned.[9]

Ostensibly it was the failure to implement the artistic policy of Centre 42 (a failure which was surely epitomised by the decision to bring in *Oh! Calcutta!*, a controversial sex show, devised by Kenneth Tynan, who had approached most of London's theatre managements before finding that Hoskins was willing to take the risk of a possible prosecution) which forced Arnold Wesker into resigning as artistic director of the Round House Trust in September 1970:

George Hoskins the administrator, and the trustees, really have no understanding of the social implications of Centre 42 and I think are much more concerned with or in love with the notion of possessing a unique architectural building which they have discovered they can exploit commercially ... they seem to be firmly entrenched in the notion of self support: they will only present work which can pay for itself. In other words, any Company that can afford to hire the building has it.[10]

Naturally, all the controversy surrounding the production of *Oh! Calcutta!* attracted large audiences and after its eight-week run it went into the West End where it ran for over a year.

Like Charles Marowitz, though for different reasons, Arnold Wesker could not believe in the integrity of artistic purpose if profits were an important consideration. His clash with George Hoskins, as we have seen, was on ideological grounds. Although they had worked together in 1963 and 1964 on devising an appeal for £590,000 to buy and equip a building for their centre, their approaches to running the Round House diverged sharply. Hoskins blamed Wesker for having created the debts incurred by Centre 42's provincial festivals. His contention was that these debts had to be paid off before any more money could be spent on the centre, and he saw only two ways of doing it: either by reverting to the use of the Round House as a warehouse or by forging ahead slowly, step by step, only converting the building as funds became available and aiming for independent artistic policy in the years to come (the 'seven-year plan' referred to earlier). Wesker saw his ideals as being eroded by the increasing emphasis on commercialism favoured by Hoskins, who found no difficulty in persuading the other trustees that the Round House could be a viable commercial proposition. The relationship between the two men had deteriorated over the years to such an extent that it was in part responsible for Arnold Wesker's resignation. It was also Wesker's emotional intensity that finally caused the conflict with the cast of his own play, *The Friends.*

A few months after his resignation, an article appeared in the *Sunday Times* (14 February 1971), stating that Hoskins was in the middle of negotiating the purchase of land to the south

Exterior of the Round House

of the Round House on which to build a property which would be let and which would in turn help to finance the necessary improvements at the Round House. The tone of the article with regard to Wesker was derisive: his ideals were dismissed as dreams and Hoskins' pragmatic approach was paraded as a triumph for the enterprise. There followed a sharp exchange of letters to the *Sunday Times* between Wesker and Hoskins in the subsequent weeks, and Wesker made it clear that he regarded Hoskins' attitude as a betrayal of friendship, a feeling which must have given considerable weight to his decision to resign. In his final letter he wrote:

> the facts surrounding a conflict do not necessarily reveal the truth, which is complicated and partly personal. Since I engaged George to help raise funds his attempts to discredit me and Fortytwo hurt bitterly, let me confess. (*Sunday Times*, 7 March 1971)

IMPLEMENTATION OF 'THE SEVEN-YEAR PLAN'

One idea Hoskins had for making money was to buy up the land around the Round House and to construct a hotel and offices on it to bring in revenue for the Trust. The *Observer* Colour Supplement (11 January 1970) ran an article in which it was stated that this commercial exploitation meant that the enterprise was now paying its way. It also stressed that the importance of the Round House lay in its use as a social centre rather than in its capacity as a theatre because it did not receive enough subsidy to develop as a theatre. During Hoskins' term as Round House administrator, children's activities were the only events consistently subsidised by Camden Council, which, though normally generous with aid for cultural work in the borough, never showed any interest in the Round House as a theatre.

The plan for a hotel on the Round House premises did not materialise, but in 1972 Louis Mintz financed a new office annexe which also contained dressing rooms, workshops and storage. This was not completed until the end of 1974, though it was opened for Steven Berkoff's presentation of *The Trial* in November 1973. These new facilities were leased to the Round House free of rent.

The Newsletter for January 1973 mentioned new stairs at the front entrance and the excavation of the vaults, for which Camden Council gave financial assistance. The earliest newsletters held in the Round House archives are dated 1972. These were simply roneoed information about coming events at the Round House. Later they became modest brochures not only advertising coming attractions and ticket prices, but also listing developments in the building works and hopes for the future of the project. They were printed fairly consistently, sometimes by the month, sometimes by the season until 1983 and were mailed to those who paid a small sum of money for the privilege (in 1973 it was 50p a year).

From 24 February to 24 March 1973 the building was closed for steel reinforcements to the floor before excavations could begin. This made room for the Theatre Downstairs, a small, studio-like space to take low-budget productions. It was eventually opened by Harold Wilson on 10 July 1975.

On 14 December 1973 Hoskins prepared a statement for the press which was obviously designed to provoke a response from the Arts Council:

The Round House Trust has made its case to the Arts Council that its magnificent spaces can only be continuously well used if it can exert greater control over the choice of shows it should present than has been possible till now. This means subsidy on the scale of the major provincial theatres, which is £1,000 per week or approximately £50,000 over a year. The Trust is now sufficiently hopeful of a change of policy by the Arts Council to adventure into the money-dangerous realms of promotion.

A letter from George Hoskins to Sir Hugh Willatt, the Secretary General (15 January 1974), answers Sir Hugh's concern over the press article, and he defends his use of the phrase 'money-dangerous realms of promotion'. His carefully worded reply re-assured Willatt that 'ventures into direct promotion will follow as far as possible your precepts "very carefully and always well within available funds". Thus our *policy* for 1974/5 remains as put to you on 15 October, while its implementation depends on the response you are able to make.'[11] Whether or not Hoskins' original public announcement made any difference to the Arts Council, the Round House received £24,500 for the year 1974–5, an increase on the previous year of £7,000.

In an article for *The Times* (28 January 1974) Hoskins once again publicised the Round House's goal of promoting or co-promoting its shows. Hoskins' words, always couched in terms of future objectives imminently to be achieved, revealed 'this will mean that in the theatre at least the Round House will have become master of what it presents'. At the end of the article he asks, 'And what if we were financially free to do whatever we liked?' His reply to his own question does not include Wesker's dream of work created at the Round House by artists working for it as part of a complex, but only that he might choose exciting productions from abroad, or attract 'outstanding directors' to work there. The aim of presenting experimental foreign companies was one which Hoskins adhered to throughout his period of administration, and it is this that made the Round House justifiably famous. As successful artistic ventures Hoskins singled out Richardson's *Hamlet*, *1789* and *Rabelais*, and included two companies, Le Grand Magic Circus and *The Red Buddha Theatre*. Only one of the productions was British. He talked also of expanding the intake of music and contemporary ballet, of which the latter was eminently suited to the environment. Twyla Tharp, Ballet Rambert and London Contemporary Dance Theatre made consistently successful use of the auditorium.

In the summer Newsletter of 1974 Hoskins again emphasised the Round House's importance as a social centre, and he still talked of opening the gallery in the near future, to serve as an exhibition space and community area. He claimed, too, that they were about to enter the 'third and last phase' of the building plan:

> The first phase ended in March 1973 when we received land, building and equipment to the worth of about £150,000. The second phase will end in December this year and will give us dressing rooms, stores, workshops, offices, studio theatre and the vaults ... The third phase which has just begun ... will take two years to finish and will cost £190,000 of which we expect public bodies and brewery loans (for the new restaurant) to find £70,000 so our public appeal will be for £120,000.

This last phase was to include new rostra and seating for the auditorium, but at no time during his administration did he entertain the idea of radically altering the stage and auditorium areas. This was left to Thelma Holt in 1979; her concern with the Round House was primarily with its theatre space and not its function as a social centre.

THELMA HOLT'S ALTERATIONS

In the spring of 1977, George Hoskins became ill and had to take leave of absence. The administration muddled along until July when it became clear that Hoskins was not going to be able to continue in his position. Thelma Holt, who had resigned from the Open Space earlier that year, was asked to organise the running of the theatre for three months, after which probationary period she was asked to stay on as the theatre's director. She agreed to stay provided the Arts Council was prepared to grant her a working subsidy for the theatre. For 1976-77 it had provided £39,000, which, in her view, was enough to maintain the building and no more. As a 'gesture of confidence' in her ability to re-animate work at the Round House it offered for the following year a subsidy of £47,500 and she decided to accept the post.[12]

For a year she continued the old policy of keeping the doors open for anyone who would pay the rent. Meanwhile she reorganised the staff who were not, in her opinion, 'theatre people' and installed a personnel of twenty-two with whom she had worked before, including Celia Gulley who had been her assistant at the Open Space. Although Holt admired Hoskins' achievement, she felt it was time that the theatre was managed by people who understood the arts and who recognised the necessity of high standards in any creative venture. Hoskins himself was a businessman and an economist, and in her opinion brought an economist's values to bear on his theatre policies.

It was Holt's contention that, because of the nature of artistic endeavour, success could not be guaranteed with every production. However, work should not be allowed to slip below a certain level because it would demoralise those concerned with it; it would also tend to depreciate those works associated with it, by virtue of being presented in the same building. The reputation of those outstanding plays which had been presented during the past ten years became submerged beneath a mass of rubbish. She blamed in particular the Sunday night rock concerts which had become a source of annoyance to the local residents and which also created bad feeling amongst the companies who used the auditorium during the week. The mess they created was giving the building a derelict air and a reputation for harbouring drop-outs and drug addicts. The problem of drug peddling was one which arose very early on in the life of the Round House, and Hoskins mentions it on page 24 of *The First Report*. Thelma Holt claimed (in interview, 19 February 1979) that when she arrived on the scene there was no longer a problem of drug trafficking, but unfortunately the Round House's reputation as a centre for drugs hung on. So her first positive move in changing policy was to discontinue the rock concerts, her second was to mount her own production, and her third was a decision to make the auditorium a more practical shape for theatre performance.

John Wells as Cokes, Henry Woolf as Wasp and Jonathan Cecil as Littlewit in
Bartholomew Fair by Ben Jonson

In some ways, Thelma Holt's ideals coincided with those of
Arnold Wesker. One of these was a desire to have artistic control over what was presented at the Round House. Not only
did she wish to choose what shows she invited in but she also
wanted to produce her own at least twice a year.[13] Her first
and only attempt was a production of Jonson's *Bartholomew
Fair*, the last full-scale venture before the conversion of the old
auditorium. Peter Barnes directed it, using a cast without well-
known stars (i.e. those who would draw in the public whatever the production). His idea was to use the whole of the
downstairs area as the fairground so that the 'action' might
continue before and after the performance of the play
proper. They borrowed a genuine fairground collection
from Wookey Hole in Somerset (donated by Lady Bangor)
and built booths and stalls which contained both food and
livestock. Typical fairground figures could be encountered
strolling around selling their wares and inviting members of
the audience to participate in various games or watch puppet

shows. Even Shakespeare was there, trying to persuade the audience to go and see one of his plays instead of his rival's! Unfortunately the fairground ambience did not extend into the performance of the play itself and the star of the show became one of the stall inhabitants – a donkey who was born shortly after the play opened. After having beguiled its audience into mingling with actors and participating in the events staged all around and in the auditorium, the production then ignored them, with only one actor, Peter Bayliss as Justice Overdo, making any attempt to involve them in the action by direct address. The production, which had started so stunningly by using all the resources of the Round House, then turned its back on them, and a conventional and unexciting rendering of Jonson's comedy ensued.

The audience were seated on wooden benches, there was sand and sawdust on the floor and programmes were mock scrolls. The stage had audience on three sides and there were wooden slatted flats and booths at the back and round the sides (the designer was Robin Don). They tended to dwarf the actors and the acoustics were bad. The actors' performances seemed to lack exuberance and size, and there was a failure to take into account the kind of building they were playing in. Environmental theatre, so well exploited by Holt and Marowitz at the Open Space, did not flourish in this production as it ought to have done, because the director did not follow through his original concept and encourage his actors to bring to the performance all that he had created before the play began.

It was bad luck that there was another production of *Bartholomew Fair* running in London at the same time. Michael Bogdanov had done a modern setting of it at the Young Vic, and although the reviews for Barnes' production compared favourably with Bogdanov's, they were not sufficiently enthusiastic to help attract good audiences. The Round House took £16,705 in box-office money for a total of twenty-seven performances. The benefit performances which took place to raise money for the Elizabeth Garrett Anderson Hospital did not even cover costs and Thelma Holt had to make a personal donation. It was undoubtedly an ambitious project for a theatre without full subsidy to attempt. It was expensive to mount and unpopular because of the difficulties inherent in the text, and it was one which Holt was unfortunately unable to repeat.

It was the decision to make the Round House a more efficient theatre, plus the idea of doing what the National Theatre had failed to do with its new buildings (that is, form a London venue for the best of the provincial shows), that made Thelma Holt look towards the Manchester Royal Exchange for inspiration. The Royal Exchange was a Victorian building (also not originally a theatre) that had been converted into an arena theatre two and a half years previously. The major difficulties to overcome were similar: bad acoustics, poor sightlines and a large space. Many of the productions which had come into the Round House had made no attempt to use the circular area and had merely cut off a section of it by placing rectangular staging over one arc. It seemed to Holt a pity that a circular building should not be given the chance to exploit all the advantages of theatre-in-the-round, and she decided that it should have its natural shape defined by a new seating plan.

Since the buildings were similar, and both managements wanted to see productions from Manchester offered a London showcase, Richard Negri, the architect who had conceived the idea for the Royal Exchange, and D.K. Jones, who had solved the Manchester theatre's acoustical problems, were asked to convert the Round House auditorium into a theatre-in-the-round.

On 6 March 1978 Thelma Holt wrote to Negri suggesting a ceiling cost of £9,000 for the project, taking £8,000 of that as their target with £1,000 to be regarded as contingency money. She mentions here the possibility of using skilled and semi-skilled workers from Camden's job-creation scheme, and the fact that they already possessed a large quantity of timber, at the time on loan to Riverside Studios.[14] Negri expressed concern in his reply (8 March 1978) that so little money was available for the project. However, when the contract between Thelma Holt and himself was finally signed on 4 January 1979 (not until the work was almost complete) the figures had not changed. Both he and D.K. Jones accepted small fees (£900 and £200 respectively) for their services.

In all, £23,535.36 was spent on the conversion and the same sum was raised from many sources (£5,000 was a personal loan from Eddie Kulukundis). The money was augmented with gifts from companies such as Sanderson's who supplied the paint free and from others who gave generous discounts.[15] Not only was the auditorium altered but also the theatre's periphery: the existing shop was dismantled, a proper box-office installed and the entrance to the gallery cleared. In Thelma Holt's words (in interview), 'only the horrors have been removed and more of the original Round House has been exposed. Nothing has been spoiled.'

Negri's plan involved a reduction in seating capacity from 940 to 600. Although this meant a drop in potential profits, shows seldom filled 900 seats, and only half of the possible occupants had been able to see properly. With the new plan every one would be able to see. The arena stage was timbered and there were six rows of stepped seating all the way round. As at the Royal Exchange, there were seven aisles which formed entrances and exits for actors and audience alike. One row of seats was to be kept in the existing gallery and the front row of seats downstairs was to be kept for sale on the day of the performance. The auditorium was to remain flexible so that if a thrust stage was needed, it might be transformed with as little as thirty-two hours' notice. The auditorium was enclosed with thick green drapes.

D.K. Jones designed a canvas umbrella baffle which was suspended from the roof above the central lighting rig. This ensured that the sound did not get lost in the huge dome. For those who complained that it hid one of the architectural beauties of the Round House, Thelma Holt's answer was that the practicalities of theatrical performance required its presence and that it was removable anyway. The centre of the rig could be lowered to any level and used as a flying stage. Although the baffle and rig were effective when in use, according to Thelma Holt they proved awkward to manipulate, which meant that in effect they were less flexible than they had been designed to be.

The Round House auditorium designed by Richard Negri, with its canvas baffle by D.K. Jones

The design of the Royal Exchange was copied almost exact-ly and the transformation completed in eight weeks. The Round House was now ready to receive its first three productions from

Manchester: *The Ordeal of Gilbert Pinfold,* adapted by Ronald Harwood from the novel by Evelyn Waugh; *The Family Reunion,* by T.S. Eliot; and *The Lady From the Sea,* by Ibsen. At the time Holt felt it was the beginning of a long-term relationship with this repertory company, which would encourage other regional reps to bring their work to London. The National Theatre had apparently formally announced that it could not afford to bring in regional theatre (*Time Out,* 16 February 1979) and there was no other theatre in London that could do it, so its function would be unique.

It proved difficult to agree on a contract between the two companies. The first draft was exchanged on 14 July, but three others were drawn up before the final contract was signed by Thelma Holt on 27 October 1978. The major changes between the first and last drafts were as follows: the final contract stated alternative arrangements if one of the projected productions fell through; it gave details of performances and matinées, staffing and pay and seat prices; it specified that the Royal Exchange should be responsible for its own publicity. The greatest difficulties were over the production of *The Lady From the Sea* because it was impossible to obtain firm dates from Vanessa Redgrave, who was to star in it. Having taken three months to find mutually satisfactory terms for the two companies, Thelma Holt wrote to Laurence Harbottle, the solicitor dealing with the contract, 'Enclosed your copy of the contract. Hurrah! I am in such a catatonic trance now that I am not quite sure what we have done, but I have not married you, have I?' (27 October 1978).

In a prepared statement for the press, the Royal Exchange called the terms of the agreement 'very generous', but relations between the two companies were not always as smooth as this suggests. For instance, ill feeling was caused when Michael Williams (general manager and associate artistic director at the Royal Exchange) wrote an angry letter to the Round House management (1 February 1979) concerning an article in the *Guardian* (1 February 1979) which he thought did not fairly acknowledge the part the Royal Exchange had played in the Round House conversion. The reply (2 February 1979) was acerbic. Although this did not entirely characterise dealings between the companies, it nevertheless explains some of the tensions which existed between them and their part in the seemingly interminable delays before signing. It also explains, to a certain extent, why it took so long for the second season of Royal Exchange productions to materialise at the Round House in April 1981.

Both managements had recognised the need to change the public image of the Round House if the project was to succeed. Thelma Holt had taken the first steps by getting rid of the rock concerts. Michael Elliott, one of the artistic directors of the Royal Exchange, saw that a publicity campaign needed to be launched and he therefore wrote to the Arts Coucil thus: 'the biggest worry of all is whether the London audience can be persuaded to go to a building which has no successful tradition of presenting straight plays ... without this transformation I cannot see how it will find a future life (12 July 1978).' He asked the Arts Council to finance a publicity officer to instigate and supervise such a campaign. Although no reply to the letter is filed in *Show File* 22, the success of the three productions demonstrates a new enthusiasm for the venue. The transcript of the press conference held on 4 January shows that in order to break even they needed to play to 84% capacity houses. In a letter to her accountants, Thelma Holt claimed that they were still playing to 60% capacity and that it was near the end of the run of the first production.

The theatre, in its new form, remained open until 1983, when its subsidy was terminated. The Arts Council had been generous to the Holt administration, though not generous enough for her to run the theatre as she wished, i.e. promoting productions which were artistically interesting but not commercial. As Camden Council would not show an interest in the financial concerns of the theatre, the Arts Council, whose policy it then was to continue to subsidise only if the theatre's local council also felt it worth supporting, withdrew their help and the theatre had to close (Paul Collins, the then director of finance for the Arts Council, in interview 16 July 1986). In the spring of 1983, with a final boost from the Arts Council, Holt was able to close the premises and pay off all outstanding debts. She has continued to independently produce plays from all over the world, winning awards, earning a CBE and in 1997 was appointed as the Cameron Mackintosh Visiting Professor of Contemporary Theatre in association with St Catherine's College, Oxford.

NOTES

1   Written for *Encore* magazine in 1958; the article is reprinted in *The Encore Reader* (1965), 96–103 (p.11).

2   *The Kitchen* and *Chicken Soup with Barley* had been written before his article appeared. The latter had had a success in July 1958 at the Royal Court.

3   Richard Hoggart, *The Uses of Literacy* (London, 1957), p.11.

4   The lecture was entitled 'O Mother is it Worth It' and is reprinted in Arnold Wesker, *Fears of Fragmentation* (London, 1970), 11–19 (p.17).

5   Frank Coppieters' dissertation, *Arnold Wesker's Centre 42*, gives a detailed analysis of the proposals, pp.87–91, RH archives.

6   A copy of *The First Report* is to be found in SF Pre-1971 A.

7   Arnold Wesker, 'The Secret Reins, Centre 42', in *Fears of Fragmentation*, 39–50 (p.47).

8   The rehearsal period up to the first night has been documented by Garry O'Connor, 'Arnold Wesker's *The Friends*', *Theatre Quarterly*, 1 (1971), no.2, 78–92.

9   For more information on *Oh! Calcutta!* see Frank Coppieters pp.299–302.

10 Wesker in interview, 'The System and the Writer', *New Theatre Magazine*, 11 (1971), no.2, 8–11 (p.8).

11 The Press Statement (14 December 1973) and Hoskins' letter (15 January 1974) are contained in 'Press Releases to September 1974', RH archives.

12 Thelma Holt in interview with the author, 19 February 1979.

13 Ibid.

14 This, and all subsequent information (unless otherwise stated) on the transactions between the Round House and the Royal Exchange during their first season, is contained in SF 22, 'General Correspondence'.

15 For a breakdown of income and expenditure see SF 22, 'Change Over'.

specialised audience, but was, as far as Brook's work is concerned, part of a development towards a kind of theatre whose popular appeal blossomed with the production of *A Midsummer Night's Dream*.[2] His later production of *The Ik* (Round House, January 1976), devised in Paris, did not need an invited audience: it received wide publicity both before and after performance, and has been well documented.[3]

ARDEN AND D'ARCY'S *THE HERO RISES UP*

In November of the same year, *The Hero Rises Up*, written and directed by John Arden and Margaretta D'Arcy, was the first full-length play to be staged at the Round House. Appropriately enough, these two playwrights were already well-known for their left-wing views and their dramatisations of political issues. Not only were their politics radical, but the two had already attempted alternative forms of theatre, and *The Hero Rises Up* was no exception. It was an experimental production which employed improvisatory techniques, both in the way it was performed and the content of the play itself. Unconventional staging was to be used to express an unconventional and unflattering view of Nelson, the national British hero. At the same time, the play was intended to show something of the nature of mankind in general, and the way in which society creates, moulds and abuses its 'great men'.

The show had been salvaged from a project for a Broadway musical with Bock and Harnick (the *Fiddler on the Roof* team), a project which had been amicably discontinued after disagreements about the meaning and interpretation of the show. The script had been written but the final contract did not materialise, so the Arden team took away their text to use as they wanted, and the others kept for themselves the lyrics and tunes they had written. It was at this stage that Arden and D'Arcy decided to make the play into a ballad opera, to be staged under their own artistic control, in order to experiment 'in various popular theatre directions that a B'dway [sic] production would have inhibited'. Arden also said that at the Round House the production team encountered difficulties rooted in the structural peculiarities of the building and the lack of technical facilities.4 There was nothing to help the echoing acoustic of the hall except a sounding board hanging from the roof, which apparently did not serve any very useful purpose, and the actors had difficulty making themselves heard. There was no team of technicians to help in any crisis, so that when on the first night the amplifiers ceased to function, the management were unable to rectify the fault. The play relies for much of the time on the music, so that the lack of the special sound effects created by Boris Howarth proved disastrous.

Howarth's musical score was semi-improvised (the published text of the play specifies certain tunes for some of the songs, but leaves the rest to the imagination of the company); the most important feature of the band was a piano stripped of its case and played like a harp, which then needed to be electrically amplified.5 When the amplifiers broke down the sound was lost and unfavourably disposed critics were quick to seize on the failure as an example of professional and artistic incompetence.

Howarth and his wife, Maggie, had previously worked informally with Arden and D'Arcy at their home in Kirby-moorside in 1966, doing music, sets and costume for the first production of *The Royal Pardon*, a show improvised round bedtime stories the authors had told their own children. *The Hero Rises Up* was an extension of the kind of work they had done together. They also worked with them again on *The Non-Stop Connolly Show* in 1975 when it was presented at Liberty Hall, Dublin. This gave a sense of creative continuity to the work of the playwrights, and Arden felt that 'the Round House production justified us in the direction we hoped we were going in'.

According to Boris Howarth, in a letter to the author (6 July 1981), all scores of the music for *The Hero Rises Up* have been lost except for two short extracts entitled 'Kite Floats' that are in his possession. In his letter, Howarth described the kind of music he had created for the production, which was essentially divided into four parts:

1. 'The Songs'. I think 50 in all, mainly adaptations of existing folk-tunes used as a vehicle for *dramatic* rather than *musical* expression. They had no formal accompaniment, but some of them may have been backed by any one or a combination of the other musical modes in operation.
2. 'Dramatic Punctuation'. A wide range of percussive textures used to enhance and counterpoint important words and gestures.
3. 'Atmospheric Texture'. Played live, but relayed quietly thru [sic] twelve speakers equally spaced around the balcony, falling like gentle rain and working subliminally...
4. 'Historical Wallpaper'. A little trio played decaying tea-room selections from classics of the period. Occasionally, at dramatic high-points, melodic and harmonic disciplines would break down and the music would be used to augment *Atmospheric Texture*.

The trio playing 'Historical Wallpaper' (piano, viola, and flute) and 'Dramatic Punctuation' (drums, gongs, bells and woodblocks) needed no amplification, but 'Atmospheric Texture' used John Cage innovations: prepared piano with the keyboard removed (the whole laid flat and played with a selection of different hammers), water gongs, toy pianos, a fire-organ (Howarth's own invention of glass organ-pipes activated by gas jets), and other small sounds, all of which needed amplification. There was also a tape bank which augmented the sound of 'Atmospheric Texture'; some instrumental pieces were added ('Kite Floats' was one of them), and also some recorded sea and boat sounds, some of which were taped on HMS Victory in Portsmouth.

The stage consisted of a rostrum, forty feet wide, placed off-centre in the circular auditorium, with two small extension stages at either side of the front of the main stage, each reached by a gang plank. Two sets of steps were placed back stage left and right and were used as entrances, though the stage could be reached from any part of the auditorium. A circular podium, on which the trio performed, was placed stage left of the main stage, and stage right there was a separate side-stage for the other sound effects. At the back of the rostrum was an enormous screen for a projected film and slide show created by Mark Boyle, which was described by Albert Hunt in *New Society* (14 November 1968) as 'merely boring and distracting'. In his letter, Boris Howarth drew an analogy between the music and the sound effects which showed clearly the relevance of the light show to the production as a whole. The music, he said, was at once an aural version of Mark Boyle's scenery and an emotional barometer of the dramatic action.

Originally the intention had been to seat the audience directly in front of the platform (the production was obviously not conceived as theatre-in-the-round despite the Round House's potential for such work), so that the film and scene titles would have been clearly visible to all members of the audience. However, because of a row that Arden and D'Arcy had had with the management of the Institute of Contemporary Arts, where the play had previously been staged, the audience numbers were so great that people were packed into the auditorium without proper seating facilities, and many of them did not experience the full impact of the visual effects. Many of the critics who arrived for the first night were without seats and naturally most of them grumbled. B.A. Young of the *Financial Times* (9 November 1968) left at the interval even though a member of the audience offered him a table-top to sit on; Harold Hobson (*Sunday Times*, 10 November 1968) and the critic for *The Stage* (14 November 1968) both expressed outrage at not being allocated seats. In his letter Arden explained that he and D'Arcy were at the time asserting playwrights' and audiences' rights against reviewers', so special seats were not reserved for critics. In retrospect he acknowledged that this was probably a tactical mistake but commented, 'It was all in the spirit of the times'. The dispute which had bedevilled the show from the start began, Arden said, because:

> they [the ICA management] were putting on another elaborate stage production at the same time in their own premises and it over-extended their then resources to be managers of both at the same time. We felt they were not exerting themselves to sell tickets for the Roundhouse but were concentrating their efforts far too much on the Mall building. (Arden's letter 1 April 1981)

In *To Present the Pretence* he defined the issues he and D'Arcy were fighting over: 'our right as co-author-directors to compose our own publicity material, our right to manage the production the way we wanted it managed, and our right to determine the type of audience we thought would be best served by the show we were putting on.'6

One of the practical ways in which Arden and D'Arcy tried to implement their own ideas about recruiting audiences was to set up a system of free seats which ensured that the Round House was full throughout the run, and people were packed so tightly that many were sitting sideways on to the stage. This meant that the film show, which was to have provided a background to the actors, could not be seen as such. Arden's own comment on this in his letter was that since the audience had got in free, he had assumed they would not grumble: 'Alas, the English public don't think like that, or, at least, a significant number of those who don't are writers for the theatre-journals: so we had some really bitchy reviews in one or two places.'

The Round House had seemed an attractive venue for a production of their play. It had been hoped that the audience would promenade and participate, though it seems as if the overcrowding of the auditorium hindered this. Even Philip Hope-Wallace, writing for the *Guardian* (8 November 1968) in sympathetic vein, remarked that despite Arden's opening speech, which invited the audience to walk around and complain if they could not hear, people remained hunched in their places. The promenading was vital to the show since Arden and D'Arcy were specifically trying to make direct contact with their audience, among whom were agit-prop and political groups. The idea was to make the play relevant to modern-day issues and not merely to present an historical extravaganza, no matter how unusual a portrait of Nelson it contained. Although the failure of the promenade effect could be attributed to audience numbers and lack of preparation time, it is possible that the conventional thrust staging inhibited the participation that the authors desired and that a more radical method ought to have been found in a building that was so different from a traditional theatre.

The play, which is subtitled *A Romantic Melodrama* and described in the published text as having used 'the style of

[147]

Henry Woolf as Nelson and Bettina Jonic as Lady Hamilton in *The Hero Rises Up* by John Arden and Margaretta D'Arcy

"popular print", legend and ballad', achieved this effect through costume design and acting. The actors wore modern trousers and footwear with overstated period jackets and hats. Maggie Howarth, in a letter to the author (6 July 1981), criticised the costume maker for not having exaggerated the costumes enough to realise the puppet-style convention that the directors required, though colours were heightened, which helped to give a feeling of the grotesque. An emphasis on large gesture was demanded of the actors to suggest that Nelson was one of the many puppets manipulated by society, and some of the actors had difficulty in performing convincingly in this manner. Henry Woolf, who played Nelson, was apparently a notable exception. The action, played against Boyle's massive backdrops, was picked out by a pair of two kilowatt follow-spots which made the actors appear to be tiny bright puppets set in front of the vastness of the sea.

Visual effects were not confined to the stage area. Maggie Howarth designed large sails, flags and banners to be hung on rigging mechanisms (all made by Inter-Action from nearby Wilkin Street), which were activated by teams of well-drilled 'sailors' from the East 15 Drama School, scuttling about below stage and on the balcony, changing canvas and setting signals. The body of the auditorium was itself transformed for some scenes from the lower deck of a fighting ship to a vast baroque pageant arena where actors carried large processional images above their heads; the foyer was transformed with a wild fig- urehead sculpture of Nelson made by John Fox (founder in 1968 of the Welfare State Theatre Company). Thus the the- atre itself was made an integral part of the production, creat- ing one of the earliest English experiments in the theatre of total environment.

It had proved a difficult task to put on an experimental production in a building which was not built for the purpose and which was still very much an unknown quantity. Backstage conditions were cold, dark and dirty and the ICA had not organised things efficiently: the Round House had been double-booked for the week's run, so that each evening, almost before the show had finished, the cast had to leave the building in order that a rock band might take over. In addi- tion to this, a conference on anarchism took place on one afternoon during the run and some damage was caused to the materials the cast had had to leave in the building. Yet, although the venture was beset with problems, none of them, according to Arden, would have been insurmountable, if there had been more time. One week was not long enough to get to grips with the peculiarities of the Round House, partic- ularly since this was the first full-length production staged there and the company did not have the benefit of anyone else's experience of the working conditions; but enough energy and atmosphere were generated for the more percep- tive critics to see the value of the work. Philip Hope-Wallace in the *Guardian* (8 November 1968) referred to the opera enthu- siastically as 'a big top, a mob theatre ... historical drama in comic strip', and the RSC offered Arden and D'Arcy work with them as a result of the production.

Though the critics had largely been scathing about it, audi- ences during the play's short run had been responsive.

Howarth said that he remembered 'long and hearty ovations and no half-empty houses', and that there was an atmosphere of excitement amongst the public. The production had its weaknesses, but Arden had tried something new: he had added pantomime and improvisatory techniques to a formally structured narrative, which confused many critics. Arden, in his letter, characterised the production as a 'do-it-yourself cultural effort' in which the local community had become involved. It had been supported by the participation of local teenagers from Inter-Action, also a Camden enterprise. They took part in crowd scenes and helped to make masks and properties. This proved a mixed blessing. According to Arden the teenagers were:

> nice kids but *very* wild, and drove our professional actors mad by their exuberance behind the scenes during the performance. One of them brought his dog in and another rode a bicycle around. Another of them said he liked playing a press-gang officer in the play because it enabled him to really show the actors what 'the violence' was like. He nearly put one of the cast into hospital. We did have a curious mixture of the professional, the amateur and the juvenile in the company: and it did present a number of problems of social integration.

It was the last time the Arden/D'Arcy team attempted to put their ideas into practice in a regular London framework. They disowned the performances of *The Island of the Mighty* by the RSC in 1972 because of a similar dispute about authors' rights during production and their later work was done on a much more independent basis.

The demand for artistic autonomy made by the co-authors was one with which Wesker sympathised, and he made it clear in the *Sunday Times* letter (21 February 1971) that he did not wish to denigrate the work that had come into the theatre: 'the Round House pursues a colourful existence and I'm not concerned to detract from it'. He had not envisaged local participation in the way that Arden and D'Arcy had accomplished it here. He saw the role of artist as separate from the role of those who would enjoy the product of the artists' creativity, and he believed there was a clear dividing line between professionals and amateurs. However, the kind of enthusiasm the show generated and the mingling of performers, playwrights and audience came closer to the spirit of Centre 42 than the other productions staged prior to Wesker's resignation.

RICHARDSON'S *HAMLET*

The *Hamlet* which followed at the beginning of 1969 was the first major production to be presented at the Round House, that is in terms of the length of contract and its box-office success. It was given a great deal of pre-performance publicity, not least because Tony Richardson, the director, published a manifesto in which he put forward the aims of his company, the Free Theatre. It was so called, not because it was offering free seats (though this was to be its ultimate goal), but because it was to free the theatre from the limitations imposed upon it by the proscenium arch. Its desire was to attract young audiences who were inhibited by the 'social habits' that go with proscenium theatre, so the emphasis was on a casual atmosphere and cheap seats. Seat prices went as low as 2s.6d., and these were subsidised by seats which cost £5 (this system of expensive seats subsidising cheap ones was adopted by the National Theatre when it first went into its South Bank building). Critics were asked to pay for their tickets. The manifesto declared that 'ideally all performances should be completely free. This is obviously for the future and depends on massive subsidy'.

The production had a mixed critical reception, though the presence of Nicol Williamson and Marianne Faithfull ensured full houses. First of all Richardson's manifesto caused controversy amongst critics who thought it naïve and misguided. Albert Hunt in *New Society* (17 April 1969) wrote a long article demolishing the arguments set out in the manifesto and criticising the production for proving as anachronistic as the productions it purported to reject. He and a number of other critics took issue with Richardson for his 'trivial' analysis of the reasons why young people do not attend the theatre (the necessity for advance bookings as well as the 'social habits'), but he was the only one to attempt an analysis of his own to counteract Richardson's claims. His argument was one which

Charles Marowitz would have endorsed: that it was naturalism which bedevilled the English stage, not the proscenium arch itself and, although the set used in the Round House was non-representational, 'all that holds the play together is a completely naturalistic portrait of Hamlet himself.'

Perhaps it was the hectoring tone of the manifesto that made the critics bristle: 'To restore impact to the theatre it must be liberated from the tyranny of any form. Each production can have its own shape of stage and audience.' It was a tone that certainly admitted no place for more traditional theatre – 'now a new revolution is needed to destroy, finally and completely, the form of the proscenium theatre' – but neither did it take into account any previous work done by experimental theatre groups all over the world (and in the Round House itself). Indeed it was this aspect that annoyed Marowitz who had worked on his own collage version of *Hamlet* as early as 1963. He saw the manifesto as a mere device to publicise the production. The claims that Richardson made were not in themselves revolutionary, as Marowitz pointed out:

> The hoopla hooched up by Richardson for *Hamlet* concerned a woolly-minded concept called 'free theater' which, after the rhetoric subsided, turned out to be a plea for open staging and a blast at proscenium theater; a crusade which is almost exactly 50 years old and which, in England, has already succeeded in places as far afield as Stoke-on-Trent and Bristol not to mention recent environmental breakthroughs at LAMDA, Donmar, the three London fringe theaters, and the Round House itself. (*Confessions of a Counterfeit Critic* p.149)

It is interesting that Marowitz is here berating Richardson, not simply for making pretentious claims about theatre in general but for making false claims about the nature of his own production, a charge that was levelled at the Open Space many times.

Some critics found that the production itself made exciting use of the Round House space, others such as Milton Shulman and Irving Wardle felt that the acting area was not used to advantage and that the stage which the company had erected was 'unlikely to do anything to break the dreaded tyranny of the proscenium' (*The Times*, 18 February 1969). The annoyance of these critics, then, was prompted by the company's failure to fulfil its unequivocal, and in the critics' view arrogant, claims. A three-sided, stepped platform was used with a projecting apron, bare of any props. At the back was a black screen; the only colour came from the flame and brown costumes designed by Jocelyn Herbert. According to her, the colour range was chosen to reflect the decadence of the court and was deliberately restricted. 'I use scenery to be evocative rather than decorative,' she added (*The Times*, 16 April 1969). Beneath the dome was suspended a ring of lamps, with no attempt to hide them. The Ghost's voice echoed through the vaults, repeating key words such as 'unnatural' and 'murder', and only bright light on Hamlet's upturned face suggested the Ghost's physical presence. Always dimly visible were the Round House's pillars and the maze of passages and doors behind them at the edge of the auditorium so that 'the audience is enclosed in the same space as the play' (*Spectator*, 28 February 1969). As Auriol Stevens reported in the *Observer* Colour Supplement (11 January 1970), the Round House is 'a space entirely dominated by the character of the building', and Richardson wisely chose to exploit this. In the same way that the sordid surroundings of the Open Space theatre helped create the prison environment of *Fortune and Men's Eyes*, so the Round House itself managed to suggest the echoing halls of a sinister castle. However, here it was a much more difficult space to contend with because it was so enormous, and Richardson attempted to achieve a degree of intimacy with his audience by using a three-sided rostrum as stage. Instead of using the round spaces the building afforded he chose to erect a platform-stage which meant that the acoustics were better and sight-lines easier to manage. According to *The Times* (18 February 1969), Nicol Williamson came right down to the audience for his soliloquies, snarled at them, and yet made no attempt to take them into his confidence.

In this production, just as in *The Hero Rises Up*, the director had tried to cope with the size of the building by diminishing it. A fixed platform was used which cut off a large section of potential acting space. Many directors who brought shows into the Round House used this rather conventional method of staging to counteract loss of sound (and too large an acting area), instead of shaping their productions in more radical ways. Even though *Hamlet* was played on a jutting platform, the actors made use of all parts of the stage for their entrances and exits, and the exceptionally wide acting arena forced the players to work at a 'gallop' so that the performance did not seem to stand still (*Observer*, 23 February 1969). *Themes on the Tempest* had attempted to exploit the vast circular void of the Round House by moving both the action and the audience from area to area. Arden had tried to do a similar thing with his audience, but because of the overcrowding and the conventional shape of the rostrum the technique had merely caused confusion.

Productions of the classics, given new treatment, were to be a feature of Round House events in the years to come. The most notable of these was the Theatregoround programme devised by John Barton for the RSC, in which his adaptation of the Henrys, entitled *When Thou Art King*, was a feature (November 1970). Prospect also brought in, with some regularity, works by Shakespeare and his contemporaries as well as new plays, having found that the Round House auditorium was suitable for the minimal sets that it so often used (August 1973, November 1974, October 1975).

THE LIVING THEATRE AND FREEHOLD

Julian Beck and Judith Malina (The Living Theatre), who were primarily concerned with new ways of integrating actors with the audience, followed closely on these first productions at the Round House with their four shows, *Paradise Now*, *Frankenstein*, *Mysteries* and *Antigone*. They had previously brought two spectacles to London that had caused quite a stir: *The Connection* to the Duke of York's and *The Brig* to the Mermaid. Now they brought over a programme which moved further away from the structured play in an attempt to 'create an event'.7 The first of these, *Paradise Now*, was developed as if it were a religious ritual involving both congregation and those aiding the rites. Richard Schechner, who interviewed the Becks for *The Drama Review*, found that the evening was conducted like the Yom Kippur service and that, like the service, it was to a certain extent a test of endurance (the show lasted between four and five hours). The Becks both denied the Jewish emphasis and stressed rather that the play was structured like any 'good ritual' (*The Drama Review*, p.26). The chanting and mingling with the audience were ideas that had been used by Peter Brook in *The Tempest*. However, The Living Theatre took the audience participation further than Brook: in Malina's words, 'Anything I say to you in the lobby is very much part of the play. If *Paradise Now* can be said to have a direction, it is that I don't have to put on any kind of an act' (*The Drama Review*, p.26). She goes on to say that friendliness is not the aim of mingling and talking to the audience, and it was the open (though acted) hostility towards her audience that antagonised so many of the critics and the public. This meant, of course, that the impact of the play was going to be felt only by those who were already prejudiced in its favour. The Becks seemed to be prepared to lose even their staunchest supporters through this method. They did not believe in revolution through persuasion, even though they termed themselves pacifists.

To Schechner, Julian Beck described the process of creating *Antigone*, the last of the four 'events' to be staged: 'the prologue to *Antigone* is real time – it takes just about that long to get hostile toward the audience, to spot each one and decide who you don't like' (p.41). The Living Theatre was bent on rousing anger in its audiences and refused to respond to the heckling which it had deliberately induced. The actors hurled insults at the audience members as they rushed through the aisles and stripped down to G-strings in an attempt to force a reaction from them. Brook in *The Tempest* tried to find expression for the violence inherent in the play and to link it to the broader question of violence in our own society, but he did not attack his audience in the process.

Of their four shows the one that pleased the critics most was *Frankenstein*. Like Brook, the company used scaffolding in the auditorium to represent different settings. The show opened with all kinds of deaths being enacted in the fifteen different cell-like compartments which the scaffolding formed. Later it functioned as the inside of the brain, a group of prison cells and the cages of a zoo. The action was accomplished largely without words, the company preferring to use choric sound (murmurings, groanings, magnified heart beats etc.) to evoke and suggest rather than to state its effects. Brook had hoped to communicate without words with a multinational company, and the Living Theatre was attempting something similar. Its version of *Antigone* was the only production which relied on words, and here it tried to solve the problem of language barriers by improvising gesture which accompanied and interpreted it. The actors also spoke all of the narrative lines in the language of the country it was performing in.

Frankenstein was the only one of the four shows to rely upon something more than the human body to make its effects, though the scaffolding itself was always swarming with human bodies. Just as the structures in a circus-ring are always being used by the performers, so that there is an interdependence between actors and apparatus, here the scaffolding formed an integral part of the action. The monster was made with a pyramid of actors which stretched up to the top of the scaffolding (about twenty feet high) whilst the silhouettes of the rest of the cast could be discerned crowding all over it. Many of the critics were impressed by this, but Marowitz in 'An Open Letter to the Becks' (*Plays and Players*, June 1969) objected to their use of 'tableaux-vivants' and 'zealous physical expressionism' which he 'associated with bad drama school exercises'. He himself used the kind of exercises that the cast performed but not as an end in themselves, only as pre-performance aids. He was, however, himself prone to overusing the technique of the tableau-vivant even in his last adaptations with the Open Space, such as *The Father* and *Hedda*.

Marowitz's letter to the Becks was by no means entirely critical. Indeed, he acknowledged them as a powerful influence on all modern theatre. 'Yours is,' he said, 'the most fertilizing and significant theatre company in the world.' The Round House was admirably suited to the kind of show the Living Theatre produced. The Living Theatre did not want a proscenium stage even though it could adapt its work to one if it had to, but it much preferred large spaces in buildings such as sports arenas or amphitheatres. During its run at the Round House there was trouble with the police who had received complaints of indecent exposure from local residents, but the performances were not actually closed down.

In November of the same year, another American company, Nancy Meckler's Freehold, brought a production of *Antigone* to the Round House, where it played as a late-night show. Like the other plays before it, this production was concerned with communication through physical means rather than through language, and movement and sound were used to illustrate the action. Although it used a stage that separated actors from audience, it also used the auditorium for various effects. Shouts of 'What is man?' echoed from the far corners of the Round House, and at the end the actors moved through the audience chanting slogans and making reference to contemporary events.

Its use of a classical text had similarities to the Marowitz collages in that it emphasised, to the exclusion of all other facets of the play, the idea of the state versus the individual. Marowitz, in most of his works, extracted a theme from his chosen text and developed and expanded it so that often the original play offered no more than a framework for his own ideas. He also included in *An Othello* and *The Shrew* scenes of modern dialogue which had nothing to do with the original. Meckler's production made only one substantial change in the text, 'all pleas to "the Gods" were turned into appeals for "Love"' (*Disrupting the Spectacle* p.26), but at the end of the play the actors drew attention to the horrors of Biafra, Vietnam and South Africa. The Living Theatre's version started by using Brecht's text, but early in rehearsal it was discarded and the dialogue was improvised. Many critics reviewing Meckler's *Antigone* disliked the interpolations because they felt that the production had already made the contemporary relevance explicit enough.

Words used sparingly were replaced by mime and movement. Emotion was expressed physically and symbolically. The body of Polynices was seen on stage throughout the performance, and each actor in the company took a turn as the corpse. At the end of the play the audience was invited to come up onto the stage and scatter dust on the body. In this way they were coerced into taking a positive though symbolic stand with Antigone against laws which deny the human spirit in mankind.

BERKOFF'S *METAMORPHOSIS*

It is interesting that many of those companies of the late Sixties and early Seventies that considered themselves experimental were attracted to using the classics. By taking the framework of a well-known play already rich in meaning for a modern audience, the work could be moulded by the company to shape new meanings which would be the more penetrating when placed in the context of the old play. The choice of material was not limited to drama, but literary works were adapted, such as Kafka's *Metamorphosis* by Steven Berkoff and the fables of Gargantua and Pantagruel adapted by Jean-Louis Barrault as *Rabelais*. Historical and contemporary events were chosen to illustrate the ills within our own society, and very soon after *Palach* at the Open Space, Le Théâtre du Soleil performed *1789* at the Round House. Both of the French productions had more success in France where the original literary works and underlying French history were much better known.

Berkoff's adaptation of *Metamorphosis* was presented with another adaptation of a Kafka short story called *In the Penal Colony*. The two productions were in sharp contrast to each other: the former, highly stylised and worked out with geometrical precision; the latter a naturalistic portrayal of brutality and violence. Berkoff obtained the approval of the Kafka Trust for the venture and, with a small company, no funding and a great deal of encouragement from Hoskins, presented his first professional production, having worked previously only with drama-school students. Unlike the Becks or Meckler, Berkoff was not interested in trying to dissolve the natural barriers which exist between audience and actor on a conventional stage, though he was fascinated by the stage space itself and believed that in order to realise the full potential of a stage such as the one the Round House offered he needed to 'carve up the stage as if it were a giant cake' and to move his actors in a mathematically worked out design.[8] The stage he used was a semi-circular rostrum with masking curtains at the back. If you were not seated centrally as one of the audience, the full effect of the 'beetle' mime was lost. The public came to the production since the critics had been enthusiastic about Berkoff's performance, which was offset by the angular scaffolding suggestive of 'an abstract sculpture of a giant insect'.[9]

The family was placed at the front of the stage, while Berkoff as the 'beetle' was walled up at the back in a box which stood throughout both the productions. It was excluded from the main lighting and was lit by spotlights. Because of this positioning, Berkoff was forced to keep miming throughout to keep the audience focused on him, and he did so even at the expense of upstaging the other characters at crucial moments.[10] It was a black and white production: the faces of the family were whitened, and in the scenes where the family freeze in different attitudes, the spotlight picked them out, so that the effect was of an old-fashioned group photograph which had caught its subjects at an awkward moment. The visual impact of the play was very strong, and the music which accompanied it was abstract and atmospheric. Barely any stage furniture was used because, in Berkoff's own words, 'The actor's body is the environment of the stage rather than the set.'[11]

Subsequent Berkoff productions at the Round House used similar techniques: *The Trial* (adapted from Kafka's novel) in 1973 and *Hamlet* in 1980 used black and white staging with bright white light, and except for some essential props such as the door frames held by the company in *The Trial* and the chairs which bounded the dark stage in *Hamlet*, the stage was bare. In *The Trial*, mime was the company's main way of suggesting both the spiritual torment of Josef K and also the nightmare setting, where a physical labyrinth of corridors was evoked by the actors bearing the door frames. Groups of figures in both the plays froze in stylised attitudes while the focus was directed elsewhere. Jonathan Hammond, writing for *Plays and Players* (January 1974), felt that Berkoff was in danger of becoming creatively sterile (his *Agamemnon* was being performed at the same time as *The Trial*, and he was, in Hammond's opinion, using the same methods on two very different plays). Box-office returns show that fewer seats were sold for *Hamlet* in 1980 than for *The Trial* in 1973.[12]

The same fate seemed to dog the Living Theatre, who on its return to the Round House in July 1979, with *Prometheus*, played to half-empty houses and unenthusiastic critics. According to one member of the audience, they were asked to re-enact the storming of the Winter Palace, but there were not enough of them to create the desired effect. Afterwards they were all encouraged to walk to Holloway Prison and stand with lighted candles, but people slunk away – Holloway Prison is a long way from Chalk Farm! Living Theatre was still shouting the same political slogans and inviting the audience to engage in 'revolutionary' activities with it, but the lack of response to its attempts at rousing the rebellious spirit suggests that it needed to develop new ways of exciting its audiences. Perhaps, too, the effects of the Thatcherite reaction to anti-establishment experiment were already in the air.

POTTER'S *THE SON OF MAN*; GENET'S *THE BLACKS*; WESKER'S *THE FRIENDS*

Plays followed in 1969 and 1970 by established, contemporary playwrights and others who had acquired a reputation for promising new works, but they failed to make much impact on the public when performed at the Round House, partly because they were not written with the theatre's unconventional performing space in mind. Dennis Potter's *The Son of Man* (directed by Robin Midgely), which had earlier caused such controversy when it was shown on BBC television because of its unorthodox portrayal of Christ as an 'aggressive' and 'blustering' man (*Guardian*, 12 November 1969), now caused little excitement. The production had originated at the Phoenix in Leicester and naturally used a proscenium stage setting as it had done there, thereby ignoring the Round House's potential. The bare platform of the steeply raked stage was dominated by two giant T-shaped crosses. Some of the action was stylised with 'Artaudian groaning sessions', and fights and floggings were enacted in slow motion (*Tribune*, 21 November 1969), but prolonged scenes of violence, obviously influenced by the Brook/Marowitz Theatre of Cruelty season, lost their impact under this theatre's vault.

An attempt was made to break the proscenium frame of the play when the audience was used as the congregation for the Sermon on the Mount. Disciples moved amongst them, asking them to join hands with their neighbours as a sign of brotherly love. According to the critics, the audience did not respond well to this invasion of their territory. The involvement with the play required on their part had not been properly established and seemed merely to embarrass them.

A similar lack of enthusiasm greeted the Oxford Playhouse's production of *The Blacks* by Genet, in November 1969. The conventional staging, which might have provided a feeling of intimacy between action and audience in another, smaller theatre, here failed to impress. Reviews were mixed and the staging was hardly mentioned by the critics who concentrated their attention upon the all-black casting and low standard of acting.

Both *The Son of Man* and *The Blacks* were booked for three weeks. Other productions that came in had much shorter runs, sometimes only three nights. It was therefore only after a great deal of persuasion that Hoskins agreed to keep the Round House free for a twelve-week run of Wesker's new play, *The Friends*. However, public response to it was so poor that it had to come off after only six weeks. Wesker blamed its failure on the critics, and in a long article in *Theatre Quarterly*, where he examined some of their reviews in detail, he analysed and defended his play.[13] Garry O'Connor, who had acted as Wesker's assistant director, published in the same number a production casebook of *The Friends* (pp.78–92) which makes it clear that problems with the show were more deep-rooted than Wesker's defence suggests.[14]

Wesker himself does not appear to have expressed fears that the Round House might have been the wrong venue, but in 'The Diary of the Production' O'Connor describes the play as 'a piece of chamber music' and goes on to wonder how it will 'fare in the Roundhouse, which is everything but intimate' (p.79). The play concerns a group of seven people in their mid-thirties who are together waiting for the death of Esther, one of the seven, who has leukaemia. It dramatises the tensions felt amongst these friends before she dies and explores their reactions after the death, which occurs at the end of Act 1. It is a wordy play which communicates emotion through long speeches, where nuances of voice, facial expression and gesture are essential to an understanding of the issues presented. The reference to chamber music is an apt one, and the *Daily Telegraph* reviewer (20 May 1970) used the same phrase. He added that the Round House did not generate the right atmosphere for the subtleties of the 'drawing room play'.

In order to diminish the alarmingly open space of the Round House auditorium, the stage area used was enormous, though conventionally constructed with the audience seated in front of it. The stage was set as one large room with its different areas characterised by outsize props: Esther's bed with a picture of Lenin behind it, huge potted plants, a carved desk and a recreation of the Crick-Watson model of the structure of DNA. Critics commented on how well the set blended into the Round House surroundings, though this could not compensate for the lack of intimacy between the characters and the audience.

It is interesting that the rehearsal difficulties the cast experienced with Wesker were similar to those that arose during his time as administrator of the Round House Trust. He could not gain the confidence of his actors, just as he could not quite persuade those with power and money to trust his Centre 42 enterprise. Full of good intentions, which ranged from taking the cast of *The Friends* to live in his house before rehearsals began, so that they could get to know each other, and trying to set up an arts centre for everyone, he managed to incur intense dislike from many in his cast. Much later, in his autobiography *As Much As I Dare*, Wesker was to write of one actor in particular, Victor Henry, cast as Roland, whose 'strength fed on the diminishment of those he felt a threat. His delight was in destruction ... Victor decided to sabotage

The Friends.[15] The lack of trust led to blazing rows between Wesker and the actors, and Wesker and his colleagues on the administration, which finally necessitated his withdrawal from the enterprise. He was even indirectly accused of plotting a Communist takeover of the arts through Centre 42.[16]

Wesker's letter to Hoskins (20 February 1970), responding to the offer of a contract for his play *The Friends*, was emotional. He accused Hoskins of not standing by a verbal agreement, made prior to the signing of the contract, that they should be offered the building free of charge on the first Sunday:

> Can't you see how monstrous it is for you to lend a building for a serious theatrical production, involving great expenditure, to people who cannot have total use of that building? We have to pack up Saturday nights like refugees.

Hoskins' reply showed annoyance yet restraint: 'it is the circumstances in which we operate - if we are to operate at all' (24 February 1970). In response to Wesker's complaint that other contractual terms were unfair, he took care to point out politely that the other companies who had performed there were content to accept the same contract (he listed their names) and he had therefore not deemed it necessary to alter it for Wesker.[17] The exasperation that these two men felt with each other could not continue much longer, and *Oh! Calcutta!* marked the end of an era, during which there had been at least an attempt to uphold some of the Centre 42 principles. By accepting this production, with all its sensational pre-performance publicity and high priced seats, Hoskins had, in Wesker's view, prostituted all Centre 42's ideals by wholeheartedly embracing commercialism, thereby dealing the final blow to subsidised theatre at the Round House. Wesker resigned; *Oh! Calcutta!* was an unqualified box-office success and, as predicted, transferred to the Royalty on 30 September 1970.

NOTES

1   SF Pre-1971 A.

2   For a detailed description of *Themes on the Tempest*: Margaret Croyden, 'Peter Brook's *Tempest*', *The Drama Review*, 13(1969), no.3, 125–8.

3   Articles on (or partly on) *The Ik* include Ann McFerran, 'The Beginner's Mind',

Time Out, 9 January 1976, 12–15; Kenneth Tynan, 'Director as Misanthropist', *Theatre Quarterly*, 1977), no.25, 20–8 (pp.24–5); David Williams, 'A Place Marked by Life', *New Theatre Quarterly*, 1 (1985), no.1, 39–54 (pp.47–54).

4   John Arden's letter to the author. Unless otherwise stated, all comments in this chapter by John Arden are taken from the letter.

5   John Arden and Margaretta D'Arcy, *The Hero Rises Up* (London, 1969), pp.8–9.

6   John Arden, *To Present the Pretence* (London, 1977), p.84.

7   Beck's own description, *The Drama Review*, 13 (1969), no.3, p.25.

8   Steven Berkoff in interview with the author, 7 July 1981.

9   Steven Berkoff, *Metamorphosis*, in *The Trial and Metamorphosis* (Ambergate, 1981), p.89.

10 It is interesting that in his revival at the Mermaid in February 1986, another actor played the part of Gregor, and although the staging was essentially the same, he remained quite still until the action required the focus on him.

11 Bruce Elder, 'Doing the Inexpressible Uncommonly Well', *Theatre Quarterly*, 8 (1978), no.31, 37–43 (p.40).

12 CF 2 (*The Trial*) and 64 (*Hamlet*).

13 Arnold Wesker, 'Casual Condemnations', *Theatre Quarterly*, 1 (1971), no.2, 16–30.

14 Unnecessarily hostile critics of *The Friends* were Albert Hunt (*New Society*, 16 July 1970) and John Russell Taylor (*Plays and Players*, July 1970).

15 SF Pre–1971 File B, '*The Friends*'.

16 Coppieters, pp.297–8.

17 Arnold Wesker, *As Much As I Dare, An Autobiography* (London 1994), pp.144–5.

'The Hoskins Years'

FOREIGN COMPANIES

With the arrival in March 1971 of Jean-Louis Barrault and his English version of *Rabelais,* a new pattern of events at the Round House was set. Foreign companies had already begun to use the premises, but from now on there was to be an emphasis on bringing in experimental work from abroad until George Hoskins retired in 1977. *Rabelais,* first performed in Paris in 1968 and subsequently brought to the Old Vic in 1969, was created in the same sort of anarchistic spirit as *The Hero Rises Up.* There was the same desire to produce a fairground atmosphere and to use the whole of the available space in an unconventional manner. Barrault's experiment was done on a much larger scale, with more money and time to prepare the show. It had first been seen at the Elysée-Montmartre, a sports arena, so that he had been ready for any difficulties the Round House might present.

The material for the show was taken from the five books by Rabelais which were presented with 'elements of La Mama, Bread and Puppet Theatre, pantomime, circus, political cabaret, and discothèque'.[1] The following extract from *Theatre Quarterly* clearly shows the use Barrault made of the auditorium:

> *Rabelais* is played on a cruciform stage standing just over three feet off floor level, the longest limb of the cross giving a possible run from end to end of sixty-one feet. The cross-piece is forty-three-and-a-half feet from end to end. At each end of the four limbs is a rectangular area – at the head, a ten-and-a-half foot square area with a three-foot-square trap in the centre. At the ends of the cross piece, and at the foot, the areas are ten-and-a-half feet by six-and-a-half feet.

Where the limbs intersect, there is an acting area seventeen-and-a-half feet square. The limbs of the cross are five feet three inches wide. Seats are arranged all round the stage, and advancing into the angles of the cross, with additional seats in the circular balcony. Vision and hearing vary drastically from different positions.[2]

This prestigious production did not have the success the company had hoped for. Perhaps this was because it had already been performed at the Old Vic in 1969, albeit in French. Possibly, too, the performances did not match up to those of the original cast, though both had included Barrault himself. The *Theatre Quarterly* article makes it clear that Barrault was intent, not on creating a new experience out of the old, but on recreating as exactly as possible the original performances (p.84). This may have had an inhibiting effect on the English actors but, ironically, the main cause of the critics' discontent seems to have stemmed from the adaptation to the Round House premises – ironically, because in theory the production was intended for a building more closely resembling the Round House than the Old Vic, where it had played to capacity houses. Most of the critics liked parts of the English version whilst complaining of the straggling and unstructured nature of the piece as a whole. The most difficult thing to deal with at the Round House was the sound (there were a great many effects used with microphones) and this increased the incomprehensibility of both dialogue and, in consequence, action. The public seemed to have been more mystified than beguiled by the spectacle. It had been hoped that the play would transfer to the West End after its run at the Round House, but it closed on 24 April after just four weeks.

Continental acting companies were more used to the idea of performing in places that were not necessarily purpose-built theatres, and it was *Rabelais* that led the way for others to come to England and perform in the one large venue that could take a non-proscenium-dependent production. In the same year, 1971, Ariane Mnouchkine brought over her Théâtre du Soleil with *1789*, and that made a greater impact on the public and critics than *Rabelais* had done. Its political and historical basis was more readily identifiable to an English

Le Théâtre du Soleil in *1789*

audience than the 'surrealistic fantasy' of *Rabelais* (*Guardian*, 19 Mar 1971), even though some critics complained that *1789*'s politics were naïve and that English audiences were not sufficiently acquainted with French history to find it interesting or comprehensible. The play shows a group attempt to reinterpret the history of the French Revolution specifically from the point of view of the working classes. In *The Times* (13 October 1971) Wardle made the point that the show was a product of the 1968 student rebellion in Paris (just as Barrault's personal involvement with the events of 1968 had informed *Rabelais*). It had come from the Cartoucherie in Paris, an old ammunition factory, and found a good equivalent auditorium in the Round House.[3]

The dimensions of the acting area that the company used were the same as a basketball court, and around the outside edge were trestles used as stages. Each was 1.5 metres long, 4 metres wide and 3 metres deep. They were bolted together and arranged in groups of two and three, joined together with planks for bridges. At the back of the trestles were hung brightly coloured curtains and painted backcloths. Actors could mount the stages by means of stairs and ladders. The audience stood in the middle area, as they had in *Palach* at the Open Space, and the impression was one of a public square surrounded by the fairground trestles of times gone by. There was a bank of seats behind the trestles, but as B.A. Young commented, not a great deal could be seen from them (*Financial Times*, 13 October 1971). This was essentially a promenaders' show with the actors using the audience to help create much of the action. The most notable scene, and one which kindled the interest of most critics, was the storming of the Bastille, where the various storytellers joined the 'mob' in the auditorium and for fifteen minutes or more there was storytelling, rising sound and drumming, and then the whole arena erupted into a 'kaleidoscopic fairground' (*Guardian*, 13 October 1971). The promenading was a success: there was enough space for the audience to choose which trestle they wished to watch at any time, and Mnouchkine had organised it so that when she wanted her audience watching in one direction, then that was where her actors would focus attention. Sometimes actors rushed through the crowd, which would rapidly part to allow them through; at other times scenes were being enacted simultaneously on different stages, and the audience's attention would be diffused. Only the fairground scene had simultaneous action on all five stages at once. Sometimes scenes were played across the crowd and spotlights were used to pick out the various centres of interest.

Both *Rabelais* and *1789* used spectacular effects, whilst the Open Space with its limited resources could not, and these two productions naturally made a much bigger impact on the public than *Palach*, largely because of advance publicity and the size of the Round House auditorium. *Palach* had employed many of the same anti-illusionist devices that the two other plays had used (in *1789* actors interchanged their roles and put on make-up and costumes in full view of the audience). All three productions had been labelled by reviewers as 'total theatre'. The critic for *The Stage* (21 October 1971) claimed that *1789* was 'the most complete example' London had seen of 'total' theatre; although this is a reviewer's generalisation, it shows the extent to which this production gained popular support for its method of presentation.

The only major criticism the play received was that its political attitudes were misconceived and the facts over-simplified in order to express a particular view of the revolution. John Weightman of *Encounter* (December 1971) was contemptuous of a play that so misinformed its public of historical events. He called it an example of the 'romantic leftism' endemic to France. The *Guardian* (13 October 1971) dismissed such criticism because the show was great popular theatre. The form of the play had proved more interesting than its political content, and Mnouchkine in interview with Michael Billington explained that the final scene, which turns the tables on the bourgeois audience and identifies them with the 'villains' of the piece, never managed to outrage the Paris audiences, who, like those at the Round House, nightly cheered the spectacle of the procession of 'Gogol-like grotesques' (*Guardian*, 25 October 1971).

In the December edition of *Plays and Players* (1971) the reviewer suggested that the Round House was 'rapidly becoming established as an ideally flexible auditorium for round-the-clock presentations of international experimental companies.' On the strength of two productions from France and the Living Theatre from America, this might seem a hyperbolic judgement, a journalistic summary of the year's events. It proved, however, a genuine insight into the future success of the Round House, where the most exciting and popular work presented was that which came in from abroad. Companies from France used it the most consistently, with productions such as *The Last Lonely Days of Robinson Crusoe, From Moses to Mao* and *Les Grands Sentiments* (Le Grand Magic Circus, 1972, 1974 and 1975 respectively); *Le Palais des Merveilles* (Jules Cordière, 1975); *Le Pavillon au Bord de la Rivière* (Théâtre de Gennevilliers, 1975); and *La Grande Eugène* (Frantz Salieri, 1976). Besides American companies such as Chaikin's Open Theatre (1973) and The Living Theatre (1969 and 1979), Stomu Yamash'ta twice brought over his Red Buddha company from Japan with *The Man From the East* (1973) and *Raindog* (1975), both of which were well received and had striking similarities to the work of some of the French groups.

Of the French groups, Jérôme Savary's Le Grand Magic

Circus was the one that returned most often to the Round House, with his second show running for sixty-six performances and playing to 51% capacity houses for the whole of its season (CF 3). Savary first started his group, under the name of Le Grand Théâtre Panique, in 1966. In 1968 'Circus' was substituted for 'Théâtre' and in 1970 it finally chose Le Grand Magic Circus as its preferred name. In the same year the group staged *Zartan, Tarzan's Unloved Brother* in New York, where it developed the style that characterised its later work. Visual images predominated; dialogue and plot, if they existed at all, were secondary. Savary had worked with the Spanish-born French playwright, Fernando Arrabal in 1966 on a production of *Labyrinth* at the Mercury Theatre, London, but he had found Arrabal's approach to theatre too literary and had broken away to create his own kind of improvised theatre. This was not the same kind of improvisation that Mnouchkine developed with her company, where everything was rehearsed, though the dialogue came initially from the actors. Savary's group relied to a large extent on spontaneous improvisation so that the content of the show varied from performance to performance and did not always end in the same way. In an interview for *Time Out* in 1972[4], Savary said 'you cannot rehearse communication' – and this was the essence of the Circus's style of playing.

Of the three productions, the first, *Robinson Crusoe*, was the most successful in artistic terms. There was closer contact, with the audience surrounding a central stage area and also four other rostra which jutted into the audience who either sat on the floor or in raked seats. Even the raked areas were included in events, as actors (often naked) clambered over and through the audience or reclined on laps. The show also had just enough structure taken from the Defoe story to give the piece coherence.

By contrast, *From Moses to Mao* had a vast subject matter (its title includes the description '5000 Years of Love and Adventure') and nothing to give it focus. The horseshoe shape of the stage for this show prevented that close contact with the audience that had been so much enjoyed in *Robinson Crusoe*. As if in an attempt to correct the mistakes of *From Moses to*

Mao, Les Grands Sentiments had a strong, clear storyline which actually inhibited much of what the company did best, namely burlesque created through the juxtaposition of contrasting images, rather than sequential plotting.

As in all his circus shows, Savary himself appeared as ringmaster. He was at once the narrator and master of ceremonies; he played various percussion instruments and engaged in disputes with the audience, but without the real belligerence of the members of the Living Theatre. It is ironic that the reviewer for the *Guardian* (21 December 1972) likened the 'non-specific chaos' of the proceedings to that produced by the Becks, whereas Savary himself disliked what they had done in the theatre. In the *Time Out* interview he firmly stated:

> The two greatest calamities of modern theatre are Grotowski and The Living. Not because of their work, but because of the influence they have had on young companies. They gave to the actors a sense of introspection instead of communication.

Savary's work was also dissimilar from that of the Living Theatre in that his aim was 'not to do political theatre but to do theatre politically'. Both the Becks and Mnouchkine had political messages in their work; Savary preferred to play for specific occasions, for instance those where the mere fact of performing made a political statement, so that he performed in Iran at the Persepolis/Shiraz Festival (when Peter Brook directed *Orghast* there) and managed to play in the streets to the people who would normally have had no access to European theatre.

Circus and pantomime were burlesqued. The company's only animals were creatures such as rabbits and hens, otherwise they were humans dressed as animals. In *Robinson Crusoe* there were a pantomime zebra and 'mad harlequins' (*Observer*, 24 December 1972) who chased each other through the audience. Often the circus acts were made to look deliberately amateurish, a quality that began by charming audiences but in later shows bored them, because the acts seemed to lose the appearance of deliberate shoddiness and to acquire one of actual shoddiness. Savary's own attitude to skill in the theatre was perhaps what, in the end, dampened long-term British interest in his work (for his last show at the Round House there was an average of only 47% of the capacity house for twenty performances). His view was expressed in *Time Out* thus:

> Anybody should be able to work with the Magic Circus. We don't have auditions. We say to people, 'If you are happy, you will be good; if you are not good, you won't be happy; if you are not happy, you will leave' ... I think a fat man walking down a street is doing corporal expression just as beautifully as Marcel Marceau, because he is expressing his own life.

Not only does this view endorse the notion that life is art and therefore good theatre, but it is also an odd assertion by one who certainly wished to startle his audience by using witty and unusual images and who capitalised on the public's desire to be entertained by something different from everyday life.

Many of the images in *Robinson Crusoe* had a surreal quality to them: after the opening announcement, an ancient Robinson gazed upon a youthful and naked version of himself lying in a hammock. He was humming Fauré and was surrounded by a television set, a radio and an electric kettle. Later a three-foot plastic foot was found in the sand and a chicken was extracted from the body of a dead savage. Scenes changed location at speed, for little or no discernible reason, and often there would be a violent change of tone. At one moment there was a carnival in progress, which then switched abruptly to a gruesome scene with Friday eating a man's entrails. Harold Hobson objected strongly to what he considered blasphemous images of Christ with his cross preparing to jump into a tub of water from a high ladder (*Sunday Times*, 24 December 1972), but these were the kind of iconoclastic images which audiences had seen before with the People Show and Portable Theatre, and in general they did not take exception to them.

The Red Buddha company employed some of the techniques described above, but was much more disciplined in the performance of its material. Yamash'ta was already well-known as one of the greatest percussion players in the world (*Financial*

Times, 1 February 1973) and, with the traditions of Kabuki theatre behind him, it was inevitable that these two precise arts should influence his work as creator/director. His first appearance in the West was at the Avignon Festival in 1972. He made a brief appearance at the ICA in August 1972 and then continued to play at the Théâtre Thorigny, Paris, until he came to London in 1973. *The Man From the East* (the company's first show at the Round House) took the theme of the Japan of yesterday and today, as seen through the eyes of an old cripple. At its climax was the bombing of Hiroshima, where the action froze and a light began to glow intensely on the horizon.

This was a production dependent on lighting effects, stylised gesture and music. It was, as most of the critics pointed out, a multi-media production, using music, mime, dance and dialogue to make its impact. Actors entered through the audience, but there was no attempt at audience participation. Yamash'ta in an interview (*Plays and Players*, March 1973) alluded to comparisons made between his work and that of Le Grand Magic Circus and said that he could not afford to have improvised action on stage since the intellectual content of his work was much more important than the visual. Here was aggressive political theatre given a popular form, where the images of death after an atomic explosion were close enough to present reality to stun the audience emotionally.

In his later production, *Raindog*, many of the same devices were used: a central stage focused the attention and screens behind it were used for specific lighting effects. Spots roamed the auditorium in time with the music (*Listener*, 20 February 1975), lending the show the appearance of a pop concert. Again a traditional Japanese story was used as the basis for the action, but this time the relevance to modern life was not obvious. Although critics acknowledged the technical prowess of the performers and director, it was felt on the whole that the show battered home its effects with over-loud music. Audience members who could not take the decibel level were unable to escape because there was no interval. There were stunning effects but they were lost because they merged with the general turbulence.

Throughout Hoskins' administration at the Round House, the place had a reputation for Sunday rock concerts, and the Red Buddha company combined elements of rock and drama, so that it played to comparatively good houses for a long season; both shows ran for two months and *Man From the East* transferred to the West End. Le Grand Magic Circus might have found it more difficult to attract the public on its first visit if the way had not been paved by *Rabelais* and the highly successful *1789*. Marowitz had used the idea of the circus ring as the setting for his collage *Hamlet* in 1969, at the Open Space; this theatrical metaphor had been extended to encompass the whole building at the Round House and became a fashion which lingered there throughout its entire history.

Not all the successful foreign companies brought over shows that used the Round House space fully. Just as *Oh! Calcutta!* succeeded in spite of the auditorium, so did *La Grande Eugène*, an elaborate cabaret act which really needed an intimate setting, and it became the longest running show at the Round House, extending its original five-week season for another three months. The show, which had been running in France since 1970, brought with it a reputation for expert drag performances, though Frantz Salieri did not like it to be called a drag show, because he wanted it to be taken as a serious theatrical experience. The production reached a sophistication rarely seen in British cabaret. The auditorium was used with a stage eight metres deep and twelve metres wide with a false proscenium arch. A substantial apron area jutted out in front of the arch, thus diminishing the seating capacity of the house from 940 to 852. The tabs were plush, there were flats standing on stage, faced with aluminium sheets, to give bright reflecting surfaces, and the cyclorama was covered with silk. In other words this was a show which had transferred from one type of environment – that of the expensive and decadent nightclub – and brought all its trappings with it, to try to recreate the original. No attempt was made to harness the cavernous spaces of the Round House to the production, and the performance sparkled from its isolated pool of light. One reviewer, trying to show how the show dazzled despite its surroundings, likened it to 'a sea-anemone on a work bench' (*Financial Times*, 28 April 1976).

Lord Delfont had put up most of the money to bring the show over, but after its initial successful season, audiences began to decline and when the box-office reached a low point in July, he asked to withdraw his guarantee. A new advertising campaign was started, the Round House functioned with a reduced staff and matinées were cut, but from then on the show floundered and it was only kept open because it was marginally more expensive to go dark in August than to continue with small losses.5 After its initial *succès de scandale* with a limited audience it was unable to sustain public interest and was no longer a viable commercial concern.

ROCK MUSICALS

The Round House had earned a notoriety early in its development with shows such as *Paradise Now* (The Living Theatre) and *Oh! Calcutta!*, and the press was quick to label it a theatre for 'dirty shows'. This public image was perpetuated throughout the years of Hoskins' administration with extravaganzas such as *The Canterbury Tales* (1972), *Decameron 73* (1973), *Feast of Fools* (1973–4), *120 Days of Sodom* (1974) and later with shows such as *La Grande Eugène* (1976) and Lindsay Kemp's *Salomé* (1977). Hoskins was prepared to risk presenting a show which might cause a public furore where West End managements preferred to wait and see what happened in Chalk Farm. He also profited from a new spate of rock musicals, which carried their own brand of notoriety, this time because of their unconventional treatment of the classics or of stories from the Bible. The Round House had already acquired a regular 'rock' audience from its Sunday night concerts and its auditorium had proved ideal for hugely amplified music. The first rock musical presented there was *Catch My Soul* (written by Jack Good), taken from *Othello* and directed by Braham Murray and Michael Elliott (it had opened in Manchester with the Theatre 69 Company and predictably transferred to the West End after its Chalk Farm run). It was followed by *Godspell* (1971), *Rock Carmen* (written by Herb Hendler) and *Joseph and the Amazing Technicolor Dreamcoat* (1972), all of which went into the West End with varying degrees of success.

These musicals did not use experimental staging techniques, but were successful because of their commercial music scores and fashionable updating of dialogue and costuming. A review of *1789* in *The Stage* (21 October 1971) had commented that the Round House 'comes into its own' with the environmental staging, and certainly until 1976 environmental shows were the kind of productions that flourished there, achieving both financial success and a high artistic standard. In order to accommodate shows of a different kind Thelma Holt had to work hard to change the Round House's public image.

NOTES

1   Bill Wallis, 'Production Case Book: Jean-Louis Barrault's *Rabelais*', *Theatre Quarterly*, 1 (1971), no.3, p.84.
2   *Theatre Quarterly*, 1 (1971), no.3, p.90.
3   *1789* has been documented in *Différent: Le Théâtre du Soleil, Supplément à Travail Théâtral* (Dole, février, 1976), pp.7–42.; Denis and Marie-Louise Bablet, *1789: Le Théâtre du Soleil* ('Diapolivre' 1979), Paris: CNRS; *Theatre Quarterly*, 2 (1972), no.8, 58–63. The text was published as a programme/text for the Round House production, by Calder and Boyars Ltd., 1971.
4   *Time Out*, 15 December 1972.
5   SF 12, 'General Correspondence', 15 July 1976.

'The Holt Years'

THE ASSOCIATION WITH THE
MANCHESTER ROYAL EXCHANGE

The season of plays from Manchester marked Holt's most serious attempt to alter the public's view of the Round House: all of the Royal Exchange productions were suitable for her new, in-the-round auditorium. The first play, *The Ordeal of Gilbert Pinfold*, was the least successful of the three, both financially and critically. All three plays deal with a central character's mental breakdown or readjustment, and in each case Michael Elliott, who directed the productions, attempted to suggest in his settings and stage effects both a symbolic and a naturalistic dimension. Elliott is reported to have said that 'nothing in the theatre can work symbolically or metaphorically unless it works concretely first' (*Observer*, 22 April 1979). The stage for *Gilbert Pinfold* was made to resemble a ship's cabin, and Michael Hordern in the title role suggested the agonised feelings of a man trapped in such a confined space. When his mental anguish was at its peak, the production showed him 'marooned' by the voices that troubled him, 'relayed from actors placed in circular arrangements in each of the aisles and then coming closer, ominously patrolling around his living space' (*Guardian*, undated). A complete musical score of weird sound effects helped create the play's claustrophobic atmosphere. It seems, however, that the production did not resolve the difficulties inherent in any play done in the round and, according to the critic for the *Guardian*, Hordern was too often positioned so that large sections of the audience could not see him clearly. A comment in the *Observer* (18 February 1979) sums up the feeling of a number of critics: 'the in-the-round staging ... compels Hordern, democratically offering everyone a view, to rotate constantly like a chicken on a spit'.

In the second production, T.S. Eliot's *The Family Reunion*, the natural hazards of staging in-the-round were avoided and Michael Elliott's policy of giving the play a solid basis in reality before attempting to realise 'the spiritual dimension', was entirely successful. The drawing-room set of heavy old settees and standard lamps, surrounded by an audience who could not help but be aware of each other, together with spotlighting effects when the dialogue changed from everyday banalities to the agonised soul-searchings of the chorus or protagonist, admirably suggested the worlds of reality and fantasy encroaching on each other.

The appearance of the Furies, huge (they were much taller than humans) and menacing, looking like members of the Ku Klux Klan as they swept in through the aisles from all sides and on to the stage, both shocked and terrified the audience. T.S. Eliot himself had no faith in the theatrical viability of these supernatural creations whom he claimed to have seen staged in every possible manner and whom he wished eventually to omit from performance, because he regarded them as a dramatic mistake.[1] His original conception was vindicated in this production where the Furies' size and number dwarfed the actors. Their sudden and palpable vulnerabilily heightened the audience's fear, already kindled by the shock of the Furies' swift and silent entrance. Even the distant, subterranean rumblings of trains, always present at the Round House, helped to produce the right atmosphere. Most critics recognised that the production had achieved a remarkable 'reconciliation between ... poetry and naturalism' (*Sunday Telegraph*, 22 April 1979). The critic for the *Evening News* (20 April 1979) was in a minority with his view that an audience all round deprived the set of its capacity to convince them that it was a drawing room.

The third and last of the plays presented in this season, *The Lady From the Sea*, was artistically less satisfying than its predecessor though, in terms of its box-office returns, it did better than either of the other two. The set, which caused a stir

amongst the critics, impeded, rather than helped, the movement of the play. Michael Elliott had created an island of
rocks surrounded by water through which Ellida splashed to
make her first entrance. The fibre-glass rocks were difficult to
negotiate and the actors looked ill-at-ease on them, with the
effect of slowing down the action and making the audience
uncomfortably aware of what might happen if actors missed
their footing. The enclosing band of water, three inches deep,
never really managed to look anything more than symbolic,
even though the actors at one point took a punt on it. This set
design did not fuse the elements of social realism and mysti-
cism that permeate the play. It functioned on a symbolic level
only, and Elliott seemed to have deliberately turned his back
on the governing principle of his production of *The Family
Reunion*.

Most accounts in the press praised Vanessa Redgrave's performance above all else. From her first, startling entrance
splashing barefoot through the water, wrapped in a towel, with
her hair dripping down her back, she captivated the audience
with her ability to make the character Ellida into a human
being, tormented by a 'mystical hunger for the sea' (*Guardian*,
17 May 1979). Michael Billington described clearly what most
other critics seemed to feel: that she 'charts exactly Ellida's
psychological crisis'. On the whole it was not felt that this central performance obscured the roles played by the rest of the
company, though Sheridan Morley, the critic for *Punch* (30
May 1979), saw the production as no more than a vehicle for
Redgrave to make her comeback to the London stage. He did,
however, acknowledge that his was a minority view.

The play ran for eight weeks, taking £97,420.72 (CF 53).
Although this was slightly less on a weekly average than *The
Family Reunion* made, it must be remembered that *The Lady
From the Sea* ran exactly twice as long. The season finished on 7
July, and it was about this time that Michael Elliott was taken
seriously ill with kidney trouble. Since the initial inspiration
for the relationship between the Round House and the Royal
Exchange had been his and Thelma Holt's, his ill-health
became a major factor in the delays that ensued before a
second season could be mounted. It had been their intention

to waste no time in preparing for another, so that the public should not be allowed to forget the success of the first season. But in August 1979 relations between Michael Williams and Thelma Holt became strained, as they failed to reach agreement on a new programme. Holt refused the suggestion of *The Cherry Orchard* and *The Lower Depths*, neither of which had opened in Manchester, on the grounds that *The Cherry Orchard* had just been revived at the National Theatre and at Riverside, and that *The Lower Depths* was a notoriously difficult play to sell.[2]

Braham Murray and Michael Williams both wrote letters stressing that if the relationship between the two theatres was to flourish then shows must be accepted on their artistic merit and not because of the stars who were in them, nor because of previous rave reviews from Manchester.[3] They had come under criticism from their local council because they appeared to be adopting a policy of pre-London runs, which the council considered the wrong role for a regional repertory theatre to play. Murray emphasised again that their first season was acting as a 'bridge-head', the first move in a game which they hoped to make a regular feature of their work in Manchester. Moves had been made to bring Tom Courtenay down in *The Dresser*, but without Michael Elliott negotiations had fallen through, and this too aggravated the tensions between Holt and Williams.

It was not until April 1981 that a new season of plays from the Royal Exchange opened at the Round House. It comprised *The Duchess of Malfi*, directed by Adrian Noble, starring Helen Mirren and Bob Hoskins, *Have You Anything to Declare?* by Maurice Hennequin and Pierre Veber, directed by Braham Murray, starring Brian Cox and Susan Littler, *Waiting for Godot*, directed by Braham Murray, starring Max Wall and Trevor Peacock, and *The Misanthrope*, directed by Casper Wrede, starring Tom Courtenay. They had all done well in Manchester, and all received good London reviews. However, the long gap between seasons predictably spoilt the chances of capitalising on the previous success, and it proved hard to reanimate public enthusiasm without the added boost that the Round House's new look had given to the first season. The newspapers seemed

Helen Mirren as the Duchess, Julian Curry as the Cardinal and Mike Gwilym as Ferdinand, in *The Duchess of Malfi*, by John Webster (from the Royal Exchange Theatre, Manchester)

unwilling to give editorial coverage to the project (profiles on the actors and company and so on) and Michael Williams clearly blamed Holt for not doing enough in the way of publicity. At a meeting called on 23 April, Holt assured the company that £6,000 had been spent on publicity, to which Williams replied that he could not see how.

Of the four plays, *The Duchess of Malfi* was the most popular, and it had been hoped that its financial success would help carry the little-known farce that followed. The leads in *Have You Anything to Declare?* were not well-known outside theatre circles at that time and, despite excellent reviews, the production took no more than £12,269.33 in box-office receipts for the whole of its four-week run (*The Duchess of Malfi* took on average £16,471.18 per week, CF 72). *Waiting for Godot* and *The Misanthrope* both did better, though the former had played first at the Old Vic, so potential audience numbers were fewer. The latter, according to Holt, contained a star who appealed only to a minority audience. Average weekly earnings for *Waiting for Godot* were £11,214 and for *The Misanthrope*, £7,263 (CF 72).

REGIONAL THEATRE AT THE ROUND HOUSE

While negotiations were in progress with the Royal Exchange, Holt continued her search for suitable regional productions, and she speedily came to an arrangement with the Crucible in Sheffield to bring in *The Glass Menagerie*, starring Gloria Grahame. This seems to have angered Michael Williams, but Holt firmly quelled the rumours that Sheffield was getting a better deal than Manchester.[4] The terms of the contract were simple: the two theatres were to split the box-office takings in half after the costs of publicity, get-in and get-out had been deducted. There was to be no percentage for the star: Holt felt she could not afford this until she was provided with the necessary subsidy, and she pointed out in a letter to the associate director, Andre Ptaszynski, that none of the stars in the Royal Exchange season had asked for this and she felt it would be unfair of her to make an exception.[5]

On the whole the reviews were complimentary, and the *Financial Times* (24 November 1979) remarked on the 'extravagant superstructure of a St. Louis fire escape ... and a grilled side walk to encircle the action,' which suitably filled the Round House void. Despite this, the company played to 43.2% capacity houses during the three-week run, so without subsidy the Round House could not afford to continue to implement the idea of provincial theatre in a London base.

It was, of course, much more complicated to arrange for a regional company performing a whole season of plays to come in than it was for a single production lasting only three weeks. Before the Royal Exchange second season began, Holt had secured *Season's Greetings* by Alan Ayckbourn and his Scarborough company and *Don Juan*, a new version of the story by Robert David MacDonald, directed by Philip Prowse at the Glasgow Citizens' Theatre. Again, hopes were expressed that this might be the beginning of a permanent relationship between the theatres. It was the hope of Giles Havergal (Director, with Prowse and MacDonald, of the Citizens') that one season of their productions a year in London would help to build up interest in audiences outside Glasgow.[6] Holt started a campaign to raise funds for the venture and *Don Juan* was staged at the Round House on 3 December 1980. There was a good deal of support for it in the press, but critics were disappointed by the play, which they found tedious, though not altogether lacking in Philip Prowse's usual sensational theatrical effects.[7]

Holt had a financially disastrous two weeks with *Season's Greetings*; most critics found that it merely repeated earlier Ayckbourn plays.[8] It was, however, instructive to see a play of his performed in London with his own repertory company and none of the usual stars included for West End or National Theatre audiences. Holt therefore invited Ayckbourn back with a musical play, *Suburban Strains*, at the beginning of 1981. When she had first invited him to the Round House, she spoke of a 'built-in audience'[9] following the success of the Royal Exchange season, but it became quite clear that she had miscalculated the long-term effects of the first Manchester season. There was no 'built-in audience'; reviews were quite good but the image of the Round House had not altered sufficiently for Ayckbourn enthusiasts to follow his work out to Chalk Farm. As he himself pointed out in a letter to Holt after the event:

> my rather genteel followers from suburban London would never normally look for my name amongst the Round House small ads. In fact you stand to be expelled immediately from my fan club if you are seen to be carrying a copy of *Time Out* even for a friend. (SF 31, 31 October 1980)

Nevertheless, for *Suburban Strains* they attempted to improve on their first production by making the Round House auditorium a little smaller and more intimate, in line with the Scarborough environment. They screened off the top two rows of seats by bringing in the green curtains, and placed a revolve on the stage area. The play failed dismally, matinées were cancelled, and after thirty-eight performances the production had taken only £13,780.83 in box-office receipts (CF 67).

[183]

Such was Holt's commitment to the idea of regional theatre at the Round House, and her belief in presenting exciting and worthwhile plays, whether they were likely to bring in the public or not, that she wrote to Ayckbourn offering him another season in 1981–2 should she receive subsidy and therefore be in a position to offer proper guarantees.[10] No subsidy was granted and the opportunity never arose. By the end of the season the Round House had run into such debt that it could not settle its account with the Royal Exchange. It paid £2,000 on 12 May 1982, and the final settlement of £2,919.29 was made on 15 March 1983 before Thelma Holt left the Round House.

SUMMARY OF HOLT'S ACHIEVEMENT

Critics of Thelma Holt's auditorium changes (Steven Berkoff was one) felt that she had taken away from London the one venue that accommodated physically extravagant productions, thereby limiting the repertoire which could be satisfactorily staged there. He saw it as a deliberate move to make the Round House into a conventional theatre which would take in pre-West End runs, gathering a public following appropriate to such conditions.[11] Holt was aware of the criticism, and her choice of subsequent productions demonstrates amply that this was not her intention.

She still invited foreign companies to perform there, and out of the thirty-one productions that came before closure (excluding concerts), at least eleven were from abroad. They tended to be smaller than those that characterised the early and mid 1970s, but this reflects changing artistic forms and tastes rather than indicating that the Round House could no longer accept experimental forms. One of the first foreign companies to use the new auditorium was the Teatr Studio of Warsaw, who used a cruciform stage shape for its production of *Dante*. The Round House was transformed into 'the underworld' and revolving stages and extravagant props were used. The auditorium was used imaginatively: in the words of the director, Jozef Szajna, theatre is 'the synthesis of all the arts' (CF 50) and, as with the old auditorium, so the new prospered best when its particular spatial arrangements were given proper consideration.

Perhaps the most prestigious of the final productions was the two-week run of *Richard III,* performed by the Rustaveli company from Georgia. Although the Russian invasion of Afghanistan took place only a month before the company was due to open in London (it occurred on 27 October 1979) and there was a good deal of anti-Russian feeling in Britain at the time, Holt did not cancel the arrangements, nor did she lose a significant amount of support for the venture, making £29,782.81 in box-office returns for only twelve performances. Holt knew that, even if she played to full houses, she could not cover the costs of bringing the company to England, and it is a demonstration of her artistic integrity that she asked it to come despite this knowledge. Having seen it previously at the Edinburgh Festival, she was determined that its performance should reach a wider public. She secured Robert Maxwell as underwriter for the show and raised funds from the private sector. She incurred displeasure from those who normally expected to receive complimentary tickets by refusing them, and she charged the, then, outrageous price of £7 and £4.50 a ticket, except for the gallery where, despite bad sight-lines, she charged £2.50.[12]

It was well worth the trouble. The critics were almost unanimous in their enthusiasm for this expressionistic interpretation of Shakespeare's tragedy with its magnetic, central performance from Ramaz Chkhikvadze (his Richard was not the fashionably attractive villain, but an absolute predator, and his Fool was an added character, from Holbein's *The Dance of Death*). The production had all the hallmarks of previous successes at the Round House, such as *1789* and Le Grand Magic Circus. The new auditorium had in no way inhibited the pageant-like movement (tumbrils and processions, both solemn and festive) and circus-like atmosphere of the proceedings. A section of the seating had been taken away so that the actors were no longer performing in-the-round. A gaping cavern was created at the back of the acting area from which characters emerged as if from the underworld, only to be swallowed up again by the tide of events. The stage area itself was covered in white

Ramaz Chkhikvadze as the protagonist in *Richard III*, Rustaveli Company

scrim and the whole was encased in a gigantic, ragged and bloody tent. Shakespeare's play had been cut and altered, with new characters added who served a symbolic function. Queen Margaret was played as a witch and malevolent manipulator of fate, and another actor played the part of the Fool who would comment on the action. This was all made clear to an English audience by the acting technique of Chkhikvadze and the stylised gesture employed by the company. Props, too, were symbolic, with a throne reminiscent of a gibbet and the crown a football kicked between all the main characters, who followed it around as if mesmerized by it. The final battle scene between Richmond and Richard was fought as they emerged through slits in an outsized map of England which was held by the rest of the cast. Much of the action, normally played for dramatic or tragic effect, was given a comic twist, so murders were accomplished through stylised mime instead of with violence and bloodshed. The Round House had proved itself once again to be an appropriate place for generating the atmosphere of the big-top.

It is interesting that, of the thirty-one productions after the conversion, only six used the fully circular area. As had happened in the past, many companies adapted the space to a three-sided stage; theatre-in-the-round calls for productions deliberately staged to suit its shape, a factor which in itself would have limited the number of shows able to use the Round House. Holt had avoided this pitfall by keeping the seating flexible. Of course she had tried to change the theatre's image, but she had never been one to bend before the demands of commercial enterprise. She sincerely aimed to make of the Round House what Peter Gill made of the Riverside Studios in Hammersmith, a venue open all day for various artistic and cultural activities, with theatre as its hub. What she wanted was to get rid of the drop-out element, so that she could encourage a wider section of society to attend. This she achieved, though the need for subsidy ultimately crippled her endeavours. She needed to have the resources to publicise her theatre with the same intensity that she had been able to achieve when she was subsidised for her conversion to the Manchester plan, and to keep the new image of the Round

House before the public. She demanded the right to fail in her artistic endeavours, just as Marowitz and Wesker had done, and like those two before her, she finally lost her enormous enthusiasm for the project in the face of insurmountable financial difficulties. Her directorship at the Round House lasted half as long as Hoskins', but their ideologies were what made the crucial difference. Hoskins' methods were based on commercial and not artistic principles, and the work coming in was of a widely variable standard.

Holt had aimed consistently for high quality, continuing with only the best of what Hoskins had achieved, whatever the financial consequences. Unfortunately the government tendency at the time was to turn its back on subsidy for anything experimental. Irving Wardle summed up what was happening in 1983:

> Culture is being barricaded inside official fortresses housing nothing less than classics of impregnable repute and proven drawing power. Free spaces for visiting foreign troupes, experimental events and what one can only call artistic hospitality are on the way out; together with the exhilaration and flashes of insight that only thrive in open conditions. (*The Times*, 3 January 1983)

Other critics lent a sympathetic voice to the Round House's plight but no pressure of this sort made any practical difference at this stage.

NOTES

1 T.S. Eliot, *Selected Prose of T.S. Eliot*, edited by Frank Kermode (London, 1975), p.143.

2 Letter from Holt to Murray, 25 September 1979. All information on the Royal Exchange 2nd Season, unless otherwise stated, is contained in SF 30.

3 Letter from Murray, 4 September 1979 and from Williams, 11 October 1979.

4 Letter from Holt to Williams, 26 October 1979.

5 Letter from Holt to Ptaszynski, 11 October 1979.

6 Letter from Havergal to Holt, 5 November 1979, SF 25.

7 Among others, *Guardian* and *The Times*, 4 December 1980; and *Financial Times*, 5 December 1980.

8 Among others, *Financial Times* and *The Times*, 15 October 1980.

9 Letter from Holt to Ayckbourn, 3 July 1979, SF 31.

10 Letter from Holt to Ayckbourn, 14 January 1981, SF 31.

11 Berkoff in interview, 7 July 1981.

12   The top price for a ticket for a show at Drury Lane Theatre Royal in the West
End was £8.00, for the Adelphi £7.00, and prices went as low as £2.00. Holt
went back to a top price of £4.00 with the productions that followed, such as
Marowitz's *Hedda* and Nikolas Simmonds's *The Strongest Man In The World.*

[14]

Conclusion

Those responsible for creating these two theatre enterprises were all people with forceful characters, a factor that helped establish the theatres' identities and reputations. Marowitz, Holt, Wesker and Hoskins all had enormous energy and enthusiasm for their work, and it must be acknowledged that this is what gave the impetus to their various undertakings. All were outspoken, but only Holt managed to remain consistently on good terms with those official bodies and wealthy personalities who might have helped her cause.

The Marowitz/Holt management could not have hoped to make a better team. Their confidence in each other's skills meant that theirs was a real joint management. Both have artistic dispositions, Marowitz as the original creative genius behind the best productions, Holt as an actress who could help him realise it. Holt also has business acumen and tact, so that she was able to smooth over any management problems that arose. She never seems to have attempted to take the limelight from Marowitz in anything to do with the directorship of the company. She had, however, ample opportunity to shine in her roles in the collages; her most remarkable performance was as Katherine in *The Shrew*. So the two did not encroach on each other's territory, but knew very well where their own strengths and weaknesses lay. It is also clear that Holt could function on her own as artistic director of a theatre (witness her years at the Round House). She left the Open Space, wishing to dissociate herself from the bad publicity created by 'the pink bath scandal' and feeling that her relationship with Marowitz at the Open Space had run its course; Marowitz then gradually wound down its activities. She nevertheless gave him help after the lease had expired on the Euston Road

Jenny Agutter as Hedda, Kathryn Pogson as Thea and Frank Grimes as Loevborg in *Hedda* by Charles Marowitz

premises by presenting two of his shows at the Round House. It is interesting that in 1972 Charles Marowitz had somewhat prophetically said:

> Something, I'm not sure what exactly, happened in '68. It had to do with the students in Paris, with Dubcek, with the Chicago riots at the Democratic Convention. It's going to continue sending out its waves until about 1978, I calculate. At that time I'd like to think that the Open Space will be closed and that something else will have taken its place. (Plays and Players, October 1972).

In fact it had a good ten years, with two more in decline – a long stretch for a fringe theatre.

Wesker and Hoskins were not temperamentally suited to each other. Wesker involved himself emotionally with his project, having put money and effort into the cause, and he took any adverse criticism personally. Unlike Marowitz, he did not thrive on controversy, and came near to a breakdown over the Centre 42 affair. The tone of his many articles on the subject reflects a kind of bewilderment at hostility shown towards him.

Wesker would not compromise his principles; Hoskins thought those principles mistaken. Hoskins survived because he decided to continue without depending on subsidy, eventually giving up owing to illness. He could not be said to have stamped his personality on the Round House, his policies were too amorphous, and the repertoire was essentially determined by the place itself. He was there for eight years as sole artistic director, but the Round House is not remembered during this period as his theatre, but simply as the Round House, and Thelma Holt did not have to contend with the problem of taking over a theatre which had become synonymous with the person running it.

The Round House was started by Wesker as a community arts centre where artists of the highest calibre would pool their work, making it available to those who could not normally afford to indulge a taste for the arts. Again it was hoped that locals would support it, though Wesker also felt that the reputation of the artists using the venue would draw audiences from all over London and ultimately gain a national following for Centre 42. The Open Space had no such pretensions. It was designed to appeal to those who were disenchanted with commercial theatre. Because it was a fringe theatre, it was aimed at predominantly young and not necessarily local audiences. Marowitz, like Wesker with his Centre 42, had always intended that his work should be subsidised. It was therefore essential to start with material that would attract full houses so that subsidising bodies could see there was a need for his theatre. At first new works that were not experimental at all but had popular appeal were produced (particularly those that contained material that would have been banned before 1968); this policy, however, created an image that was not what Marowitz had intended, though he was quite capable of capitalising on it. Only for brief periods was he able to present the work he really cared for.

Wesker wanted his work to influence the everyday lives of people who could not normally afford to enjoy the arts, and who had no tradition of doing so, but he was also concerned with raising the standard of their taste, so that it was not enough to give them the kind of entertainment they expected to enjoy. He never had the chance to put his policy into effect, but his choice would not have been made on commercial lines. Hoskins opposed Wesker's approach, and, after Wesker had left, allowed in any company that would hire the building, so the Round House built up its image in a haphazard fashion. The kind of shows that gravitated towards it had their similarities, and it became obvious which kind of plays were suited to the auditorium. In general they were company-created and relied on spectacle to make their impact. From the start, works with an anti-establishment bias were performed there, and the Round House gradually gained a reputation for being a centre that attracted what some considered 'undesirable' characters (i.e. those who were looking for alternatives to the bourgeois ethos and who by their lifestyle undermined established society), a reputation which was expunged only after Thelma Holt had been there for a year.

Despite this reputation, it housed many productions of interest which were genuinely experimental, even though it did not have an official policy of encouraging such works. New plays made little impact there. Brenton and Barrie Keeffe had conspicuous failures with Joint Stock in August 1977, playing to 29% and 22% capacity houses respectively (CF 38). *Epsom Downs* was well-suited to the Round House auditorium, but the place had not established a reputation for interesting new works by political playwrights, and the public did not come. In his official statement of policy, Marowitz had talked of mixed-media events at the Open Space, but it was really the Round House that captured the market for this sort of theatre, because its large performing area could easily accommodate it. Both the Round House and Open Space survived a long time, precisely because, at certain times during their lifespan, they offered a genuine alternative to the West End: the Open Space as a result of management policy, the Round House primarily because of its building.

It can be considered difficult to sustain artistic integrity once it is diluted with commercial concerns; this was the view taken by Wesker, who refused to stay with the Round House when he saw the measures that Hoskins was prepared to take to keep it open. Marowitz did not share this view and tried for a while to produce commercially viable work at his theatre. Wesker believed that only full subsidy could produce artistic works of real worth, and when it became clear that neither the trade unions nor the Arts Council would give it, he gave up and let Hoskins go his own way. The Arts Council did give grants to certain productions and activities, but as Paul Collins, the then Director of Finance for the Arts Council, said, recognition of the place as an arts centre came only in 1971-2, when it received its first substantial award of £7,500, and even that was not enough to maintain work of a non-commercial kind.[1]

For Marowitz subsidy meant an opportunity for laboratory theatre, i.e. theatre that could experiment with forms as a learning process for actor and director, where the finished product was not necessarily going to appeal to the ordinary public, as opposed to theatre enthusiasts.

A characteristic form that experimental theatre took in the late 1960s and early 1970s was that of the 'happening'. This type of event, often interrupting another, challenged an audience's preconceptions about the nature of theatre. The audience was provoked in to playing a positive role in proceedings; in the process its role as spectator and the actor's role as communicator were redefined. One of the ways of exploring this idea was to use a stage or stages on which different actions were taking place simultaneously, or to make the auditorium and stage space the same. Instead of an apparent narrative line, a series of theatrical images would be presented suggesting various themes. Sometimes the action and dialogue were so haphazardly improvised that the final effect was amateurish and confused. Often it was the spectacle itself which made the impact, and not the minimal dialogue.

Marowitz's attitude to this kind of experimental work was ambivalent. On the one hand he used many of the above methods in his collage work, on the other he profoundly disliked what he considered to be an obsession with 'techniques for their own sake' (*Plays and Players*, July 1971). The groups he named in the article as guilty of this excess were the Pip Simmons Group and Freehold, both of which performed at his theatre.

It can be seen from most of his own work at the Open Space that his way of working on experimental forms was very controlled, and limited by a carefully planned script. Even *Palach*, with all its improvised scenes and its many stages, was carefully orchestrated by Marowitz and Burns. Spectacle was sometimes allowed to predominate (as in *The Four Little Girls*), but it co-existed with the careful cutting and shaping of the text. Although audiences at his environmental shows were invited to participate in the action, they were not harangued, bullied or even cajoled into actively working with the actors. Actors and audience did not interact, because there was a text which did not alter according to audience response; the exception to this was *Palach*. Marowitz's interest was not with theatre as therapy, nor was he concerned to stimulate an awareness of social and political ills, as were so many of the directors of contemporary experimental groups (among them Brook with his production of *U.S.*, the Becks with their work at the Round House, Pip Simmons and Nancy Meckler), where the audience was charged with the responsibility for those ills. His concern was with theatre as an art form which he wished to reinvigorate, and not with theatre as a means towards social change. Experiment, for Marowitz, meant not so much a reassessment of the relationship between the actor and audience, as between the audience and the classical text, i.e. the work of art itself, though when he probed further into the nature of experimental theatre, he could also produce inspired work like *The Four Little Girls*.

Marowitz said many times that experimental work was only authentic when prepared by a permanent group of actors who had a communal sense of purpose and a desire to work and rework their (or rather his) ideas, with no sense of urgency for commercial success. He was not a director who believed in allowing the actors a great deal of freedom; the conception of the piece was his, and he carefully regulated its execution. One of the reasons he could be difficult to work with was his unwillingness to consider a view contrary to his own. Although this sometimes made him enemies, it also meant that he developed an individual and original style which distinguished all his work. He was probably better at working with actors for short intensive periods than over a long stretch of time, which would produce all sorts of inter-personal tensions. The excellence of his pre-permanent company productions of *Hamlet* and *A Macbeth* (1969) is testimony to his ability to make the most of an *ad hoc* group's acting skills.

Marowitz decided to keep his theatre working, despite lack of sufficient subsidy, and over the years the subsidy increased erratically. It can be seen from the figures to be found listed in the Arts Council Library that there was a big jump in the size of the grant both times that Marowitz formed a permanent company: 1971-72, £8,820, and 1972-73, £14,950; 1974-75, £26,754, and 1975-6, £39,310. After that grants declined, and there is no record of them after the end of the financial year 1977, when the Arts Council helped the company move into new premises.

It can also be seen that, as subsidy to the Round House increased, so the standard of work presented there became consistently higher, though not necessarily more adventurous. Under Hoskins the plays that came in changed, to some extent, with the tide of fashion. During Thelma Holt's administration the most important development was the continuity of worthwhile productions. The Open Space was never granted the money it needed to maintain a permanent company, and when it was unable to finance another theatre building, the whole enterprise folded. During the period when subsidy improved, the repertoire became more Marowitz-orientated, with a preponderance of his own work being presented.

A great deal of the money available to the Round House and the Open Space was raised from the private sector. Marowitz made money by establishing a reputation for himself in Europe and America, where he took his Shakespeare collages and *Artaud at Rodez*. Some of these shows originated abroad; *An Othello* was written by request for the Wiesbaden Festival in 1972, and *Hedda* for the centennial festival of the Bergen National Theatre in 1978, where it had a very successful run with a transfer to Oslo. In England (in 1973, 1974 and 1975) he presented *Hamlet* and *The Shrew* in conjunction with workshops for the Open University, where they formed part of the teaching programme. When he toured his collage work it was nearly always done together with special classes for university or drama-school students; he worked extensively with David Hirst and his undergraduates at Birmingham University on his own collages and on Artaudian theory. Thelma Holt used her considerable skills at persuading companies and individuals to sponsor work, notably to finance the Open Space's opening and Marowitz's own productions. She also raised money for the Round House to bring the Rustaveli Company to England, to bring provincial shows to London, and to support the building conversion which she embarked on at the end of 1978.

Obviously the buildings and geographical situation influenced the fortunes of the two theatres. The Round House was accessible to all Londoners as well as to Camden residents, but its situation outside the central theatre area meant that non-local audiences needed to travel farther and along less familiar routes. The Open Space, which was closer to the West End (near Oxford Street), had no local audience as such. It was very well situated to capture a lunchtime public (those who worked in the area, or those who were simply wandering by) but audiences were expected from all over London, particularly those who read the 'alternative theatre' pages in *Time Out*. Although the Open Space was closer geographically to the West End, it was, paradoxically, the Round House that supplied the West End with successful transfers (for example *Oh! Calcutta!*, *Catch My Soul*, and *Godspell*), cashing in on the fashion for sexually explicit shows (post-1968) and rock musicals. At the outset of the Open Space project two plays transferred to bigger theatres, *Fortune and Men's Eyes* to the Comedy, and *Blue Comedy* to the Yvonne Arnaud in Guildford, which helped the company financially, though it did not become a feature of its future policy. Ten years later, *Sherlock's Last Case*, which had done well in 1974 and toured the United Kingdom, was taken up and produced on Broadway where it played for almost a year. That commercial success came too late to help the Open Space, but it must have been an unusual, if not unique example at the time, of a London fringe play being successfully presented on Broadway.

The theatre buildings themselves determined the repertoire

of plays performed, though the Open Space in particular used its very limited space imaginatively and in a great variety of ways. The theatre's name was not meant to denote a large area, but a flexible one, open to unlimited creative use. Its lack of sophistication and stage equipment was its virtue rather than a disadvantage and, even here, with a production like *The Four Little Girls*, the company managed to transform the theatre's drab appearance into a magical world. It had proved possible both to use the environmental dinginess to enhance a production (*Fortune and Men's Eyes*) and to create a wholly different locality, though the cost of building it was considerable.

The Round House is so vast that it has never been possible to hide its features; it is a building with an architectural personality of its own. Unless, therefore, a company was prepared to use fully what it had to offer, the incongruities were too apparent for comfort (e.g. *The Friends*). Only shows such as *La Grande Eugène*, whose intrinsic originality was enough to persuade an audience to attend, managed to survive in spite of their surroundings. It is clear that companies got to know the strengths and weaknesses of the building, so that, for instance, intimate naturalistic dramas ceased to be performed there.

Both the Round House and the Open Space made successful use of direct audience contact. *Sam, Sam* at the Open Space used music-hall turns for its main character; shows at the Round House often integrated actors with the audience, where the technique was more appropriate than at the Open Space, because of the large auditorium. The Open Space and the Round House both attempted to develop the idea of 'total theatre' which had gained popularity through Richard Schechner in America, but Marowitz was the first to develop the idea of 'environmental' theatre in 1968, at the Open Space, with *Fortune and Men's Eyes*, and he continued sporadically to do so until 1971 with *The Four Little Girls*. The Round House was turned into a circus big top many times (sometimes for real circuses like Gerry Cottle's in 1976 and the Pickle Family Circus in 1981, and sometimes creating a metaphorical circus ring for shows like Brook's *Themes on the Tempest* and Le Grand Magic Circus). Perhaps Thelma Holt made the fullest use of an environmental technique when she produced *Bartholomew Fair* in 1978.

The very nature of these two buildings, a Victorian engine shed and a basement that had served as an old people's centre, demanded a different approach to theatre. The one, tiny and intimate, worked best when the emotions of its audience were fully engaged in the action. This demanded total concentration from the actors and a high standard of acting. The other, vast and impersonal, worked best when rousing its audience to participate exuberantly in the staged events.

The physical condition of the theatres had a part to play in their history too. The Round House had structural faults which needed attention. When the first *Hamlet* was presented there the Council would not allow the company to use the gallery for the Ghost, and it had to be content with lighting effects instead. It was later repaired, and during the Hoskins era money was constantly being raised to keep the building in working order. These funds were used, not only to finance repairs, but also to make improvements (to the rostra, the seating and so on), all of which was an added financial burden for the management. The Open Space initially furnished its auditorium with movable seating and rostra and the bare essentials for lighting a show; it made very few improvements during its ten years in Tottenham Court Road. Marowitz worked well with simple equipment and relied on his actors to provide the effects for a production. The Round House extravaganzas often required special lighting and sound effects which the various companies would supply themselves (for example for *Rabelais*). Richardson's company installed a lighting board for *Hamlet* which it left there for the Round House's future use.

The actual appearance of the theatres from the outside must have played a part in their success and failure. The Round House is an imposing building which stands with its entrance opening on to a main road. It was not a daunting building to enter, and there was no mistaking its function because of the posters which adorned its walls. The Open Space had peculiarities which might have deterred potential audiences. Its premises were placed next to a cinema showing continental films and pedestrians might be forgiven for thinking it was another like it, particularly since the photographs outside often showed naked bodies, so that those entering would either have been people who knew what they wanted to see, or strip-joint clientèle who had made a mistake.

The abolition of censorship in 1968 was a key factor in determining the types of production presented at the Round House and the Open Space, and the managements took advantage of it. Both enterprises provided channels for the work being done by companies from Europe, America and even the Far East, which helped put London at the heart of world theatre, with its desire to move away from proscenium presentation and the convention of audience as passive spectators. The abolition of our theatre censorship laws meant that they were able to exploit the new freedom to choose their productions from wherever companies were pushing back the boundaries of what was allowed. Although not always willing to be experimental, they were always present as a reminder that theatre needs to be a constant barb in the side of the establishment.

The new wave of experimental theatre after 1968 found a natural home in these two theatres. The hippy drug culture of the 1960s for a time attracted a certain kind of audience to the Round House, which was counter-productive in terms of encouraging a local public. The Open Space never at any time aspired to being a social centre, and because of its more central position did not suffer in the same way. It was also a club theatre, which meant in theory that the public needed to join for a small fee before being allowed in. This was a necessary step for the theatre to take in order to circumvent all the usual theatre regulations to which it was impossible that the theatre should conform. It would also have eliminated casual audiences, except that it was not very strictly enforced (as in the *Flesh* police raid), and it was legally possible for membership to be effective on the same day if one arrived early enough. It had the added advantage of providing a source of regular and identifiable income.

The Round House did not form a club, but the public could pay for a regular newsletter, and it had the coffee bar open all day, with a bar open during licensing hours for anyone who cared to drop in; there was also a casual restaurant which often sold good food. It was not meant only for those attending a play performance and, according to Thelma Holt, many of the people using the bar facilities at the Round House had nothing at all to do with the theatre and would not have dreamed of going to see the plays.[2] Wesker thought of the Round House as a home for all the arts, a 'cultural centre' which suggested hopes for encouraging new audiences to attend performances. Unfortunately, Wesker's enterprise lasted only two years though it had taken much longer than that to initiate his scheme.

The press, both national and local, gave each new venture a great deal of support, both in the form of publicity and of an initial willingness to attend shows. This did not mean that they were uncritical of policy and plays – often quite the reverse – but they helped each theatre to become known to a wider public. The Open Space was run by two people who were very much in touch with new ideas on theatre and with what might attract a contemporary audience. They offered (when they were able to) something original and controversial. Controversy attracts the public, and the reviewers were often in violent disagreement about the merits of a production, an aspect that Marowitz was not slow to encourage. Even here the spirit of change waned, the Marowitz experiments became predictable and interest in his work decreased.

The Round House's most successful presentations were those which returned to the forms of popular entertainment (such as the circus and the open-stage conditions of the Elizabethan theatre). However, they were not simply resurrections of old forms, but those forms used in exciting new ways with a particular voice for a twentieth-century audience.

Theatrical performance is by nature ephemeral yet undeniably influences future generations. More than any other art form theatre can reflect the changing tastes and conditions of contemporary society. Thus the most successful post-war plays could be said to embody the desire for a secure and undemanding mode of life, whereas the challenges to the status quo after 1968 (with student protests and the political changes in the world at large) are mirrored by innovations on the fringe.

Theatre is also at the mercy of the changing times, and if it does not express those changes it becomes redundant. This is what happened at the Open Space, though it is arguable that, had Marowitz been able to find a new building for his company, his work might have gained some of its old sense of purpose. The enormous cost of upkeep at the Round House necessitated large sums of money before any theatrical activities could begin, and the Arts Council was finally not willing to pay. The scale of the Open Space venture was much smaller than that of the Round House; it operated in more modest surroundings, and Marowitz wisely chose to emphasise the need for imaginative acting and resourceful production techniques, thus presenting 'poor theatre' at its best. The fight for survival seems to have contributed to this theatre's success as well as to its final closure in that there was a determination to make use of every available expedient. It was the theatre's misfortune that the Holt/Marowitz partnership terminated, because the will to prevail evaporated with it.

It was also a time when government funds were forthcoming, and there was official recognition that new theatrical enterprises needed Arts Council help. Though both managements complained about lack of funding, they benefited considerably from the new enthusiasm for fringe events. In the same way, they were clearly victims of cutbacks in government spending during the late 1970s and early 1980s.

Subsidy provides the right to fail; in harsh economic conditions, the fringe, which was once essential for providing an outlet for new work, is now much less in evidence. The demise of the Open Space and the Round House is linked with the gradual erosion of subsidised London fringe theatre. Given that the arts are vital to the quality of people's lives and that theatre is one of those which could reach large numbers of the population, there is a need for the government to recognise its diversity and to show a practical concern for its continuance. The Open Space theatres have been demolished; the Round House still squats at the intersection of Adelaide Road, Haverstock Hill and Chalk Farm Road in NW1. Its circular shape and conical roof are a landmark in the area, a testimony to the Victorian era and an enduring herald of new possibilities. We are reminded that the course of British and even world theatre has been enriched and changed by the existence of these two enterprises, and what can be learnt from their histories should be instrumental in creating new and significant theatre for the future.

NOTES

1   Paul Collins in interview with the author, 16 July 1986.
2   Thelma Holt in interview with the author, 19 February 1979.

Afterword

Since 1983 the Round House has been the object of many different schemes. One was a conspicuous failure. In April 1983, Camden Council and the GLC put in a bid to use it as a Black Arts Centre.[1] Other ideas were mooted and in June of that year it was offered to a consortium of trade unions for use as a conference and cultural centre. However, by September Camden Council had offered to buy the building for £300,000 and, together with the GLC, would fund the repair and conversion costs. It was hoped that other organisations such as the Arts Council, local authorities and charities would help fund the running of the enterprise.

In 1984 Remi Kapo, the project coordinator, produced a feasibility study in which he stated that the aim of the centre was to 'become London's first high profile, mainstream arts centre where London can see the Black community's contribution to the arts'. The facilities required were ambitious: cinema, theatre, recording studios, art gallery, library and so on. Money was put into the centre, but nothing ever materialised and in October 1988 Kapo resigned after allegations of financial malpractice had been made in a programme entitled *01 For London*, broadcast by Thames Television on 29 September 1989. Kapo took them to court and on 12 July 1989 the 'Statement in Open Court' pronounced, 'These allegations were toally unfounded'. Kapo was awarded damages but plans for the Black Arts Centre were finally abandoned.

After this there were proposals to use the place again as a theatre, a rehearsal space and a cinema. In 1990/1 Brian Rix and Melvyn Bragg obtained English Heritage approval to create an arts centre there, but they failed to gain the necessary listed building consent because they planned to remove four cast iron columns to improve the stage area. The proposal that came closest to success was from the RIBA who planned to buy the building in order to exhibit drawings there, and an appeal was launched by the British Architectural Library Trust to raise £2,000,000. The scheme was given listed building consent in 1996 but was refused Lottery funding because the plans entailed too many changes to the building's original architectural features. It too foundered.

In 2004, the Round House, now the Roundhouse (it was usually written as two words in the early days though there were aberrations), fights on under the aegis of the Norman Trust, a registered charity dedicated to children and young people, set up in 1986 by Torquil and Anne Norman, who acquired the freehold of the Roundhouse in 1996s. Torquil Norman is its charismatic chairman and benefactor, whose initial £6.5 million (*Evening Standard*, 29 April 2004) led the way for future funding of the project. On his Advisory Board, among others, are Laurence Harbottle, the lawyer with a strong theatrical practice who consistently helped Thelma Holt when she was at the Open Space, Sir Richard Eyre and Lord Attenborough. The Trust has the goal of bringing together all the arts in a 'Creative Centre' for young people, who will be directly concerned with their implementation.

In section 5 of *The Round House Conservation Plan* it is stated that the undercroft is to be used as the creative centre for young people and the large space of the ground floor is to continue to house different types of production, though in each case the spaces are to be provided with 'state-of-the-art acoustics, lighting and seating configurations limited only by the imagination'. During school holidays, productions in the main performance area are to be aimed at young audiences. The building is in the process of being stripped down to its original structure; when I visited in June 2000, there were builders painstakingly searching for any structural weaknesses in the balcony (it has since been removed), and in the labyrinth of passages in the Roundhouse's undercroft, a duel was being fought by young local actors preparing for some gothic drama to be performed that night.

Successful shows such as *Stomp,* the Chinese State Circus and productions by Artangel and De La Guarda are regularly brought in to help finance the venture just as they were in the days of George Hoskins, and Joan Littlewood's *Oh, What A Lovely War!* (directed by Fiona Laird for the National Theatre in April 1998, when it went on tour in a tent before arriving at the Roundhouse in August) gave it the first sustained production since Thelma Holt closed the theatre in 1983.

Holt's dream of hosting serious drama from the provinces was given another chance of success in March 2002 when the RSC decided to use it after quitting its Barbican home. Almost twenty years after her auditorium had been demolished a new one was constructed which echoed hers in its design, with seating around a circular stage area. This time, however, the seats did not rise from the stage floor but started quite high up, reaching in a steep rake into the rafters. The circular stage was surrounded by a high, perpendicular wall, with a ledge running round it about halfway up, and well above the heads of the actors. It could be reached by steps from the stage and used as another level where the action could take place. These steps also led into the auditorium itself, so that in certain scenes direct contact could be made with the audience. The height of the wall focused both sight and sound (it was rather like looking into a well); there was no bad seat in the house, and the domed roof of the Roundhouse, with its circular lighting rig suspended below it, was allowed to be a part of the production. For *The Winter's Tale* (directed by Matthew Warchus and designed by Vicki Mortimer), fairy lights were draped beneath the rig and were lowered over the action in the second half to help create the atmosphere of celebration during the festival scenes in Bohemia.

The cheapest seats at £12 were advertised as 'promenade' places though audiences were not allowed to walk around as they had been expected to at Brook's *Themes on the Tempest.* Instead spectators could stand around the acting area below the ledge or sit or lie upon the floor close to the wall. For the opening scene of *The Winter's Tale* some were even allowed to sit at cafe tables since it was set in a 1940s restaurant in America (a similar idea was used by Bogdanov in the RSC's version of *The Venetian Twins* in 1993). They were invited to dance during the sheep-shearing festival of the second half, but that was the only time they mingled with the cast. They formed, as far as the rest of the audience was concerned, part of the stage spectacle (a slightly daunting prospect as there was nowhere to hide), a reminder that they were spectators and not a part of the action. The circular arena was bare, with a kind of parquet flooring which easily represented restaurant floor, dungeons and rural landscape with the help of imaginative lighting. The largest exit had a high, stark arch which also formed a platform surrounded by ugly iron railings suggestive of prison bars or a stadium where spectators needed to be restrained. When Paulina came from the prison with the newly born baby into the presence of Leontes, the shadows cast on the scene by these railings suggested the fascist state that Sicilia had become under its tyrant-king. In the judgment scene Hermione was alone in the centre of the arena, chained to a pole like a bear in a bear pit, and the audience could sense the massive odds against her and her seemingly inevitable destruction.

The dark and cavernous space of the Roundhouse, more or less unchanged from the Holt days, lent itself most easily to the first half of the production, steeped as the play is in the evil forces of jealousy and political tyranny. Warchus turned it into a black-and-white film from the forties dominated by the American Mafia (all the actors, some of whom were American, had American accents) and just before the interval, at Shakespeare's instruction, 'exit pursued by a bear', a monstrously large grizzly appeared that stalked Antigonus before 'dining' on him. The accompanying music and storm effects suggested gothic horror gradually giving way to the comedy of the scenes with the old shepherd and his son. The first laugh of the evening occurred as the old man, totally involved in his own thoughts, stepped over the huge bag holding the baby, without even noticing it. The passage of time (16 years) and the change of location were stunningly evoked by Florizel sending a live hawk from the high platform above the stage to the other side of the circle where it soared into the vaults and disappeared.

Lighting changes in the second half helped to alter the

atmosphere to that of pastoral joy. Instead of harsh spotlights which picked out lone figures disappearing down dark, labyrinthine passages, and strobe lighting which suggested a king 'in rebellion with himself', a warm yellow glow created warmth and sunlight, and the live country and western music changed the production from threatening scenes of *film noir* to the musical comedy of *Seven Brides for Seven Brothers*. With the final scene's emphasis on a magical resurrection (fore-shadowed by a scene in dumb show at the beginning) we returned to the dark of the earlier scenes, but the glow from the lamps carried by the silent circle of courtiers and royal family that formed the onstage audience present at the cere-mony, was warm and reminiscent of the atmosphere created by candles carried by the cast and audience at the National Theatre's *Nativity* (part of *The Mysteries* first directed by Bill Bryden in 1980). This first RSC production at the Round-house since 1970, when the company brought the Theatre-goround Festival there, harnessed the difficult space to their conception of *The Winter's Tale* as a play dependent on a mix-ture of different dramatic genres that express most appropri-ately different aspects of its message. In this production the action glides smoothly from one to another, while at the same time making the play's structure recognisable to young audi-ences to whom film is a more familiar medium than theatre. It is puzzling that it met with apathy from the critics who certain-ly helped to discourage attendance.

The Tempest (directed by Michael Boyd and designed by Tom Piper) was greeted more warmly. Once again the Round-house was used as a big top with the actors as acrobats swing-ing onto the platform from the rafters, or erupting into the action from below through traps in the boards. The ledge pro-vided intimacy with the audience as much of the action took place on it. Prospero told Miranda the long story of her back-ground standing on it just inches away from the first row of seats. The set was composed of hanging ropes and ladders that were lowered and retracted as required, and lighting and acro-batics were used to suggest the mystery surrounding the island, the depths of the sea, and the magical storm. Pros-pero's entrance was made on a swing that was lowered from on high, his long purple robes billowing around him, reminiscent of Brook's celebrated *A Midsummer Night's Dream*.

All three productions were publicised as promenade performances, but it was Adrian Noble's *Pericles* (designed by Peter McKintosh) that used this element most successfully. Here the audience felt as though they were at an exotic eastern bazaar where, amidst the bustle of life, a storyteller was inviting each one of them to draw round and listen. The usually dark spaces of the Roundhouse were a blaze of warm light and the atmosphere was alive with noise and excitement. This was a production reliant on visual effects (some borrowed from circus events, others evocative of sixties pop festivals) which Michael Billington found too showy (*Guardian*, 8 July 2002), but audiences seemed to love. By the time the season drew to a close they seemed to have found their way over to Camden Town and houses were full. The critic in the *Independent* (5 May 2002) claimed that Lord Alexander, chairman of the RSC, believed that the location was too rough for its audiences. Another spokesman said the choice of plays was to blame for generally poor attendance. Two of the productions (*The Winter's Tale* and *Pericles*) were exceptionally well adapted to the theatre building, and the fact that the season was not a financial success was perhaps as a result of the turmoil within the RSC management at the time. Aesthetically this was the Roundhouse at its best: circus, flamboyant storytelling, gothic terror, promenading, and palpable contact with the audience. One of the actors to whom I spoke fervently wished that this could be the RSC's permanent new home.

But the Roundhouse has its own momentum, and there is a sense of purpose driving the new venture, similar to that surrounding Centre 42: its emphasis on involving local talent is different (the education of Camden's underprivileged youth into the performing arts is Norman's central aim), but the high hopes, energy and commitment against all the odds are there, as they were for Wesker. A new story is emerging: the Roundhouse will not go away.

1   All information on the different schemes for the Round House, before Torquil
    Norman took it over, are from Camden Local Studies and Archives Centre,
    Round House Project Pack.

Appendix

CHRONOLOGICAL LIST OF PRODUCTIONS AT THE OPEN SPACE

(LN) = Late-night; (LT) = Lunchtime

Date	Title	Author	Director/Company
11 July 1968	*Fortune and Men's Eyes*	John Herbert	Charles Marowitz
22 July 1968	(LT) *Come*	Open Space Company	Charles Marowitz
8 August 1968	(LN) *Keep Tightly Closed in a Cool Dark Place*	Megan Terry	Roger Hendricks Simon
21 October 1968	*Blue Comedy* (two short plays, *Madly in Love* and *Hank's Night*)	Paul Ableman	Charles Marowitz
1 November 1968	(LN) *One Autumn Evening*	Friedrich Dürrenmatt	Fredrick Proud
13 November 1968	(LN) *The Ringa Ranga Roo*	Eliza Ward	Eliza Ward
17 November 1968	(LN) *An Exhibition of Stammering and Stuttering*	Jack Shepherd & Roger Booth	Jack Shepherd
3 December 1968	*The Lunatic, The Secret Sportsman & The Woman Next Door*	Stanley Eveling	Max Stafford-Clark
17 December 1968	*Come & Be Killed*	Stanley Eveling	Michael Blakemore
26 December 1968	(LN) *Cirkus*	Hakan Strangberg	Hakan Strangberg
31 December 1968	*Fucknam*	Tuli	Kupferberg
9 January 1969	(LN) *The Puny Little Life Show*	The Scaffold	The Scaffold
30 January 1969	(LN) *War*	Jean-Claude van Itallie	Roger Hendricks Simon
4 March 1969	*One is One & All Alone & Ever More Shall Be So*	Julian Chagrin	Julian Chagrin

Date	Title	Author	Director/Company
25 March 1969	*The Fun War*	Geoffrey Bush	Charles Marowitz
25 March 1969	*Muzeeka*	John Guare	Charles Marowitz
17 April 1969	*A Whitman Portrait*	Paul Shyre	Paul Shyre
24 April 1969	(LN) *Metamorphosis*	Kafka, adapted by John Abulafia	John Abulafia
20 May 1969	*A Macbeth*	Shakespeare, adapted by Charles Marowitz	Charles Marowitz
6 June 1969	(LN) *The Law Circus*	David Mairowitz	David Mairowitz
24 June 1969	Programme of Pop Films		
7 July 1969	Theatre Seminar		
7 July 1969	*Hamlet*	Shakespeare, adapted by Charles Marowitz	Charles Marowitz
12 August 1969	*The Body Builders*	Mike Weller	Roland Rees
	Now There's Just the Three of Us	Mike Weller	Roland Rees
26 August 1969	*Rats*	Israel Horowitz	Walter Donohue
	The Indian Wants the Bronx	Israel Horowitz	Walter Donohue
2 September 1969	*Birdbirth*	Leonard Melfi	Roland Rees
	Halloween	Leonard Melfi	Roland Rees
8 September 1969	*The Hunter and the Bird*	Jean-Claude van Itallie	Roger Hendricks Simon
	Ex-Miss Copper Queen on a Set of Pills	Megan Terry	Roger Hendricks Simon
	The Loveliest Afternoon of the Year	John Guare	Roger Hendricks Simon
	Botticelli	Terence McNally	Roger Hendricks Simon
20 October 1969	*Don't Gas The Blacks*	Barry Reckord	Lloyd Reckord
16 November 1969	*Are Critics Necessary?* (seminar)		
4 December 1969	*Leonardo's Last Supper*	Peter Barnes	Charles Marowitz
	Noonday Demons	Peter Barnes	Charles Marowitz
6 December 1969	Open Space Movies		
19 January 1970	*Alas Poor Fool*	Neil Mundy	Nicholas Young
19 February 1970	*Hot Buttered Roll*	Rosalyn Drexler	Charles Marowitz
	The Investigation	Rosalyn Drexler	Charles Marowitz
4 March 1970	(LN) *New Victorian Line*	Tony Jason	Leslie Rocker
16 March 1970	(LN) *Bleak Moments*	Mike Leigh	Mike Leigh
12 May 1970	*Find Your Way Home*	John Hopkins	Kevin Billington
18 June 1970	*A Macbeth*	Shakespeare, adapted by Charles Marowitz	Charles Marowitz

Date	Title	Author	Director/Company
6 July 1970	(LN) *Box & Cox*	John Mortimer-Maddox	Tony Haygarth
27 July 1970	*The Civil War (rock concert)*	Bill Russo	
24 August 1970	*The Chicago Conspiracy*	John Burgess & Charles Marowitz	Charles Marowitz
15 September 1970	*Superman*	Pip Simmons Co.	Pip Simmons
24 September 1970	(LN) *Creatures of the Chase*	Willard Manus	Walter Donohue
27 October 1970	*Stuff*	The Scaffold	The Scaffold
11 November 1970	*Palach*	Alan Burns	Charles Marowitz
16 December 1970	(LN) *XXXXX Nativity*	Billy Hoffman & John Vacarro	Wherehouse La Mama
12 January 1971	(LN) *PC Plod*	The Scaffold	The Scaffold
19 January 1971	*Curtains*	Tom Mallin	Michael Rudman
22 February 1971	(LT) *Gum & Goo*	Howard Brenton	Janet Henfrey
15 March 1971	*The Cuban Missile Crisis*	John Ford	Albert Hunt
16 March 1971	*Flash Gordon & the Angels*	David Mairowitz	Walter Donohue
20 March 1971	(LT) *Icarus's Mother*	Sam Shepard	David Benedictus
29 March 1971	(LT & LN) *Grant's Movie*	Mike Weller	David Benedictus
20 April 1971	(LT) *The Difference*	Peter Bergman	Charles Marowitz
29 April 1971	*A New Communion for Freaks, Prophets & Witches*	Jane Arden	Jane Arden
10 May 1971	(LT) *Tira Tells Everything There is to Know About Herself*	Mike Weller	Walter Donohue
	(LT) *Ritual of the Dolls*	George McEwan-Green	Walter Donohue
26 May 1971	*The Critic as Artist*	Oscar Wilde, adapted by Charles Marowitz	Charles Marowitz
30 May 1971	International Association of Theatre Critics Congress		
12 June 1971	*Sweet Eros*	Terence McNally	Charles Marowitz & Mick Rodger
	Next	Terence McNally	Charles Marowitz & Mick Rodger
19 August 1971	*The People Show No 39*	The People Show Group	
29 September 1971	*My Foot My Tutor*	Peter Handke	Ronald Hayman
29 September 1971	*Home Front*	Martin Walser	Ronald Hayman
5 October 1971	(LT) *Your Humble Servant*	Robert Robertson	Robert Robertson
20 October 1971	*Lay By*	Portable Theatre Co.	Snoo Wilson
27 October 1971	(LT) *George & Moira Entertain a Member of the Opposite Sex to Dinner*	John Grillo	John Burgess

Appendix

Date	Title	Author	Director/Company
16 November 1971	*Bluebeard*	Charles Ludlam	Charles Ludlam Theatre of the Ridiculous
18 November 1971	(LT) *A Sky Blue Life*	Howard Brenton	Walter Donohue
15 December 1971	*The Four Little Girls*	Pablo Picasso	Charles Marowitz
9 February 1972	*Sam Sam*	Trevor Griffiths	Charles Marowitz
15 February 1972	(LT) *Edward – The Final Days*	Howard Barker	Roger Coward
3 March 1972	*Sylveste Again: Yet Another Evening with Sylveste McCoy (human bomb)*	Ken Campbell	Ken Campbell
6 March 1972	*The Writers' Lot* (seminar)		
22 March 1972	(LN) *The Creditors*	Strindberg	Roger Swain
22 April 1972	*Hamlet*	Shakespeare, adapted by Charles Marowitz	Charles Marowitz
2 May 1972	(LT) *How Beautiful With Badges*	Howard Brenton	Walter Donohue
7 June 1972	*An Othello*	Shakespeare, adapted by Charles Marowitz	Charles Marowitz
17 July 1972	*The Tooth of Crime*	Sam Shepard	Charles Marowitz & Walter Donohue
3 August 1972	(LT) *Phoenix & Turtle*	David Mowat	Peter Watson
11 September 1972	*Alpha Alpha*	Howard Barker	Peter Watson
7 November 1972	(LT) *Playing with Fire*	Strindberg	Peter Watson
21 December 1972	*The Old Man's Comforts*	Perry Pontac	Charles Marowitz
18 January 1973	*Man of Destiny*	Bernard Shaw	Charles Marowitz
19 February 1973	*Woyzeck*	Georg Büchner	Charles Marowitz
6 March 1973	(LT) *Rozencrantz & Guildenstern*	WS Gilbert	Stuart Mungall
3 May 1973	*The Cage*	Rick Cluchey	Rick Cluchey
3 May 1973	(LT) *The 47th Saturday*	William Trevor	Jeremy Young
23 May 1973	*Bang*	Howard Barker	Ron Daniels
13 June 1973	*The Houseboy*	Irving Wardle	Charles Marowitz
16 July 1973	*Excuses Excuses*	David Edgar	Christopher Parr
15 August 1973	(LT) *The Local Stigmatic*	Heathcote Williams	David Farnsworth
12 September 1973	*And They Put Handcuffs on the Flowers*	Fernando Arrabal	Petrika Ionescu

Date	Title	Author	Director/Company
1 November 1973	*The Shrew*	Shakespeare, adapted by Charles Marowitz	Charles Marowitz
14 November 1973	(LT) *Apropos of the Falling Sleet*	Dostoyevski, adapted by Robert Stephens	Robert Stephens
9 January 1974	*Ashes*	David Rudkin	Pam Brighton
13 February 1974	*The Collected Works*	David Mowat	Peter Stevenson
3 April 1974	*Marriage de Luxe*	Serge Behar	The Roy Hart Theatre
3 April 1974	*Biodrama*	Serge Behar	The Roy Hart Theatre
3 April 1974	*Ich Bin*	Paul Portner	The Roy Hart Theatre
1 May 1974	(LT) *A' Nevolent Society*	Mary O'Malley	Francis Fuchs
24 March 1974	*Sherlock's Last Case* *	Matthew Lang	Charles Marowitz
17 October 1974	*Schippel*	Carl Sternheim	Mike Ockrent
5 December 1974	*The Kid*	Robert Coover	Chris Hayes
18 December 1974	*The Snob*	Carl Sternheim	Charles Marowitz
7 January 1975	(LT) *Mr Poe*	Robert Nye	John Abulafia
1 February 1975	*Claw*	Howard Barker	Christopher Parr
12 March 1975	*The Trial of Mary Dugan*	Bernard Veiller	
19 March 1975	*Celebration*	Keith Waterhouse & Willis Hall	Bernard Krichefski
28 May 1975	*Measure for Measure*	Shakespeare, adapted by Charles Marowitz	Charles Marowitz
24 June 1975	(LT) *Prisoner & Escort*	Charles Wood	Nikolas Simmonds
3 July 1975	Meira Shore (folk singer)		
22 July 1975	*Iphigenia in Tauris*	Goethe	John Prudhoe
29 July 1975	(LT) *Down Red Lane*	B.S. Johnson	John Abulafia
August 1975	*Hamlet*	Shakespeare, adapted by Charles Marowitz	Charles Marowitz
28 August 1975	(LT) *Rosalind*	J.M. Barrie	James Mason
14 October 1975	(LT) *The National Theatre*	David Edgar	Peter Stevenson
2 November 1975	*Ten Long Years*	Roger Hibbit	
8 December 1975	*Brecht-Tucholsky -Frank Wedekind Evening*	Eve Meier	Eve Meier
17 December 1975	*Artaud at Rodez*	Charles Marowitz	Charles Marowitz
23 December 1975	*The Shrew*	Shakespeare, adapted by Charles Marowitz	Charles Marowitz

*   In his anthology of plays, *Potboilers* (London 1986), Marowitz amusingly disclosed that he was
     the author of *Sherlock's Last Case*.

Appendix

Date	Title	Author	Director/Company
11 February 1976	*Anatol*	Arthur Schnitzler	Charles Marowitz
17 February 1976	(LT) *Dialogue Between Friends*	Garry O'Connor	Peter Watson
9 March 1976	(LT) *Sense of Loss*	Alan Drury	Timothy West
27 April 1976	(LT) *Logue for Lunch*	Christopher Logue	
3 June 1976	*Love Us & Leave Us*	Peter Terson & Paul Joyce	Paul Joyce
July 1976	(LT) *Christie in Love*	Howard Brenton	Andrew Carr
1 July 1976	*Hanratty in Hell*	Andrew Carr	Charles Marowitz
12 August 1976	*Seven Girls*	Carl-Johan Seth	Carl-Johan Seth
17 May 1977	*Variations on the Merchant of Venice*	Shakespeare, adapted by Charles Marowitz	Charles Marowitz
5 June 1977	Interview with Glenda Jackson and Charles Marowitz		
6 July 1977	*Mecca*	E.A. Whitehead	Jonathan Hales
18 July 1977	*Cirrus* (rock concert)		
19 July 1977	(LT) *Split*	Mike Weller	David Freeman
7 September 1977	*Twelfth Night*	Shakespeare	Michael Gearin-Tosh
17 October 1977	*Suicide in B flat*	Sam Shepard	Kenneth Chubb
18 November 1977	*Censured Scenes from King Kong*	Howard Schuman	Colin Bucksey
1 February 1978	*A Day for Ever*	Michael Sharp	Madhar Sharma
28 February 1978	*Penta* (dance group)		
14 March 1978	*Steps, Notes & Squeaks* (dance)		Maina Gielgud
20 March 1978	*Orpheus*	Stephen Rumbelow	Stephen Rumbelow
22 April 1978	*Cool Million*	Robert Walker	Robert Walker
29 May 1978	*The Ball Game*	Tom Thomas	John Fortune
4 July 1978	*Jazz Cabaret*	Mike Westbrook	
11 July 1978	*Three Black & Three White Refined Jubilee Minstrels*	L.O. Sloan	L.O. Sloan
27 July 1978	*Boo Hoo*	Philip Magdalany	Charles Marowitz
18 October 1978	*Endgame* / *Krapp's Last Tape*	Samuel Beckett / Samuel Beckett	Rick Cluchey / Samuel Beckett
12 December 1978	*A Respectable Wedding*	Bertolt Brecht	Mike Ockrent
7 February 1979	*Brimstone & Treacle*	Dennis Potter	Robert Chetwyn
21 March 1979	*Venus in Furs*	Moving Being	Geoff Moore
17 April 1979	*PS Your Cat is Dead*	James Kirkwood	Richard Marquand

Date	Title	Author	Director/Company
June 1979	*Fifty Words: Bits of Lenny Bruce*	Danny Brainin	Danny Brainin
18 July 1979	*A Life in the Theatre*	David Mamet	Alan Pearlman
24 August 1979	*A Mime Master Class*	Miklos Kollo	Miklos Kollo
12 September 1979	*The Private Life of the Third Reich*	Bertolt Brecht	Nikolas Simmonds

Beginning 22 October 1979 Weekly Play Readings:

	Title	Author	
	In Austria I will	Andrew Carr	
	A Visitor for Xmas	Barbara Creagh	
	Dirty Tricks	Michael Gill	
	Before Dawn	Kerim Arawi	
	Daddy	Keith Dorland	
	A Turn for the Worse	Peter Tegel	
	Fladge & Vadge	Brendan Gregory	
	Home & Dry	Jo Shallis	
17 November 1979	*The Father*	Strindberg	Charles Marowitz

CHRONOLOGICAL LIST OF PRODUCTIONS PRESENTED BY THE OPEN SPACE IN OTHER THEATRES

Date	Venue / Title	Author	Director/Company
16 August 1971	Nottingham Playhouse		
	Jump	Larry Gelbert	Charles Marowitz
26 August 1971	transfer to Queen's London		
6 January 1973	King's Head, London		
	Rule Britannia	Howard Barker	Charles Marowitz
July 1973	Belgrade, Coventry		
	Macbett	Eugene Ionesco	Charles Marowitz
25 February 1980	Jeannetta Cochrane, London		
	Ubu Roi	Jarry, adapted by Spike Milligan	Charles Marowitz
8 July 1980	Round House, London		
	The Strongest Man in the World	Barry Collins	Charles Marowitz
5 August 1980	Round House, London		
	Hedda	Ibsen, adapted by Charles Marowitz	Charles Marowitz

CHRONOLOGICAL LIST OF MAIN-HOUSE PRODUCTIONS AT THE ROUND HOUSE

Date	Title	Author	Director/Company
17 July 1968	*Themes on the Tempest*	Shakespeare, adapted by Peter Brook	Peter Brook
6 November 1968	*The Hero Rises Up*	John Arden & Margaretta D'Arcy	John Arden & Margaretta D'Arcy
17 February 1969	*Hamlet*	Shakespeare	Tony Richardson
4 June 1969	*Frankenstein*	Julian Beck & Judith Malina	Julian Beck & Judith Malina for The Living Theatre
6 June 1969	*Mysteries*	Julian Beck & Judith Malina	Julian Beck & Judith Malina for The Living Theatre
9 June 1969	*Paradise Now*	Julian Beck & Judith Malina	Julian Beck & Judith Malina for The Living Theatre
11 June 1969	*Antigone*	Sophocles, translated by Judith Malina	Julian Beck & Judith Malina for The Living Theatre
30 June 1969	*Jenny*	Shane Connaughton	Gavin Richards
9 July 1969	*Metamorphosis*	Franz Kafka, adapted by Steven Berkoff	Steven Berkoff
9 July 1969	*In the Penal Colony*	Franz Kafka, adapted by Steven Berkoff	Steven Berkoff
August 1969	*The Preacher*	Alex Oduro	
13 August 1969	*Romeo and Juliet*	Shakespeare	Monica Norton
9 September 1969	*Macbeth*	Shakespeare	David Weston
12 November 1969	*Son of Man*	Dennis Potter	Robin Midgley
December 1969	*Oh, What a Lovely War!*	Joan Littlewood	Kevin Palmer
19 November 1969 (LN)	*Antigone*	Sophocles	Nancy Meckler
26 December 1969	Roberts Brothers Circus		
3 February 1970	*The Blacks*	Jean Genet	Minos Volanakis
2 March 1970	*Oh Democracy* *The Knights*	Aristophanes, adapted by George Eugeniou	George Eugeniou
16 March 1970	*Keep Tightly Closed in a Cool Dark Place*	Megan Terry Roger	Hendricks Simon
23 March 1970	*This Foreign Field*	Alan Sillitoe	Bill Martin
19 May 1970	*The Friends*	Arnold Wesker	Arnold Wesker
2 July 1970	*Carnival*	Independent Theatre	

Date	Title	Author	Director/Company
27 July 1970	*Oh! Calcutta!*	Devised by Kenneth Tynan	Kenneth Tynan
3 November 1970	*When Thou Art King*	Shakespeare, adapted by John Barton	John Barton
5 November 1970	*Arden of Faversham*	unknown	Buzz Goodbody
9 November 1970	*King John*	Shakespeare	Buzz Goodbody
23 November 1970	*Dr Faustus*	Christopher Marlowe	Gareth Morgan
4 December 1970	*A Midsummer Night's Dream*	Shakespeare	Peter Brook
7 December 1970	*Richard III*	Shakespeare	Terry Hands
8 December 1970	*Hamlet*	Shakespeare	Trevor Nunn
21 December 1970	*Catch My Soul*	Jack Good	Michael Elliot
21 December 1970	(LN) *The Black Box*	John Epstein	John Epstein
18 March 1971	*Rabelais*	Jean-Louis Barrault	Jean-Louis Barrault
4 May 1971	*Confrontation in the Roman Forum*	Hans Keuls	Warren Jenkins
8 June 1971	*Maybe That's Your Problem*	Lionel Chetwynd	Charles Dennis
13 July 1971	*Titus Andronicus*	Shakespeare	Keith Hack
2 August 1971	*Pork*	Andy Warhol	Andy Warhol
8 September 1971	*Skyvers*	Barry Reckord	Pam Brighton
12 October 1971	*1789*	Le Théâtre du Soleil	Ariane Mnouchkine
17 November 1971	*Godspell*	Stephen Schwartz	John-Michael Tebelak
7 February 1972	*Lila: The Divine Game*	Rufus Collins	Joe Donovan
23 February 1972	*Black Macbeth*	Shakespeare, adapted by Peter Coe	Peter Coe
2 March 1972 1	(LN) *The Deformed Transformed*	Lord Byron	Stephen Rumbelow
28 March 1972	*Quetzalcoatl*	Berta Dominguez	David Cohen
11 May 1972	*The Wheel*	Bettina Jonic & Charles Robinson	Geoffrey Reeves
31 May 1972	Murray Louis Dance Company		Murray Louis
13 June 1972	*Gizelle Tomorrow*	Graziella Martinez	Graziella Martinez
26 June 1972	*The Cambridge Footlights Revue*	Barry Brown	Barry Brown
13 July 1972	*Rock Carmen*	Herb Hendler	Irving Davies
4 September 1972	Korean National Dance		
20 September 1972	*Mother Earth*	Ron Thorson	Terry Palmer
9 October 1972	*England's Ireland*	Portable Theatre	David Hare & Snoo Wilson
24 October 1972	*Stand and Deliver*	Wolf Mankowitz	Wendy Toye

Date	Title	Author	Director/Company
8 November 1972	*Joseph and the Amazing Technicolor Dreamcoat*	Tim Rice & Andrew Lloyd-Webber	Frank Dunlop
9 November 1972	(LN) *To a World*	Iris Scaccheri	Iris Scaccheri
20 December 1972	*The Last Lonely Days of Robinson Crusoe*	Le Grand Magic Circus	Jérôme Savary
29 January 1973	*The Man From the East*	Stomu Yamash'ta	Stomu Yamash'ta
30 April 1973	*Kingdom Coming*	Bill Snyder	John Acerski
3 June 1973	*Pilgrim's Progress*	John Bunyan, adapted by Peter Albery	Denis Carey
4 June 1973	*The Mutation Show*	Joseph Chaikin	
2 July 1973	*The Mother*	Bertolt Brecht	Jonathan Chadwick
3 July 1973	*The Cambridge Footlights Revue*	Stephen Wyatt	
23 July 1973	Nigerian Dancing Troupe		
6 August 1973	*Decameron*	Peter Coe	Peter Coe
28 August 1973	*The Royal Hunt of the Sun*	Peter Shaffer	Toby Robertson
30 August 1973	*Pericles*	Shakespeare	Toby Robertson
5 September 1973	*Twelfth Night*	Shakespeare	Toby Robertson
25 September 1973	*Decameron*	Peter Coe	Peter Coe
22 November 1973	*The Trial*	Franz Kafka, adapted by Steven Berkoff	Steven Berkoff
29 November 1973	*Agamemnon*	Aeschylus, adapted by Steven Berkoff	Steven Berkoff
20 December 1973	*Feast of Fools*	Jim Hiley	
25 January 1974	*From Moses to Mao*	Le Grand Magic Circus	Jérôme Savary
17 April 1974	Ballet Rambert		
15 May 1974	Twyla Tharp Dance		
29 May 1974	*Les Veuves*	François Billetdoux	François Billetdoux
11 June 1974	*Go West Young Woman*	Pam Gems	Sue Todd
31 July 1974	*Les Capoeiras de Babia*		Brazillian Dance Company
9 September 1974	*Henry IV Part 1*	Shakespeare	Kenny McBain
10 September 1974	*Henry IV Part 2*	Shakespeare	Kenny McBain
11 October 1974	*120 Days of Sodom*	Marquis de Sade, adapted by Giuliano Vasilico	Giuliano Vasilico
23 September 1974	Matt Mattox Jazzart Dance Company		
12 November 1974	*The Highwaymen*	Friedrich von Schiller	H Pilikian
27 November 1974	*Henry V*	Shakespeare	Kenny McBain

Date	Title	Author	Director/Company
29 November 1974	*Henry IV Part 1*	Shakespeare	Kenny McBain
30 November 1974	*Henry IV Part 2*	Shakespeare	Kenny McBain
6 December 1974	(LN) *The Exception and the Rule*	Bertolt Brecht	Gareth Jones
18 December 1974	*Autosacramentales*	Calderon de la Barca	Victor Garcia
14 January 1975	*Sankofa* (dance)	G. Kwame Dzikunu	
6 February 1975	*Raindog*	Stomu Yamash'ta	Stomu Yamash'ta
2 April 1975	Ballet Rambert		
3 June 1975	*The Taming of the Shrew*	Shakespeare	Mervyn Willis
29 July 1975	*Renga Moi*	Abafumi Company	Robert Serumaga
30 September 1975	*Le Palais des Merveilles*	Jules Cordière	Jules Cordiére
13 October 1975	*Pilgrim*	John Bunyan, adapted by Jane McCulloch	Toby Robertson
13 November 1975	*Le Pavillon au Bord de la Rivière*	Le Théâtre de Gennevilliers	Bernard Sobel
25 November 1975	*Black Explosion*	Black Theatre of Brixton	
2 December 1975	*The Journal of Anaïs Nin*	Moving Being	Geoff Moore
16 December 1975	*Les Grands Sentiments*	Le Grand Magic Circus	Jérôme Savary
15 January 1976	*The Ik*	Colin Turnbull, adapted by Peter Brook	Peter Brook
31 March 1976	*The Journey*	Philippa Burrell	John Baliol
24 April 1976	*La Grande Eugène*	Frantz Salieri	Frantz Salieri
14 October 1976	*Ondeko-Za* (dance)	Tagayasu Den	
3 November 1976	Gerry Cottle's Circus		
21 December 1976	*Mr Punch's Pantomime*	David Haughton	Lindsay Kemp
31 January 1977	*Flowers*	Jean Genet, adapted by Lindsay Kemp	Lindsay Kemp
28 February 1977	*Salomé*	Oscar Wilde	Lindsay Kemp
2 May 1977	*Illuminatus!*	Robert Shea & Robert Anton Wilson	Ken Campbell & Chris Langham
8 June 1977	*The Red Devil Battery Sign*	Tennessee Williams	Burt Shevelove
5 July 1977	Ballet Rambert		
7 August 1977	*Epsom Downs*	Howard Brenton	Max Stafford-Clark
8 September 1977	*A Mad World My Masters*	Barry Keeffe	William Gaskill
4 October 1977	*Sleak*	C.P. Lee	Charlie Hanson

Appendix

Date	Title	Author	Director/Company
29 November 1977	*Do You Love Me?*	R.D. Laing, adapted by Edward Petherbridge	Edward Petherbridge
29 December 1977	*The Importance of Being Earnest*	Oscar Wilde	Tenniel Evans
23 February 1978	*Streamers*	David Rabe	Leslie Lawton
22 March 1978	*The Hunch*	Hauser Orkater	
1 June 1978	*Big Sin City*	The Heather Brothers, Neil, Lea and John	
11 July 1978	Ballet Rambert		
3 August 1978	*Bartholomew Fair*	Ben Jonson	Peter Barnes
13 February 1979	*The Ordeal of Gilbert Pinfold*	Ronald Harwood	Michael Elliott
28 March 1979	*Don Quixote*	Giovanni Paisiello	Tom Hawkes
3 April 1979	*Varieté Varieté*	Oskar Schlemmer	Helfrid Foron
17 April 1979	*The Family Reunion*	T.S. Eliot	Michael Elliott
15 May 1979	*The Lady from the Sea*	Ibsen	Michael Elliott
10 July 1979	*Prometheus*	Julian Beck & Judith Malina	Julian Beck & Judith Malina for The Living Theatre
3 August 1979	*Dante*	Dante, adapted by Josef Szajna	
18 September 1979	*A Midsummer Night's Dream*	Shakespeare	
2 October 1979	London Contemporary Dance Theatre		Robert Cohen
12 November 1979	*The Glass Menagerie*	Tennessee Williams	Peter James
3 January 1980	*The Pig Organ*	Richard Blackford & Ted Hughes	Michael Hackett
13 February 1980	*The Weavers*	Gerhart Hauptmann	Paul Marcus
28 January 1980	*Richard III*	Shakespeare	Robert Sturua (Rustaveli Company)
7 April 1980	*Only in America*	Ned Sherrin	Ned Sherrin & David Yakir
28 April 1980	*Hamlet*	Shakespeare	Steven Berkoff
3 July 1980	*The Strongest Man in the World*	Barry Collins	Nikolas Simmonds
31 July 1980	*Hedda*	Ibsen, adapted by Charles Marowitz	Charles Marowitz
9 September 1980	*Life Swappers*	Robert McGough	Simon Gammell
14 October 1980	*Season's Greetings*	Alan Ayckbourn	Alan Ayckbourn
3 December 1980	*Don Juan*	R.D. MacDonald	Philip Prowse

Date	Title	Author	Director/Company
4 November 1980	Circus Oz		
16 December 1980	*The Canterbury Tales*	Chaucer, adapted by Phil Woods	Michael Bogdanov
2 February 1981	*Suburban Strains*	Alan Ayckbourn	Alan Ayckbourn
31 March 1981	*The Duchess of Malfi*	John Webster	Adrian Noble
13 May 1981	*Have you Anything to Declare?*	Maurice Hennequin, Pierre Veber	Braham Murray
10 June 1981	*Waiting for Godot*	Samuel Beckett	Braham Murray
1 July 1981	*The Misanthrope*	Molière	Caspar Wrede
25 August 1981	*Iphigenia in Lixourion*	Petros Katsaitis	Spyros Evangelatos
30 September 1981	*Mephisto*	Klaus Mann, adapted by Gordon McDougall	Ariane Mnouchkine
14 December 1981	The Pickle Family Circus		
24 February 1982	*Edward II*	Brecht	Roland Rees
7 April 1982	*Zarathustra*	Ariadone Company of Japan	Ko Murobushi
4 May 1982	*Othello*	Shakespeare Floorboards Theatre Company	
26 May 1982	*Gormenghast*	Mervin Peake, adapted by Jonathan Petherbridge	Jonathan Petherbridge
26 May 1982	*Gioconda & Si-Ya-U*	Nazim Hikmet	Paul Zimet
6 July 1982	*Tristan and Isolt*	Sidney Goldfarb	The Talking Band of New York
9 August 1982	*The Cherry Orchard*	Anton Chekhov	Mike Alfreds
15 September 1982	*Mariedda*	Akroama of Sardinia	
11 November 1982	*Diary of a Hunger Strike*	Peter Sheridan	Pam Brighton

Bibliography

OPEN SPACE THEATRE

Primary Sources

PUBLIC RECORDS

Open Space Archives, Theatre Museum, Russell Street, London WC2E 7PR. They contain:

a. Cuttings books 1–20
b. Miscellaneous administrative papers
c. Photographs
d. Programmes and publicity
e. Prompt copies:

    Arrabal, Fernando, *And They Put Handcuffs on the Flowers*, translated by Charles Marowitz and John Burgess (sound and lighting plot)

    Büchner, Georg, *Woyzeck*, adapted by Charles Marowitz

    Ibsen, Henrik, *Hedda Gabler*, adapted by Charles Marowitz as *Hedda*

    Ibsen, Henrik, *Hedda Gabler*, adapted by Charles Marowitz as *Hedda* (actor's copy)

    Ionesco, Eugène, *Macbett*, translated by Charles Marowitz (lighting plot)

    Magdalany, Philip, *Boo Hoo*

    Marowitz, Charles, *Artaud at Rodez* (lighting plot)

    Pontac, Perry, *The Old Man's Comforts* (actor's copy)

    Shakespeare, William, *Macbeth*, adapted by Charles Marowitz (actor's copy)

    Shakespeare, William, *Macbeth*, adapted by Charles Marowitz (director's copy)

    Shakespeare, William, *Measure for Measure* (actor's copy)

    Shakespeare, William, *Measure for Measure* (director's copy)

    Shakespeare, William, *Othello*, adapted by Charles Marowitz as *An Othello* (lighting plot)

    Shakespeare, William, *The Taming of the Shrew*, adapted by Charles Marowitz as *The Shrew*

f. Unpublished play scripts:

    Barnes, Peter, *Laughter* (early draft)

    Brenton, Howard, *How Beautiful with Badges*

    Büchner, Georg, *Woyzeck*, adapted by Charles Marowitz (early draft)

    Collins, Barry, *The Strongest Man in the World*

    de Ghelderode, Michel, *Red Magic*, translated by George Hauger

Griffiths, Trevor, *Sam Sam*

Ibsen, Henrik, *Hedda Gabler*, adapted by Charles Marowitz as *Hedda* (early draft)

Ionesco, Eugène, *Macbett*, translated by Charles Marowitz

Jarry, Alfred, *Ubu Roi*, adapted by Spike Milligan

Magdalany, Philip, *Boo Hoo* (3 scripts)

Marowitz, Charles, *Artaud at Rodez* (early draft)

Marowitz, Charles, sketches: *The Burning Issue, Empathy, Mort and Levy, The Reunion, Sight–Seers, The Street Corner*

Marowitz, Charles, *The Tea Party*

Pontac, Perry, *The Old Man's Comforts*

Schnitzler, Arthur, *Anatol*

Shakespeare, William, *Hamlet*, adapted by Charles Marowitz (3 early drafts)

Shakespeare, William, *Macbeth*, adapted by Charles Marowitz (early draft)

Shakespeare, William, *The Merchant of Venice*, adapted by Charles Marowitz as *Variations on the Merchant of Venice*

Shakespeare, William, *The Taming of the Shrew*, adapted by Charles Marowitz as *The Shrew* (early draft)

Shepard, Sam, *The Tooth of Crime*

Wardle, Irving, *The Houseboy* (early draft)

Weller, Mike, *Now There's Just the Three of Us*

NEWSPAPERS AND JOURNALS

Burgess, John and Charles Marowitz, 'Charles Marowitz Directs *An Othello*', *Theatre Quarterly*, 2(1972), no.8, 68–81

Dacre, Kathleen, 'Charles Marowitz's *Hedda* (and *An Enemy of the People*)', *The Drama Review*, 25(1981), no.2, 3–16

Marowitz, Charles, 'Artaud at Rodez', *Theatre Quarterly*, 2(1972), 58–62

Marowitz, Charles, 'The Marowitz Macbeth', *Theatre Quarterly*, 1(1971), no.3, 47–49

Marowitz, Charles, 'An Open Letter to the Becks', *Plays and Players* (June,1969)

PLAY TEXTS

Barker, Howard, *Stripwell* and *Claw* (London, 1977)

Barnes, Peter, *Leonardo's Last Supper*, in his *Collected Plays* (London, 1981)

Barnes, Peter, *Noonday Demons*, in his *Collected Plays* (London, 1981)

Brenton, Howard, *Christie in Love*, in *Plays for the Poor Theatre* (London, 1980)

Büchner, Georg, *Woyseck*, trans. John Mackendrick (Eyre Methuen, London, 1979)

Burgess, John, and Charles Marowitz, *The Chicago Conspiracy*, in *Open Space Plays* (Harmondsworth, 1974)

Burns, Alan, and Charles Marowitz, *Palach*, in *Open Space Plays* (Harmondsworth, 1974)

Guare, John, *Muzeeka*, in *Off–Broadway Plays 1* (Harmondsworth, 1970)

Herbert, John, *Fortune and Men's Eyes*, in *Open Space Plays* (Harmondsworth, 1974)

McNally, Terence, *Sweet Eros*, in *Off-Broadway Plays* 2 (Harmondsworth, 1972)

Marowitz, Charles, *Artaud at Rodez* (London, 1977)

Marowitz, Charles, *Hedda*, in *Sex Wars – Free Adaptations of Ibsen and Strindberg* (London and New Hampshire, 1982)

Marowitz, Charles, *The Marowitz Hamlet* (London, 1968)

Marowitz, Charles, *The Marowitz Shakespeare* (London, 1978)

Marowitz, Charles, *Measure for Measure*, in *The Marowitz Shakespeare* (London, 1978)

Marowitz, Charles, ed., *Off-Broadway Plays*, vols.1 and 2 (Harmondsworth, 1970 and 1972)

Marowitz, Charles, ed., *Open Space Plays* (Harmondsworth, 1974)

Marowitz, Charles, *An Othello*, in *Open Space Plays* (Harmondsworth, 1974)

Marowitz, Charles, *Potboilers: Sherlock's Last Case, Ah, Sweet Mystery of Life!, Clever Dick* (New York and London, 1986)

Marowitz, Charles, *Sex Wars – Free Adaptations of Ibsen and Strindberg* (London and New Hampshire, 1982)

Marowitz, Charles, *Variations on the Merchant of Venice*, in *The Marowitz Shakespeare* (London, 1978)

Picasso, Pablo, *The Four Little Girls* (London, 1970)

Weller, Mike, *The Body Builders*, in *Off-Broadway Plays* 2 (Harmondsworth, 1972)

Weller, Mike, *Now There's Just the Three of Us*, in *Off-Broadway Plays* 2 (Harmondsworth, 1972)

INTERVIEWS (with the author)

Brenton, Howard	3 July 1985
Burgess, John	25 July 1985
Don, Robin	22 March 1985
Donohue, Walter	19 June 1984
Griffiths, Trevor	4 December 1984
Holt, Thelma	19 February 1979, 21 February 1984
Marowitz, Charles	3 December 1981 (lecture)
Marowitz, Charles	18 June 1983
Marowitz, Charles	2 June 2004
Merrison, Clive	10 April 1985
Pearlman, Alan	15 November 1978
Simmonds, Nikolas	19 March 1982
Storry, Malcolm	17 May 1985

Secondary Sources

Ansorge, Peter, *Disrupting the Spectacle* (London, 1975)

Billington, Michael, *One Night Stands* (London, 1993)

Gottlieb, Vera and Colin Chambers eds., *Theatre in a Cool Climate* (Amber Lane Press, 1999)

Haynes, Jim, *Thanks for Coming* (London, 1984)

Itzin, Catherine, *Stages in the Revolution: Political Theatre in Britain Since 1968*
     (London, 1980)
Knight, G. Wilson, *The Wheel of Fire* (London, 1961)
Lahr, John, *Acting Out America* (Harmondsworth, 1972)
McMillan, Joyce, *The Traverse Theatre Story 1963–1988* (London, 1988)
Marowitz, Charles, *The Act of Being* (London, 1978)
Marowitz, Charles, *Burnt Bridges* (Kent, 1990)
Marowitz, Charles, *Confessions of a Counterfeit Critic* (London, 1973)
Marowitz, Charles, Tom Milne, Owen Hale, eds., *The Encore Reader*
     (London, 1965)
Marowitz, Charles, *The Method as Means – an Acting Survey* (London, 1961)
Marowitz, Charles, *Prospero's Staff* (Bloomington and Indianapolis, 1986)
Marowitz, Charles, and Simon Trussler, eds., *Theatre at Work* (London, 1967)
Rees, Roland, *Fringe First, Pioneers of Fringe Theatre on Record* (London, 1992)
Wintle, Justin, *The Fun Art Bus, An Inter-Action Project by Ed Berman*
     (London, 1973)

ROUND HOUSE

PUBLIC RECORDS
Round House Archives, Theatre Museum, Russell Street, London
     WC2E 7PR. They contain:
a.   Contract Files 1–86
b.   Cuttings books 1–106 (Round House); 1–7 (Music Shows); 8–13
     (Round House Downstairs); 1–4 (Kids' Shows)
c.   Photographs
d.   Programmes and publicity
e.   Reports:
     Centre 42, Annual Report, 1961–1962
     The First Report, December 1965–31st March 1971
f.   Show files 1–40 (Round House); 1–15 (Round House Downstairs)
g.   Unpublished thesis: Coppieters, Frank, *Arnold Wesker's Centre 42*
     (University of Ghent, 1972), Theatre Museum, Russell Street,
     London WC2E 7PR
h.   *Miscellaneous stage and seating plans* (the list copies the numbers on the
     rolls of plans in the RH archives):
1.   Twyla Tharp Ballet (*Aquarius*), *The Journey*
2.   *Hamlet, The Mother, From Moses to Mao, The Royal Hunt of the Sun, Pericles,*
     Moving Being
3.   *Autosacramentales, Mutations, Terminal, Night Walk*
4.   Round House
5.   *La Grande Eugène, The Ik*
6.   *Bartholomew Fair*
7.   Round House
8.   Moving Being
9.   *Bartholomew Fair*
10. *Cambridge Footlights Revue,* Le Grand Magic Circus, *The Trial, 120 Days of*
     Sodom
11. Round House
12. *La Grande Eugène, The Ik, The Journey,* Le Grand Magic Circus, Moving

Being, *Le Pavillon au Bord de la Mer, Epsom Downs,* Gerry Cottle's
   Circus, *Illuminatus, Salomé, Flowers, Feast of Fools, The Trial, Decameron
   73, The Royal Hunt of the Sun, Pericles, Pilgrim, The Highwaymen, Les
   Veuves, 120 Days of Sodom,* The Brazilian Dance Company, Twyla Tharp
   Ballet, Ballet Rambert, *Mr Punch's Pantomime, Ondeko-Za*

13. Workshops

14. Red Buddha Theatre, *The Red Devil Battery Sign,* Twyla Tharp, The
   Brazilian Dance Company, *The Highwaymen,* Le Grand Magic Circus,
   Henry IV (1 and 2), *The Trial*

15. *La Grande Eugène,* Moving Being

16. Red Buddha Theatre, *The Taming of the Shrew, The Ik, Le Pavillon au Bord
   de la Rivière, The Highwaymen*

17. *Don Quixote, The Family Reunion, The Ordeal of Gilbert Pinfold,* Murray
   Louis Season

18. *The Taming of the Shrew, The Tempest, Hamlet, Richard III, Timon of
   Athens, Measure for Measure*

19. *The Journal of Anais Nin*

20. *Le Pavillon au Bord de la Rivière, Le Pavillon au Bord de la Mer,* The Black
   Theatre of Brixton, *The Journey,* Red Buddha Theatre, Le Grand
   Magic Circus, Moving Being, *Candide*

21. *Joseph and the Amazing Technicolor Dreamcoat, Pilgrim,* Moving Being, *Renga
   Moi, La Grande Eugène*

22. Red Buddha Theatre

23. Ballet Rambert

24. Round House

25. *Hoppla Wir Leben*

26. *La Grande Eugène*

27. Round House

28. Joint Stock, *Salomé, Flowers, Mr Punch's Pantomime,* RSC, *Illuminatus,
   The Ik,* Ballet Rambert

29. Round House

30. Gerry Cottle's Circus, Moving Being, *Season's Greetings, The Lady from the
   Sea, The Canterbury Tales*

31. Round House, *Autosacramentales*

32. *The Red Devil Battery Sign, Ondeko-Za*

33. *Ondeko-Za, The Trial, The Red Devil Battery Sign, Macbeth, The Wheel,*
   Prospect Theatre Company, *Feast of Fools,* Twyla Tharp, *Quetzalcoatl*

34. Le Grand Magic Circus, *The Journey, Le Pavillon au Bord de la Rivière,
   Venus and Superkid, Pilgrim, Le Palais des Merveilles, Rabelais, Renga Moi*

35. *The Trial, Feast of Fools, Pericles, 120 Days of Sodom,* Round House, Red
   Buddha Theatre, Ballet Rambert, *Go West Young Woman,* Prospect
   Theatre Company, *Decameron 73*

NEWSPAPERS AND JOURNALS

Adler, John, Michael Bath and Tim Appelbee, eds., 'The System and the
   Writer', *New Theatre Magazine,* 11(1971), no.2, 8–11

Berkoff, Steven, 'Three Theatre Manifestos', *Gambit International Theatre
   Review,* 8(1978), no.32, 7–20

Campos, Christophe, 'Experiments for the People of Paris', *Theatre*

Quarterly, 2(1972), no.8, 57–67

Croyden, Margaret, 'Peter Brook's *Tempest*', *The Drama Review*, 13(1969), no.3, 125–128

McFerran, Ann, 'The Beginner's Mind', *Time Out*, 9 January 1976, pp.12–15

O'Connor, Garry, 'Arnold Wesker's *The Friends*', *Theatre Quarterly*, 1(1971), no.2, 78–92

Tynan, Kenneth, 'Director as Misanthropist: on the Moral Neutrality of Peter Brook', *Theatre Quarterly*, 7(1977), no.25, 20–28

Wallis, Bill, 'Production Case Book: Jean-Louis Barrault's *Rabelais*', *Theatre Quarterly*, 1(1971), no.3, 83–97

Wesker, Arnold, 'Casual Condemnations', *Theatre Quarterly*, 2(1971), no.2, 16–30

Williams, David, 'A Place Marked by Life: Brook at the Bouffes du Nord', *New Theatre Quarterly*, 1(1985), no.1, 39–54

PLAY TEXTS

Arden, John, and Margaretta D'Arcy, *The Hero Rises Up* (London, 1969)

Berkoff, Steven, *The Trial* and *Metamorphosis* (Ambergate, 1981)

Le Théâtre du Soleil, *1789*, translated by Alexander Trocchi, in *Gambit*, 5(1971), no.20, 9–52

CORRESPONDENCE

Arden, John	1 April 1981
Herbert, Jocelyn	22 April 1981
Howarth, Boris, and Maggie	6 July 1981
Richardson, Tony	17 March 1981

INTERVIEWS (with the author)

Berkoff, Steven	7 July 1981
Collins, Paul	16 July 1986
Holt, Thelma	19 February 1979
Little, George	12 July 1981

Secondary Sources

Arden, John, *To Present the Pretence* (London, 1977)

Leeming, Glenda, *Wesker on File* (London, 1985)

Page, Malcolm, *Arden on File* (London, 1985)

Rostagno, Aldo, Julian Beck and Judith Malina, *We, The Living Theatre* (New York, 1970)

Shellard, Dominic, *Kenneth Tynan: A Life* (Newhaven and London, 2003)

Wesker, Arnold, *As Much As I Dare, An Autobiography (1932–1959)*, (London, 1994)

Wesker, Arnold, *Fears of Fragmentation* (London, 1970), including the following essays: 'The Allio Brief', 52–62; 'O Mother is it Worth It?', 11–19; 'The Secret Reins, Centre 42', 39–50

Wesker, Arnold, 'Let Battle Commence', in Charles Marowitz, Tom Milne, and Owen Hale, eds., *The Encore Reader* (London, 1965), 96–103

Bibliography

GENERAL SECONDARY SOURCES

Beck, Julian, and The Living Theatre, '*Paradise Now*: notes', *The Drama Review*, 13(1969), no.3, 90–107

Bablet, Denis, ed., *Différent: Le Théâtre du Soleil, Supplément à Travail Théâtral* (Dole, February 1976)

Bablet, Denis and Marie-Louise, *1789: Le Théâtre du Soleil* ('Diapolivre' 1979), Paris: CNRS

Bradby, David, *Modern French Drama 1940–1980* (Cambridge, 1991)

Bradby, David, and John McCormick, *People's Theatre* (London, 1978)

Brecht, Stefan, 'Revolution at the Brooklyn Academy of Music', *The Drama Review*, 13(1969), no.3, 47–73

Brook, Peter, *The Empty Space* (Harmondsworth, 1972)

Craig, Sandy, ed., *Dreams and Deconstructions: Alternative Theatre in Britain* (Ambergate, 1980)

Davison, Peter, Rolf Meyersohn and Edward Shils, eds., *Literary Taste, Culture and Mass Communication*, 8(Cambridge, 1978), *The Drama Review*, 30(1965), edition devoted to 'happenings'

Eyre, Richard and Nicholas Wright, *Changing Stages: A view of British and American Theatre in the Twentieth Century*, (London, 2001)

Findlater, Richard, *The Unholy Trade* (London, 1952)

Hammond, Jonathan, 'A Potted History of the Fringe', *Theatre Quarterly*, 111(1973), no.12, 36–46

Goorney, Howard, *The Theatre Workshop Story* (London, 1981)

Hoggart, Richard, *The Uses of Literacy* (London, 1957)

Innes, Christopher, *Holy Theatre: Ritual and the Avant-Garde* (Cambridge, 1981)

Itzin, Catherine, *Stages in the Revolution: Political Theatre in Britain Since 1968* (London, 1980)

Lee, Vera, *Quest for a Public: French Popular Theatre Since 1945* (Cambridge, Massachusetts, 1970)

McDermott, Patrick, 'Portrait of an Actor, Watching: antiphonal feed back to the Living Theatre', *The Drama Review*, 13(1969), no.3, 74–83

Schechner, Richard, 'Containment is the Enemy', *The Drama Review*, 13(1969), no.3, 24–44

Shellard, Dominic, *British Theatre Since the War* (New Haven, 2000)

Suvin, Darko, 'Reflections on Happenings', *The Drama Review*, 14(1970), no.3, 125–144

Time Out, 'Guide to Underground Theatre', *Theatre Quarterly*, 1(1971), no.1, 61–65

Trussler, Simon, *New Theatre Voices of the Seventies: Sixteen Interviews from Theatre Quarterly 1970–1980* (London, 1981)

Wistrich, Enid, *'I Don't Mind the Sex, It's the Violence': Film Censorship Explored* (London, 1978)

Index

Page numbers with illustrations are indicated by italics.

Names in parentheses after play titles indicate directors.